Nov 1984

Dear Michael,

Happy Birthday! Hope you use it, pages such as 1/3 are especially important!

Lots of love from
Louise xxx 🍀

The Guinness Guide to
Game Fishing

William B. Currie

GUINNESS SUPERLATIVES LIMITED
2 CECIL COURT, LONDON ROAD, ENFIELD, MIDDLESEX

Editor: Anne Marshall

ISBN 0 85112 208 6

British Library CIP Data
Currie, William Brown
The Guinness guide to game fishing.
1. Salmon fishing
2. Trout fishing
I. Title   II. Game fishing
799.1'2   SH684

Published by
Guinness Superlatives Limited
2 Cecil Court, London Road,
Enfield, Middlesex

Guinness is a registered trademark of Guinness Superlatives Limited

Design and Layout: Geoffrey Hart Associates

Printed and bound by
South China Printing Co. Hong Kong

Colour origination: Newsele Litho Limited

Contents

Acknowledgements

The author gratefully acknowledges
invaluable assistance in producing this book
from Arthur Oglesby
and Michael Shepley for
angling photographs from their files.
Thanks are also due to the
British Field Sports Society for
information on fishing seasons

Above all, the author would like
to thank Wendy Mackay and Ruth Eaton
for their help in typing the manuscript
which involved them in the terminology
of sporting English, in the
names of Highland rivers and lochs
and in the the names of flies
baits and lures decidedly remote
from normal business language.

Preface

This book is an expression of some of the delight I have had in game fishing over the past quarter of a century or more. But it is, like many other deeply felt personal things, more than just a record of how pleasant it is to fish, and to be where the game fish are. It takes on something of the triple goals of poetry noted by the ancients to be *ut doceat, ut moveat, ut delectet* – to teach, to move the reader, and to promote beauty. In the chapters which follow I have tried to teach others, mainly by involving them in my own fishing, its logic, its challenges and its successes and failures. I have, I hope, included enough of my own experiences to show that I have been thrilled by the sport, and through this I hope others find something of the excitement of this most mysterious and wild of sports. In what I have written I would like others to detect that an important element in game fishing is where it is enjoyed – in largely unspoiled and naturally beautiful country. Above all, in writing for others new to the sport or, like me, always hungry for new experiences and ideas in it, I would like some of the real feelings of achievement and the unutterable feelings of failure which the sport brings to be communicated. Fishing runs from superb fulfillment to abject humiliation, with many degrees of each ranged between. It is thus a sport of the whole range of feelings. It is also a sport which promotes thought, however, and hearty bankside argument is never far from us. A sport which is all these things is worth more than one book can bring to it. I have had to leave much out. I hope, however, that the essence of the game is here – or at least the game as I see it. But I hope every reader builds his own view, and gets as much pleasure as possible from the sport, for it has endless pleasure to give.

Section One
The Game Fish and their Habitat

Trout

There is a Latin saying that wherever you find trout you also find beauty. This is, of course, a highly-loaded statement. It tells you that the author was a man of the Northern Hemisphere, and almost certainly knew Europe as his home. For him, as for many of us, beauty in landscape means unspoiled mountain and hill and heath. These are regions of fast-flowing streams of pure, highly-oxygenated water. In chemistry the streams trout love are usually neutral or mildly acid. The temperatures associated with the habitat of the trout are the product of a temperate climate with reliable rainfall. The author of the Latin saying was not a Scot, or a Norwegian, but he might well have been, because the trout thrives in northern Europe, especially in the north-west where natural beauty means rugged heath, pine forest, rock and fast, often wild streams. This coincides with an area in which there are often great regions of low population density, low industrialisation and low pollution. The trout, in a word, is a fish of the European wilderness and its value to a leisure conscious world is very high. As a wild creature, the trout fits in beautifully with current pressures towards conservation of the environment. We are scoring plus marks all the way. We are almost able to write a new universal statement about trout – that it is associated with natural landscape of a high order of beauty, that man enjoys it in a

blameless way, and that the protection and development of the trout in its natural habitat is a work of all-round benefit to society.

In more scientific terms we can show that the distribution of trout is slightly wider than that, but it is not by any means a world-wide fish. Frost and Brown in their excellent book *The Trout* provide us with a map of the world with areas in which trout are indigenous and areas to which they have been introduced. The natural home of the trout, which they have enjoyed for some seventy million years, covers the whole of Europe, except the southern part of Italy, Spain and Greece. It includes Iceland in the north-west, and the highlands of north Africa in the south. On the east the trout inhabit the streams of the Caucasus and waters east of the Caspian Sea, but not including Kashmir and the Himalayas. In the north, trout live in the European and Asian Arctic areas, straying east of the boundaries of Europe by a limited distance only.

The leisure and food value of trout have led to it being introduced to many world waters. The brown trout of the eastern seaboard of the United States and Canada and other areas of the north American continent are good examples of this. The trout travelled with the colonists to central and southern Africa, to Australia and New Zealand, to Kashmir and the hill waters of India and Ceylon,

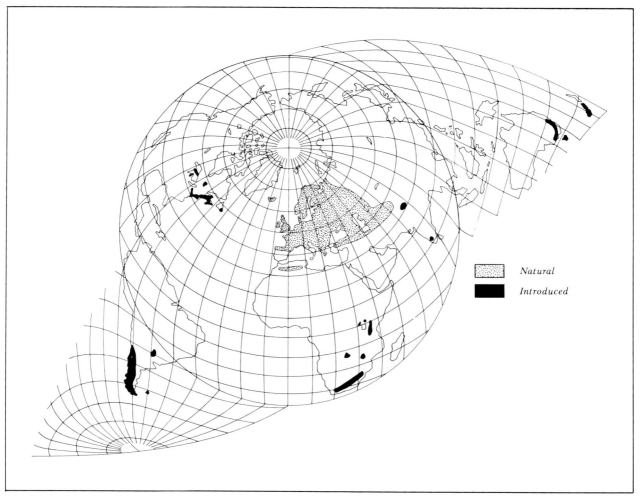

Natural

Introduced

The distribution of brown trout

and the fish has also been extensively introduced to the waters of the Andes right down through Chile to Tierra del Fuego.

In a much more relevant sense, trout have also been increased in distribution on our own doorstep. Scotland and Ireland and the north of England and Wales are the hill and heath areas where trout have managed to thrive, even during the pressures of the Industrial Revolution. But trout have been progressively introduced or re-introduced to natural lakes and rivers in other parts of England and Scotland. The great leap forward which has been taken in stillwater fishing in the UK since the formation of drinking water reservoirs in the thirties, but which has moved forward with impressive speed since 1960, has led to the stocking of midland and southern English reservoirs, ponds, gravel pits and lakes with brown trout (and rainbows) and this has not only vastly increased the availability of trout in England, but has changed the art of stillwater fly fishing by making it available to anglers from a broader spectrum of fishing backgrounds than before. As a Scot, I often travel down to East Anglia to get

some sport with big trout. Forty years ago trout fishers travelled north to find their sport in the Highlands of Scotland. We have added a whole new dimension to trout fishing in stillwater within my fishing lifetime.

One of the curious features of trout is that the waters they grow best in are often not the best waters for their spawning. The best example of this is probably the chalk streams of Hampshire and Wiltshire – waters such as the Test and the Wylie. These waters did hold trout naturally, and the slightly alkaline chemistry of these waters grew large fish. But the spawning is poor and an extensive stocking and conservation policy has been in operation on these waters for over a century. Compare this with a small Highland loch in, say, Sutherland. There the trout live in a mildly acid environment. They are well supplied with spawning streams with excellent gravel in the hill burns for breeding. They rapidly over-populate the lochs with fish which cannot find enough food for quick growth in these rather infertile lochs and the result is well known – lochs populated with old, small trout of three or four to a pound. Nature is prolific, but a balance is struck when the food supply for a given population of trout supports fish of a given average size. If the stocks were drastically reduced in these acid lochs, one would be surprised by the quality of individual trout caught in them. Trout in acid waters are popularly believed to grow more slowly than trout in neutral or alkaline waters, but this has been shown not to be the case. Niall Campbell, in a scientific study, was able to show that a mildly acid loch in Caithness produced growth rates similar to 'sweeter' waters elsewhere when the stock was limited. The marvellous thing in that study for me, as an angler, was that trout taken from a rather deprived water near Loch Glutt – the upper Thurso river – grew like balloons when they were put in Glutt, and they did this regardless of their age. Scottish trout would grow to sizes similar to those common in stocked and managed English waters, if the balance between population and food supply was right.

However, what is very obvious is that the waters of the English red sandstone plains, and clay vales and chalk areas are much more fertile than waters in Scotland. Thus, more trout of a larger size can be supported in a given area of water. These waters, however, have to be artificially stocked. It is very advantageous to manage and stock a water where there is no spawning. You calculate the crop of fish as you might calculate an agricultural crop. Wild fish remain special, with great qualities for the angler, but they are numerous and small. Stocked fish provide larger trout for us all with careful management.

The brown trout is the most widely distributed of the game fish. It is a naturally shy, secretive, wily fish and can be most challenging to catch (Jens Ploug Hansen)

In this chapter so far the word 'trout' has been used to describe what is a very diverse fish indeed in its varieties and races. Trout vary in size from mature 2oz (57g) fish in acid lochans in the Highland of Scotland to 2lb (0.9kg) average fish in the chalk streams and reservoirs of England. Many waters have an even higher average. At the other end of the scale, trout which turn to predation of their own kind, and other fish, can grow huge in the Scottish and Irish lochs. These *ferox* can be 20lb (9kg) or more in weight, yet they are trout. (See p. 213-24.)

(Jens Ploug Hansen)

Between 2oz (57g) and 20lb (9kg) lies not only an incredible range of catchable fish, but also a great spectrum of markings of fish, body shapes, flesh colour and habits. It is little wonder that some of the early biologists thought there ought to be Linnaean sub-species and varieties identified. Linnaeus himself identified the river trout, *Salmo trutta*, and he went on to name another two species, *Salmo eriox* the sea trout, and *Salmo fario*, the brook trout. These names are misleading and I am listing them for historical reasons. Ten different species of trout were identified in the nineteenth century by Günther, the noted fish biologist, using Linnaean categories and these species of trout are of interest to us, because there was an obvious connection between the species and angling experience. Günther names as different species the eastern and western sea trout, the Orkney and Galway sea trout, and in addition to the common trout, *Salmo fario*, he listed the great lake trout, *Salmo ferox*, the snail-eating trout with the thick stomach – the gilaroo – *Salmo stomachicus*, and among other local trout he gave a separate Latin name (*Levenensis*) to the Loch Leven trout.

One cannot fish for trout without being amazed and often delighted by the difference in appearance of the fish one catches. The trout in my boyhood country, Ayrshire, was known widely as the yellow trout, and not the brown trout. In Quebec, Canada, I was fascinated to find the fish called the grey trout. In fact the trout of the peaty lochans of Scotland is often dark brown to near black in colour. Some trout have a scattering of small black spots, some have squarish black spots with a few red spots and some have round black and red spots ringed in pale colour. Hopkins's famous poem 'Pied Beauty' has a memorable reference to 'rose moles all in stipple upon trout that swim'.

One could go on describing local races of trout, and still finer distinctions such as trout from one particular bay in a loch where spots were bigger, bellies whiter or yellower, fins blacker or redder and so on. The trout's obliterative shading, as the scientific phrase labels it, obviously varies according to the needs of a given environment. Trout from clear waters are greener and clearer in colour, and those from dark, peaty waters are darker. It is Nature's camouflage. In your bag, the trout will change colour, but not spot configuration.

One of the most treasured books in my collection of angling works is P D Malloch's *Life History and Habits of the Salmon, Sea-Trout, and other Freshwater Fish* (1910). Malloch was a very careful observer and a superbly well informed man on all matters relating to trout and salmon. His book contains a brilliant series of pictures of trout (and salmon) taken at the turn of the century and I know of no better introduction to the range and variety of trout types. The plates are black and white, naturally, but are full of excellent detail. It may be possible to see this book in the major libraries of the UK and some may still survive on the second-hand market. Malloch comes out strongly in favour of there being only one kind of trout: '. . . but from a close study of all these trout for the last forty years, I have come to the conclusion that there is only one species of trout in Great Britain'. This statement, in a work elaborating the differences found, is of maximum significance. This is the position taken up by trout biologists now and it is unquestionably the most productive view to take.

Trout live in freshwater, but they can tolerate a fairly high degree of salinity. Thus, in the tidal reaches of many rivers trout feed in the brackish waters which may change in salinity from tide to tide from fully fresh to very salt. These tidal trout, sometimes called slob trout – a dreadful word – are often very different in appearance from their brothers in the river. They are often silvery, nearly like sea trout. They are usually large, since their feeding is rich and their dependence on river temperature is reduced. They live and look like sea trout, and in some measure they are taken by anglers when they are fishing for esturial sea trout.

I have had some fine sport with tidal trout, and I think of the Thurso as a place where this was memorable. One could fish dry fly with great results there. The tidal trout behaved liked browns on these occasions. Sometimes tidal trout however, behave like any predatory sea fish. In Orkney I have caught them in the sea itself off burn mouths and there they have taken such unlikely baits as mackerel strip.

The trout year is regulated by the spawning cycle on one hand and the availability of food on the other. Trout spawn in the winter, usually in November, and the eggs hatch about a hundred days later in the cold waters of the spring. The hatched alevin carries the egg sac with it as a food supply and as this is absorbed, in say three weeks, is gradually weaned, as it were, and takes natural river food. Loch trout live in the burns until they are at least fingerlings before going down to the stillwater below.

After spawning, trout are weak and thin and they take several weeks to come back into condition. When the legal trout season opens in March (it varies locally) trout are usually not worth fishing for, unless you are in a very favoured, mild area where the trout can get weeks of feeding in after spawning, before the due date. I have caught good fish in March in the mild south-west of Scotland and Argyll but these are highly exceptional areas where tropical palm trees grow by the seaside and where the North Atlantic drift warms air and land. Trout are not usually fit to be fished until mid or even late April. A mild year is obviously better than a cold year. Equally, if fishing a water where there are takable trout introduced to stock the fishery in the spring, quite respectable trouting may be enjoyed in early April – if the weather is benign. Also if trout water is artificially fed, there may be no problems. But wild fisheries are really rather unrewarding when the fish are weak. You may catch them, but who wants a bag of kelts?

In May, the trout rapidly regain their form and move in the streams from the gentle and protected lies associated with their weak condition to the faster water. I have seen trout back into the fastest streams by mid May. This is the time of maximum feeding and often of the best sport. There is a kind of annual naivete around during this prolific feeding and recovery period and trout are much more willing to take the angler's flies then than later in the summer. Further, the flies of May are larger; the midges have not yet arrived to be a curse to us. About this time the trout also begin to rise to surface food more readily than they do in colder water. The evening rise begins to show up and to assert itself. Large fish are still fairly unwary in late April and May and I have seen some of the best fish of my season coming to the net well before the end of the month.

As the year progresses, trout feed, become lethargic in the warmer waters of summer, and revive again when September comes. By now they are well developed in spawn and they begin to move in the river towards the spawning streams, and in the loch they begin to congregate off the mouths of tributaries. The fish may show off these spawning streams from late August onwards and while they are there, they feed vigorously. They wait at the mouths of these streams or in the lower reaches until the water temperature and height is right, and in late autumn they run upstream and pair off. The female cuts a kind of nest in the gravel and when the time comes, deposits her eggs in it. The male fish lies beside her and fertilises the eggs with his milt. The eggs are then covered over and left to the hazards and protection of Nature. From the moment the eggs are laid, it is a fight for survival. Other fish, including trout, queue up to eat the eggs as they are laid. Birds take the eggs and also pick off the spawning and spawned trout, since they are very exposed in shallow water in small spawning streams. When the eggs hatch, the little alevins are the prey of everything which can catch them. Only a vast over-production of eggs (about 900 per pound of fish) is adequate to produce survivors and ensure that trout go on as a species. In hatcheries, however, man can produce vastly increased efficiency of spawning. He can ensure that all eggs are fertilised, which Nature cannot do; he can ensure that infected eggs are taken out of the hatch, thus eliminating the spread of disease. Man can prevent predation, and can artificially feed the fry (the young trout). He can then rear the fish to whatever size and age he wishes and introduce them to the fishing water when conditions are right. This is the basis of our reservoir and pond fisheries in England. We sometimes call such fisheries, put-and-take fisheries, since there is no natural spawning. But stocking either on a supplementary basis, or to improve the strain of trout, or to give the water fish of a better size, is practised widely. I wonder whether there is a single water in the UK outside the remote north west of Scotland where trout stocks have not been assisted in some way.

Sea Trout

Trout and sea trout share a broadly similar life cycle, except that the fish is migratory. One should modify this statement at once, however, since the brown trout is also strongly migratory. It moves upstream to spawn, and in lochs it moves to identifiable spawning grounds in the tributaries. But sea trout feed in the estuaries and coastal waters, and during summer and autumn, migrate up freshwater streams and through lochs to populate the inland waters with their numbers. It is a most welcome invasion, since the river is transformed when it has sea trout to offer sport on trout tackle. These spectacular, larger cousins of the brown trout may run to 6 or 8lb (2.7 – 3.6kg) – or much more – and they provide a challenge and a form of sport for which an extensive section has been included in this book. Like the brown trout, the sea trout ripens in spawn and cuts its redds (gravel egg nest) in the hill streams side by side with the brown trout. The kelt sea trout may die, but they do have a fair survival rate since the fish are able to feed in freshwater both before and after spawning, unlike the salmon which cannot feed in freshwater. Sea trout descend the rivers in spring and begin to feed again at sea. In a year, or possibly two, they again make the spawning journey upstream and the cycle is repeated. Mean-

The sea trout. This 6½lb (3kg) fish from the River Endrick in Scotland was taken by fly at night

while, the eggs hatch into alevins, just like trout, and from this they grow into parr, which look remarkably like small trout, living and feeding beside them. In two or in maybe three seasons, the parr make a downstream migration to the sea and begin their period of voracious feeding and rapid growth which will add anything up to 3lb (1.4kg) to their weight in a year.

Sea trout have interesting differences from salmon, in their return to freshwater. Sea trout come from the inshore seas, and stocks have been shown to remain within a short distance of their breeding streams, unlike the salmon, which travels to the ends of the earth. Sea trout do feed in freshwater, however, where salmon do not, or cannot. This has some importance for the kelt sea trout, – the sea trout which has shed its spawn – since the fish is able to feed and make up some of its condition in freshwater. This appears to improve the survival rate of sea trout after spawning, in sharp contrast to salmon. We thus find sea trout returning again and again to the rivers to spawn. The scales of big sea trout show that they are often old fish, with many spawning runs to their credit. The record is, I believe, an 18½-year-old fish with eleven spawning runs into freshwater.

Thus, sea trout in a given river system like the Ewe-Maree system or the Shiel, develop well where there is a good ratio of larger fish, with good weights, making easy returns to the sea and showing multiple returns to spawn. The systems

we have noted here and elsewhere in this book where short rivers and large lochs characterise the inland waters, appear to be ideal for sea trout security and recovery and it is there that the largest fish are usually encountered. Maree has, in the last twenty or thirty years, produced fish within an ounce or two of 20lb (9kg). The largest I have come across was a sixteen pounder, but I have seen records of many fish in the teens of pounds from these waters.

UDN, the disease which affected all game fish in the sixties and early seventies, thus took a great toll of sea trout by taking away not just the current spawning run but the whole hierarchy of generations of sea trout, and with them the large fish which gave many of our waters such character. I am happy to say that in the three seasons immediately preceding the writing of this book, my own catches have again shown the return of the larger fish – sea trout up to 7lb (3.2kg) and well supported by five and four pounders.

The sea trout which returns to freshwater after only one year of sea feeding is called the finnock or whitling (or any one of a dozen other local names). This sprightly little fish may run to ½ or ¾lb (0.2 to 0.3kg), and in certain remarkable cases where the coastal feeding is good may in fact go much higher. Finnock, however, are, to me, silvery, darting, lively half pounders which have the infuriating habit of wriggling off the hook. I tend to return them to the water since they are the developing stock of the river. These are dealt with in more detail in a later section on sea trout fishing.

Sea trout feed along the shallow water of the coast coming right into the estuaries of burns and rivers and in Scotland one often sees them 'veeing' the surface among the seaweed. It is tempting to fish for them in the sea, and in the north, particularly in Orkney and Shetland, there is some excellent sport to be had fishing in saltwater. Elsewhere, sea trout take occasionally in saltwater to the west and south in Scotland, but it would be misleading to say that any consistent sporting possibility exists in these waters, except in Orkney and Shetland. My teenage son landed a splended 3½ pounder (1.6kg) in the sea off Kintyre; it does happen, but it is a bonus, and not a regular occurrence.

Some sea trout finnock winter in our larger rivers, like the Tay, Spey and Ness and can be caught on their way downstream in April and May. They are welcome surprises on a trout rod in spring, but again I advocate a strict limit, since these very fish will form part of the returning mature stock of fish, possibly in the late summer of the season you catch them as finnock in spring.

The Salmon

The drama of the salmon's life cycle is well known. Writers and film-makers have covered the subject well, and have sometimes anthropomorphised the fish, making it take on human characteristics. The great focus of interest is the return to the river from a distant sea-feeding location, probably off Greenland, through the gauntlet of the nets at sea and in the estuaries. Then, when the river is in flood, the fish are seen forging up through rapids and over waterfalls. It is spectacular stuff. But what grips me as an angler is how the salmon make this run for most of the time almost in secret. Running fish do show, of course, but multitudes of salmon glide upstream in ordinary heights of river, passing through shallows and over thin shingle bars with hardly more than a ripple on the surface. They are big fish for the streams they run, yet one is hardly conscious of the urgent upstream run, except at waterfalls in high water.

Salmon are astonishing creatures in their return to the river. At sea they are voracious feeders, following the krill and the herring and the whole range of creatures of the plankton (ie the small sea creatures which drift with the plankton and feed on it). Then, in the winter a certain percentage of fish stop sea feeding and make their way over a thousand miles of the North Atlantic, rounding the Orkney Isles and moving down the east coast of Scotland. Some run the Helmsdale, some the Brora and some the Conon, Ness and Spey and Tay and other waters round the east coast of Scotland, including the Tweed. These are the springers and the earliest of them appear in Ness and Tay by Christmas. When fishing opens on Tay in mid January, for instance, there are always fresh fish to be caught right through the river and in the Loch above, which is over 50 miles (80km) from the sea. True, these early fish are not plentiful, and after the first burst of fishing they disappear, possibly being fished out in some pools; but they run steadily throughout the spring, through January and February when Spey and Tweed bring fish in, through March when they run in increasing numbers, and into what you and I would call spring in May. The amazing thing is that batches of fish stop sea feeding at the same time, leaving millions of salmon still feeding, and return to the river. But this is not all. These fish return to the river of their birth, and probably to the pool of their birth to spawn. It is one of the great sagas of Nature.

Spring fish are highly prized in the angling world. They are solid and well formed and are usually taken in a very fresh condition. They are also taken first during the season and they are fished for in conditions which are far from spring-like. My happiest memories of fishing for spring salmon are in ice and snow, in crisp frosty weather and in lashing sleet. One April day on the Thurso hail was beating down, but the day fished well and I had three excellent salmon on the fly on beat fifteen below the bridge at Loch More.

I can remember my springers far more clearly than I can my summer fish. The long Sutherland pool was whipped into a storm by the upstream wind and the snow which came on and blew horizontally as I backed the pool up. On my second time through I hooked a twelve pounder – a magnificent feeling.

Springers run slowly in the cold waters of the early season, but they run far, going right up into the headwaters of the river system and lying there, safe, we hope, in holes in the bed of the moorland stream, or unnoticed in a loch. They remain there until the autumn comes, and in November they spawn.

The extraordinary fact that the salmon does not eat at all from the time it leaves its ocean feeding grounds until it returns again to the sea after spawning, presuming that it survives, is often talked about. Some 5 per cent of salmon survive the return to the river, the long wait, the spawning, and the descent of the river. It is an incredible time to spend without feeding. In fact the fish cannot feed; its digestive tract is in a state of atrophy when the fish makes the return to the river. This is without doubt the most perplexing thing to the newcomer to game fishing. How can a salmon which cannot eat naturally be tempted to take bait or fly? The club rooms of Britain have grown tired of debating this, but the fact remains. Salmon on their return to the river can be tempted to take a fly, a spun bait, a spoon, a prawn or a similar lure. Some behavioural impulse is possibly responsible for the salmon at least taking the fly into its mouth.

Interestingly, the salmon behaves as if it were two different fish when it returns to the river. At first it is rather like a sea fish, running the full flood of the river and showing when it arrives in a pool. This spree lasts for a few days and during that spree, if salmon rest in your pools or take up residence, they are not difficult to catch. But leave them for a couple of weeks and the bright silver sheen tarnishes and the fish changes its whole personality. It becomes difficult to tempt, it seems to be fitful and it splashes about in a restless way. Yet, from time to time when conditions are right, it will rise to the fly like a trout. In warm

13

conditions, the salmon almost seems to relive its own early years as a parr in the river. It rises to small flies fished near the surface of the river.

In a biological sense, the return to the river brings a most complicated behavioural package in the salmon. Experience and study give you some clues to the fish's behaviour, but we are still very much in the dark in explaining the salmon's reasons for taking or not taking lures. I believe my own fishing has been greatly helped by thinking of the salmon as a sea fish when it is in fresh water for the first few days, still ready to take large lures and flies and still remembering the flashing, darting food of the ocean. The salmon which has been in the river for some weeks, however, is best thought of as a fitful, restless parr and should be fished for as if it had reactions not unlike a trout.

Salmon congregate on the redds (spawning beds) in mid autumn and they spawn, often noisily and splashily on the thin gravel reaches of the hill streams. Some salmon penetrate to what are little more than hill drains. There their eggs are fertilised and hatch in something over a hundred days, producing an alevin like a trout. The alevin becomes a fry and darts about, also just like a trout. For two or three years the fry, known now as parr lives the life of a small trout and looks and behaves rather like one. There are subtle differences, of course, as anglers need to know, since it is illegal to take a salmon parr while trout fishing. The temptation is probably highest for a boy, who might want to keep the 6in (15cm) 'trout' he has caught. Parr are slimmer than trout, bluer in colour and have distinct bars or finger markings on the flanks. The tail is more forked than a trout.

Differences between salmon parr and small trout

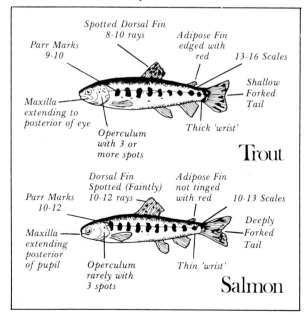

But these are fine details; there is no doubt that small trout and salmon parr look alike. One thing I learned as a boy was that if you hooked a small fish and lifted it out of the water on the leader, parr would wriggle and shake all the way up to the hand, but trout would usually curl their tails stiffly round to the side and hang motionless while they were being hoisted. Not a very scientific distinction, but a ready rule of thumb for a boy without very much experience of fish. If in doubt, of course, please return the fish to the river. A trout the size of a parr is too small to take anyway, and a parr the size of a trout will, if properly returned to the water perhaps produce a 20 pounder in a couple of years time.

Parr turn into smolts in the spring of the year in which they descend the river. The fish becomes silvery and the parr marks almost disappear. The fish shoal in the pools and make the hazardous trip down to the sea. Some are taken by birds, and some by pike and other fish as they go. Some are killed in the turbines of hydro-plants and some get into shallow water and become stranded. What a loss it is to get parr to the 6in (15cm) stage and then lose them. It is not known what the parr do when they reach the sea. At that point we lose track of them and they make that astonishing journey from the river to the distant ocean feeding ground which they have never seen. No matter how scientific one is about the migration, this point always seems to have an aura of magic in it. A returning salmon has a powerful body, and it has two years of sea sense to guide it. It can outswim many of its enemies. But the parr is a tiddler . . . yet it gets there. Without that remarkable journey the whole cycle would be broken and the salmon would die out.

There have been some interesting experiments in rearing salmon in freshwater, and recently in saltwater, from the smolt stage. I was once told to fish a little loch in western Sutherland near the Kirkaig river where some parr, not more than a bucketful, had been put in at smolt stage over a year earlier. There was no outlet from this loch and it was little fished. I fished it as if for trout, and I caught one of these landlocked salmon parr. It was a beautiful fish – slim and hard and coloured like a little sea trout. It weighed about 1lb (½kg) – not a great weight for a fish which can put on 10lb (4½kg) in a year at sea. Parr will grow as fast as the best trout and, because of their vigour, will probably outfeed the trout. Given an adequate food supply (and that is a very tall order) a parr will put on in captivity something approaching its sea weight. Salmon farming in the sea does produce well formed, but usually small, grilse of 3

Above: This fish was taken fresh in to the river from the sea and the marks of its freshness, the sea lice, are clearly seen on its flanks just above the ventral fin (Jens Ploug Hansen)

Right: These two fish were taken successively from the Junction Pool of the Tweed at Kelso. The larger fish weighed 19lb (8.6kg) and the smaller fish, a fresh run grilse, weighed 5lb (2.3kg) (Michael Shepley)

to 5lb (1.4 to 2.3kg) in this time and there is every reason to believe that the science of salmon farming will one day produce growth rates similar to those of the natural ocean environment.

A salmon may return to the river after only one winter of sea feeding. At this stage it is called a grilse. I had a grilse on my trout rod quite recently. It was a beautifully shaped fish, 4¾lb (2.2kg) and shaped like a mature salmon save for the slightly slimmer wrist above the tail and the slightly forked tail. It still had a whisper of the parr about it. Grilse are marvellous sport on the trout rod. They are great runners and jumpers and often break loose. On salmon tackle, with the big double-handed rod and the heavy line, the fish cannot show its paces properly. Of course, you cannot predict when the next salmon take will be a 5lb (2.3kg) grilse and when it will be a 20lb (9kg), high-backed fresh fish. You would have a long and hair-raising party with a twenty pounder on a trout rod.

Some salmon remain at sea for two winters and return to the river as small springers of 7lb (3.2kg) or so in say March of the year after they might have returned as grilse. Some salmon take longer to grow at sea and may return after their fifth winter at sea as forty pounders. The average size of springers varies from river to river, but my own experience is that springers tend to be just below 10lb (4½kg) on average. In recent years I have noticed a drop-off in weights. I have seen fewer of the heavy springers on Tay and Spey, although there are small numbers of substantial fish still taken. I have never been present, for example, in my thirty years of salmon fishing, when a springer of over 30lb (13.6kg) was taken. I have seen a small number of fish between 25 and 30lb (11.3 to 13.6kg) come ashore and in the lower twenties there are correspondingly more. For me, any fish over 15lb (6.8kg) is a large salmon and in the three years up to the date of writing this book – to give you a gauge of size – my own best springer was 18½lb (8.4kg) – a memorable and most handsome fish.

Anglers speak a great deal of very large salmon and you might be forgiven for believing that the year was full of large fish. It is not. I was fishing the Tay at Murthly in the summer of 1979 and I was shown the lie behind the big rock where Miss Ballantyne caught her British record rod-caught salmon in 1922, weighing 64½lb (29.3kg). Every locality in Scotland (and Ireland) has its story of formidable fish taken on rod and line and often not properly recorded and therefore not taken as a record. I have no doubt that fifty pounders do exist today, and two or three have been taken on Tay in my lifetime, usually in autumn. A fish of that size is outstandingly big and anything over about 35lb (15.9kg) attracts very wide interest. Very large fish are extremely difficult to handle, especially at the end of the fight when they are tired, and you are tired and beginning to think that you might actually land the giant. I get worried when I see large tails weakly flapping during the end game. I saw one of my own largest salmon come in, absolutely beaten from the Bridge Pool at Kelso on Tweed. As it moved over a shallow sand and gravel bar it flapped its tail and the hook fell out of the worn holds instantly. Large fish usually live to tell the tale, if only for practical reasons – they are hard to get out.

The cycle of spawning, river life, ocean feeding and return is, like a chain, only efficient if it is unbroken. In fact it is slightly more complicated than that. We must have enough pairs of ripe salmon on the redds to keep the numbers up. Most river authorities carry out careful redd counts and on some of the Scottish rivers there are counters at salmon passes or dams. We are making very important strides in keeping records of the salmon, because in recent years it has become imperative

Returning a kelt, taken in early April, to the Teviot. After the salmon has spawned in freshwater, if it does not die in the process, it slowly makes its way back to the sea as an unclean fish – a kelt. These fish regain something of their original colour as they drop downstream, becoming 'well-mended' and they might be mistaken by the novice for fresh fish

to monitor the stock sizes, average weights and other indices of salmon survival. The salmon is under assault on the high seas where commercial netting is now being carried out on the feeding grounds, formerly undiscovered and undisturbed. International agreement has limited this high seas activity and one almost feels that reason has prevailed. Inshore, however, reason has not yet prevailed. Salmon have been taken commercially in several ways around the coasts and in the estuaries for as long as anglers have been fishing inland. Bag nets are set at fishing stations round the coast and in this form of fishing a leader guides passing salmon into the bag which is anchored just offshore. In the estuaries themselves, sweep netting is used to take salmon, and in some of the larger rivers like Tay and Tweed this form of netting is used in freshwater itself well up the watercourse. These traditional forms of netting salmon are carefully regulated by law and, although you will hear grumbling from time to time when anglers say their fish are being stolen, I think it is safe to say that the interests of coastal and estuary netsmen and rod fishers coincide. Drift netting in coastal waters is a new problem, however. In this form of fishing, large lengths of net are hung over likely areas of water through which salmon migrate and the fish gill themselves in the suspended net. There has been legislation to forbid this in Scottish waters since 1962 when the Hunter report* made a recommendation that this should be done. Unfortunately there is no legislative control of drift netting south of the Scottish border at the time of writing and this has the effect of allowing the Northumbrian netsmen to take salmon more or less *ad lib* while their colleagues just north of the border cannot.

It is generally accepted that drift netting must be controlled throughout the whole UK fishing area. Salmon breed in the river and are the subject of many conservation measures while they are in freshwater. Anglers and owners of fisheries and associations with special interests in the salmon keep a careful watch on the fish, carry out research directed towards its welfare, monitor and fight pollution and in general ensure that the rod and coastal net crop is of reasonable proportions. A drift netting boat is taking the river-bred fish, is depriving the traditional netting stations of their harvest, and is destroying the valuable river fisheries by taking their stock. A salmon is more valuable when it is caught in a river by an angler than when it is netted out at any point in its return. A rod fisher pays for his beat, employs gillies or boatmen, stays in a country area, supports the fishing tackle industry and, on average, pays possibly £20 per pound for the fish caught, when it is assessed as gross expenditure for the catch returned. The commercial value of salmon rises annually, but even at £4 per pound nowhere approaches the value to the community of the rod-caught fish. It is interesting to see how estuary nets and coastal netting interests have joined with angling interests in pressing for high-seas legislation. In my view the survival of the salmon lies in that direction.

Grayling and Char

Trout, sea trout and salmon form the great majority of game fishing. We could add grayling, which we will write something about later in the book, and that little known and little seen fish the char. Grayling are anglers' fish and do provide some skilful winter sport which complements the trout fishing of the summer, but stocks of grayling are limited in extent and seem to me to be on the decline. The grayling was widely introduced to waters in the nineteenth century and it has spread and established itself in several waters. It is common in Yorkshire, in the Teviot and lower Tweed, in the Tay, but more so in its tributary

*Scottish Salmon and Trout Fisheries, Command Paper No. 2096, HMSO, London (1962)

A bag of grayling taken on fly

the Isla, in the Nith and Clyde and in certain other rivers. The fish is a spring spawner and is seldom fit to catch before mid June. Ideally, grayling should be sought in clear winter weather. The fish is a salmonid, but its branch of the family, *thymallus*, is different in appearance and shape from trout. The fish reminds one more of a roach in its appearance. It is silvery to grey in colour and has a coarse scaly skin. A great dorsal fin dominates its profile. Sometimes when you are playing a grayling you will see it fighting through a stream with its dorsal fin erect and it is a most impressive sight. I have fished grayling in the wilds of Finnish Lapland and have had some tremendous tussles with fish of up to 4½lb (2kg), but these are exceptional. Most British grayling are under a pound (½kg). They are handsome fish with flecks of black dashes on their silver sides and with a delicately sculpted tail.

The char is a rare fish in the UK. It exists in certain deep lochs in Scotland and in the lakes of Cumbria, but it is a little encountered fish. Char belong to the family *salvelinus* and the British char are related to the *fontinalis*, the brook trout of North America, which we have described in a later section of this book. The Scottish char looks to me similar to the char I caught in the lakes and streams of Finnish Lapland, except that the Finnish char were very highly-coloured fish with red bellies, often tomato red, and with a scattering of yellow spots on the the flanks. The pectoral fins of char are piped in creamy white, producing a very handsome fish indeed.

Char in stillwater in Scotland spend most of their year feeding at great depths and indeed, I believe, are caught in Cumbrian lakes by using a lure trailed behind a boat and taken to a considerable depth by heavy lead weights. In June and July, however, in Scottish lochs you will see char dimpling the surface at dusk, especially if it is a very still evening. One night on the way home from fishing salmon in late May on Loch Maree my companion and I came across dimpling char and we were able to take two before the light fell away. They were smallish fish in the half-pound class, rather weak in the fight, but very handsome to take because of their colours. The vertical migration which takes place in early summer brings some good char up to anglers' lures and again on Loch Maree I have heard of a char of 3lb (1.4kg) taking a sea trout dap.

I had some splendid char up to 2lb (0.9kg) in weight in Lapland waters and they seemed to me to be great sport on trout flies. What I liked about these char was their naivete. They would take wet flies cast to them on still, glassy lochs just as readily as they would seize flies dropped on to runs in the tundra streams. Char also take small spinners and worms in Lapland, but they give their best sport on fairly light fly tackle. No one would seriously advocate char as a main part of the game fishing scene, but once in a decade you might be out on a Scottish loch in May or June and recognise the tiny dimpling rises of these fish. They can be exotic and memorable sport for a dusk hour. I encountered these tiny dimpling rises again when I fished forest ponds in Maine where the *fontinalis* rose at dusk, and at that moment Maine, USA, Loch Maree and the remote waters of Lapland were linked by that shy, exotic but memorable little fish.

Rainbow Trout

It would be impossible to leave the description of British game fish and their environment without mentioning our greatest import, the rainbow trout. The rainbow, *Salmo gairdnerii*, was brought to Britain in the late nineteenth-century and was stocked mainly in ponds and lakes in southern England but some were also introduced to rivers. Today, the rainbow is the foundation of our southern put-and-take stillwater fisheries. They are particularly suited to life in the ponds, reservoirs and lakes in the midlands and south of England, since rainbows have a higher tolerance

Left: **A good grayling taken on fly (Jens Ploug Hansen)**

of high water temperatures and of lower oxygen levels than brown trout. I have seen them rising vigorously in ponds in 70°F (21°C) water which would have either killed off, or sickened, brown trout. Rainbows have also the great asset of being very efficient protein converters, ie they show fast and substantial growth when there is food available for them to eat. In waters with very rich bottom food, such as midland and southern English reservoirs, where there is an environment which is alkaline producing good snails, shrimp, masses of fly life and other protein in the shape of coarse fish fry, rainbows grow to double figures of pounds. A growth of 7lb (3.2kg) in three years has been recorded in the British Isles. Certainly in waters with reasonable conditions, rainbows put on 2oz (57g) a month from March to August and with luck will continue an autumn growth rate which will produce a 1½lb (0.7kg) in the calendar year. Fish which grow like this obviously provide put-and-take trout fisheries with a most valuable, replaceable resource.

Rainbows breed in a few natural waters in the UK. Blagdon is one of them, but even in waters where natural breeding takes place the fisheries have to be stocked. Indeed, the success of stocked and managed fisheries in British stillwaters partly lies in the fact that the rainbows do not breed, and the stock, catch and death rate can be closely calculated. It becomes a crop, adjustable for average size of fish, age of fish, numbers of fish, etc. I very much enjoy fishing for rainbows around the 2lb (0.9kg) mark in the ponds and reservoirs of England, but for me it is a kind of holiday.

I travel south from my wilder waters in the north to have the chance to catch a few good-sized trout. But recently I was interested to meet a southern English angler who had a fat rainbow fishery on his doorstep and who was over the moon because of the fishing he was enjoying on the Mull of Kintyre on holiday – little dark ½lb (0.2kg) brownies. He said he was just a little bit tired of taking his limit of two pounders, as similar as peas in a pod. I didn't see it that way, but he reminded me of other anglers who had said something similar about rainbows. One member of the English fly fishing team said that he valued his Hebridean 12oz (340g) fish far more highly than his local rainbows, although the English fish were bigger. I am sure these anglers, and others like them, are just enjoying a break and are loving their short contact with wild fish. Or is there a quality which stock bred fish lose? I have always found stock bred fish reasonably hard to catch, often crafty and certainly very powerful. Are they like penned deer, as opposed to the rangy, timid, fickle, wild deer of the hills? I would not like to take this idea too far. Without the stocked rainbow, most of our English ticket fisheries would be non-existent, and without these fisheries, the revolution which has brought a million new fly fishers into the sport would hardly have taken place.

Rainbows have also been introduced to Scottish waters. Some waters have a good reputation for their stocked fish, but they are usually smaller in average size than those of English lakes. Lochs like Fitty, near Dunfermline, have developed good fisheries with stock mixed between browns and rainbows. Many ponds and reservoirs throughout Scotland use the rainbow as a stock booster. They have some excellent characteristics. They come into spawn in the spring and recover by the middle of the summer and provide excellent late fly fishing for trout which can last right into November.

Rainbows tend to remain virgin over their first two winters and this means that one can have early season fishing for trout in good condition which may run to over a pound (½kg). On Coldingham Westloch, near Berwick, I have had virgin two-year-old fish in early spring which weighed over 2lb (0.9kg). Brown trout are thin and weak and poor sport in the cold waters of April; a boost from vigorous fat rainbows of ¾ to 1lb (0.3 to 0.5kg) is most welcome.

In some Scottish waters rainbows show very poor or even negative growth rates because there is just not enough protein available to feed them. This clearly limits the kinds of environment into which rainbows can be introduced effectively. I was very much struck by this when I fished one or two small lochs on Speyside where rainbows of about 12oz (340g) had been introduced to acid

Two rainbow trout from a stocked lake in Suffolk. These fish are typical of the put-and-take rainbows which are now very common in ponds, lakes and reservoirs throughout England and Wales. The fish grow quickly and rise well to fly and, although not native to the British Isles, have adapted very well to the British habitat

lochs. For about a fortnight after introduction they were great fun, but we were just fishing out the stockies. Then, once the remainder of the fish had settled down, they became very difficult to catch, and probably were trying to get such food as they could on the bottom. I caught two rainbows simultaneously on one of these lochs, one from this year's stocking, as it were, and one from last year's. This year's fish was 12oz (340g), silvery and fat and full of life. Last year's fish was about the same size, but thinner, dark in colour, weak and in poor shape. Rainbows fade away in Scottish lochs, unless the waters are especially favoured with heavy food concentrations – there are some like that, but most are unsuitable for rainbows, in my opinion as an angler.

Rainbows have earned themselves the name of being disappearing fish. You stock several hundred in year one and you catch a percentage of them. In year two you get a small percentage of better fish, but nothing like the proportion you would have reaped from a stocking of brown trout. In year three you catch almost none of the original stocking. The ones you do catch are big, often astonishingly so. In Portmore loch near Edinburgh, where there is a mixed fishery of high quality, the big rainbows which come in from time to time are 7lb (3.2kg) or more in weight and are often as fat as barrels.

Some of the big rainbows I have seen in Portmore loch, near Edinburgh, and elsewhere suffer from fin rot, blindness and general wear – all possibly just manifestations of old age. Yet brown trout which are older – albeit smaller – do not show these weaknesses. Rainbows, it seems to me, grow faster, live shorter lives, degenerate sooner and seem to have a short life and a fat and merry one.

Rainbows are at their best in their first two years of life, with possibly a third year added for the larger fish we take on stillwater. After that, the fish go down, become bottom feeders, grow huge and provide only a minimum of contact with anglers. Brown trout may live to be seven years of age or more. They, too are capable of fast growth when circumstances are right. In Scotland we know of lochs which will put on 12oz (340g) a year, but in general a few ounces a year is all you can expect.

Rainbows also disappear by migrating. They escape from ponds and lakes wherever possible and they are sometimes caught miles from their pond of origin. We pick them up in Spey, obviously escaped from some local pond, usually upstream. I wonder whether a breeding stock will be established in Scottish rivers as a result. There are breeding stocks of rainbows in various English rivers, including the Dove in Derbyshire. We know that rainbows are breeding in the feeder streams of the Lake of Menteith. The establishment of a breeding fishery – a wild fishery – in lochs and rivers of Scotland would be of great interest. I have caught wild rainbows in the waters of New York State where they had been planted (they are originally from the Pacific-flowing waters of British Columbia) and these fish were about ¾lb (0.3kg), were thinner and wilder looking than stew-bred fish, and were excellent fun to catch. While I am wary about tampering with the environment by introducing a new fish to a Scottish loch and river system, I take the view that this has happened, willy nilly, and the prospect of a resident stock in Spey or Tay is intriguing. One thing is certain, they will be very different fish from the rainbows from fish farms, which are to wild fish what 'caponised' chickens are to pheasants in the field.

A final note on the environment in which game fish thrive. I cannot think of any case where the whole area has not improved because of the development of a game fishery. Attitudes to the land surrounding the fishery improve when there are trout in the loch or pond; trees are planted, litter is cleared, a new keenness comes into conserving the natural wildlife and to getting the surroundings of the fishery into tune with the sport. Where a wild fishery is loved and cherished, the countryside code is firmly established, but the whole development is geared towards people enjoying the place and the sport. It is true that game fish and natural beauty are inseparable, but part of the beauty is the care and intelligence man puts into making his fisheries work. This is equally true of a trout stream in a Highland glen where the wild resource is cared for in the idiom relevant to the environment just as it is for the stocked pond. As I see it, game fish in addition to being a great pleasure to catch, are a social catalyst encouraging interest in, and benefiting our countryside. The care of game fisheries is linked with vigorous campaigns against pollution of rivers and lakes, is associated with wide conservation schemes and is part of the better use of leisure time in our countryside. We are lucky to have the resource to develop in Britain and I hope our attitudes to game fishing go on developing as they have been doing for many years. Our game fisheries are the envy and admiration of other countries which have allowed their natural environment to become wasted. If we are vigilant and practical we will maintain this lead and it is partly towards this aim that this book has been written.

Fishing sedge at dusk on a summer evening on Gladhouse Reservoir, near Edinburgh

Section Two
Catching Trout

Introduction

It is not so very long ago since trout fishing, to the average angler in England, meant 'game fishing'. It meant exclusive fly fishing in restricted, highly-preserved waters for a fish generally regarded as out of reach of the ordinary man. One thinks of the exclusive chalk stream fisheries of Hampshire and the reputation of rivers like the Test and the Itchen when one looks back the twenty or thirty years to what now seems to me to have been another world. It is true that there was rougher and much more accessible fishing for trout in the dales of Yorkshire and in other rivers of the north of England. There were rivers in Devon and lakes and rivers in Wales which ordinary mortals fished, but the flavour of trout fishing as sport in England up to the opening of the new stillwater fisheries in the midlands was one of exclusiveness and inaccessibility and privilege.

This tradition never affected Scotland or Ireland. There the natural, prolific local fish was the trout, backed up by the sea trout and the salmon. In Scotland it was, and still is, the coarse fisher who is the eccentric. In Scotland the term 'going fishing' usually means going fly fishing for trout. But the picture has changed a great deal on both sides of the border. In England there are still the highly-preserved chalk stream fisheries, but trout fishing elsewhere has been democratised. The development of reservoirs, ponds and natural lakes as stocked trout fisheries has brought a great range of high-quality trout fishing on to the market and this has opened up the sport to what one might call converted coarse fishers, with one's tongue in one's cheek, and to an army of newcomers to the sport.

The revolution has gone further, however. The quality of trout, both browns and rainbows, which the English reservoirs produce, is far above the quality of the wild fish grown in Scotland. If that is too strong an argument, at least few would deny that the average size of the English reservoir fish is larger than stillwater fish in Scotland. The environment is, of course, different, and that may be a very important consideration for some trout fishers, but nobody could deny the brilliance of the sport which has been brought to the local English angler in the stillwater fisheries of the midlands and the south-east. A line of testimony might not be out of place here; I was born, bred and schooled as a Scottish trout, sea trout and salmon fisher, but I did have the opportunity of living and working in south-eastern England for a couple of seasons and of getting to know a number of the new stillwater fisheries in the area. The sport I had was terrific and I learned a great deal about trout which no Scottish water could have taught me. I developed techniques of fishing which have affected both my trout and my sea trout fishing in

Scotland since. In a kind of reverse migration, I now go south in May or June to pick up some really good trout fishing in Ardleigh or Hanningfield or Grafham. I go on loving my lochs and rivers and I am on them as often as I can possibly manage, but I recognise that I am dealing, in Scotland, with a different kind of fishing resource. Trout are wilder and smaller. The waters are different in setting and chemistry; the weather is different and the fish behave in a different way. In the section of this book which follows, I will try to characterise the whole range of trout fishing, and I shall try to present it as a non-exclusive sport, because that is what the picture is, for those with eyes to see.

Trout in Flowing Water

Trout thrive in streams and rivers throughout Europe and North America wherever there is reasonably clean water, well oxygenated, and a food supply adequate for the demands of the fish. In many ways the trout in a stream is the typical fish, although in Scotland there are far more fish in stillwater than in flowing water. Trout like fast flowing water and they are well adapted to dealing with shallow varied streams where rushes and glides and pools succeed each other. They will happily live in 6in (15cm) of water where the current pours and swirls round stones. In this fast, streamy and often fairly infertile environment, they pick up two main kinds of food, in the form of snails, shrimps and other items of a similar kind, and stream-borne food such as the nymphs of flies and the hatching and hatched flies themselves. Bottom food is either inimitable, or rather difficult to match – although I have various shrimp imitations in my fly boxes – and fly fishing as we understand it is really concerned with the aquatic fly as it nears and performs its hatching stages.

When we think about flowing water we give ourselves wide scope. There are the Scottish rivers like Don, Tay and Tweed where there are good heads of trout rising in the streams and glides and pools; the smaller waters of Scotland and the north of England, Wales and Devon where the fish thrives and provides interesting and often very challenging sport with delicately fished flies. There are the famous chalk streams of Hampshire and Wiltshire where clear water glides through the water meadows, and trout of considerable size rise fastidiously to surface flies, giving the dry fly fisher his biggest challenge. Elsewhere, in quite unlikely streams sometimes, in canals (which are really stillwater) and in field drains and in the most unlikely places, trout crop up. I used to be fascinated by the conduit which links Loch Katrine and Glasgow. For probably 30 miles (48km) this great stone channel runs, bringing Glasgow its water. Much of this conduit is roofed in to provide a vast stone pipe some 10 feet (3m) in diameter. In that pipe you will find a population of trout some of which must spend much of their lives in gloom.

Fishing for trout in flowing water is broadly divided into two parts. You can fish your fly wet, that is in the water, or you can fish it dry, that is floating on the surface of the water. The wet fly broadly covers the underwater stages of the development of the aquatic fly – the larvae and the nymphs. These nymphs hatch by crawling out of the stream or by rising up through it to cast their final shucks or skins and emerge as the mature insect. Trout feed heavily on the underwater stages of flies and traditional methods of wet fly fishing broadly imitate them. It is interesting that some of the methods of wet fly fishing imitate underwater food in an unscientific way, eg. local trout fishers have found certain types and colours of wet fly effective when presented in a certain manner to trout. Traditions are founded on happy accidents. For example, in Scotland we have fancy flies dressed with silver and gold tinsel and red tags and colours not easily found in natural insects. Some of these fancy flies are astonishingly consistent takers of fish. Occasionally, one finds that a fly which seems dressed in this way, turns out to be imitating some insect or a stage of that insect's development in a most effective way. For example, the Blae and Black has a red tail. Fancy? In a way, yes. But also accurate when you think of it as the reddish shuck of the chironomid trailed by the emerging nymph. A red-tailed fly may after all be imitative.

Where Trout Lie

Before we talk about tactics and tackle, something must be said about trout lies. The fish do not lie randomly over the width and up and down the length of the stretch of river you are fishing. Trout take up lies for physical reasons – to shelter them from the fast water which would require considerable energy to cope with – and for good feeding reasons. Much of the food a trout finds is borne to the fish by the stream. The trout which has the most strategic lie will gain most. That is why you find trout lying in streams often in the shelter of boulders, or where the natural configuration of the bed gives them an area of respite from the force of the water, yet keeps them well to the fore in taking the bounty the water brings down.

There is a hierarchy in streams. The fattest

(Jens Ploug Hansen)

trout is likely to have the fattest place. Indeed, if you are skilful and lucky, you might fish steadily upstream and take several fish from a stream going up in quality as you progress. I did this once, unforgettably, on a stream in the lower Thurso. I was dry fly fishing with a small Tup's Indispensible parachute fly and I picked up a brace of half pounders at the stream tail. Then, in a flurry of sport I took a series of fish on the same fly, steadily getting better in quality as I went upstream. The fish all turned downstream when I hooked them, obligingly not disturbing the water above. I took twelve in a short time, and the best fish was a marvellous trout of 1¾ lb (0.8kg). I have never matched this hour of glory since, but the principle remains. Trout lie where it is most advantageous for them to do so and the best fish lie in the most productive food-bearing places. Remember too, that when you have taken a good trout from a known lie today, you might well expect to take another from it tomorrow since trout are great opportunists and will fill a vacant place in the food hierarchy as soon as it becomes vacant.

There are typical lies which you soon become familiar with. Let me mention a few. Boulders provide a quiet area of water behind them, and trout lie there, not so much in the totally sheltered water, as in the insides of the shelter, hard against the stream. They dart into the stream to pick up morsels of food as they pass. When the boulder is submerged, trout still lie behind it in a similar way, but it is far more difficult to read the pattern of the lies from the surface mark of the boulder. Wading a stream is excellent training. How often one finds that the boil on the surface of a stream relates to a submerged boulder several feet upstream of the surface mark. The whole of the river is affected by this visual lag. What we see on the surface has to be repositioned to give us an accurate map of the stream bed. Reading a stream like this, and in other ways, is a vital part of the successful trout angler's art. It would require a whole series of illustrated discussions to provide a primer for reading a river and even then, the teaching of the art would be far better learned through experience, especially wading and fly fishing a trout stream. One special facet must however be mentioned here before we go on. A stream presents us with waves. At first sight you might think that these waves are merely the result of water flowing quickly, and that is at least half true. But waves on a fast stream themselves form a pattern of standing waves and these affect where trout lie. Standing waves apply pressure to, say, a gravel bed at different points down the length of the run. These pressure points clear gravel and form a slightly wavy bed. Trout can lie in the hollows of the bed, in comparative shelter, harboured in the dip.

Trout lie in places which are food-bearing. Thus, you will find trout downstream of a tributary bringing in extra food. In some cases food can be concentrated in one place by the stream itself, especially where the force begins to go out of the run and eddies and pools are formed. Look for concentrations of food, such as nymphs, in backwaters where the surface looks glassy. A glassy surface means higher surface tension and consequently, more difficult conditions for the nymphs to break through. Trout move about in glassy areas picking up gummed nymphs. These areas

are equivalent to slicks in lochs which we will talk about in the stillwater section of this book.

Finally, remember that food can be blown on to rivers. Wind can funnel down on to pools and can carry flies from bankside vegetation. I have seen winged ants brought down on to rivers like this in summer. Moths and heather insects are common windborne food. The great gnat, the Jenny longlegs, can arrive tantalisingly on lochs and rivers by the agency of wind, and no reading of a river should ignore this source of food.

Trout like one further thing in choosing a lie – security. Danger comes from above in the trout's life, either in the form of birds or marauding animals or, quite simply, man. A lie which is perfect in every way, but is vulnerable or easily disturbed will not be tenanted. A lie under bushes, or close to one's own sheer bank where access and casting are difficult is a certain bet for a good fish. The clearer and gentler the water, the harder it is to approach trout. In the limestone streams of the Pindus in Greece, for instance (to take an exotic example) you can see trout in the pools in an embarrassingly clear way. A seen trout is often an uncatchable trout. The water between angler and

Downstream wet fly fishing for trout at Westerdales on the Thurso River, Caithness (Michael Shepley)

the trout acts as a curtain, and the rougher the water the better the angler's cover. In gentle, clear glides one has to take avoiding action, one must wade delicately and fish delicately with as long a line as one can handle if trout are to be tempted.

Wet Fly Fishing

Basic Tackle

The fundamental requirements of a wet fly trout rod are that it can cast the line effectively, control the flies properly as they fish, and can play the fish you hook. A multitude of rods in natural fibres like cane, and synthetic fibres like glass or the newer carbon fibre will carry out these functions well. I like to choose rods which have multiple functions. To be practical, a rod, for me, must double as a good river rod, a loch rod and a sea trout rod. I have described my loch tackle in detail in a later part of this section (*see* p.80), my preference being for a rod of built cane, 9ft 6in (2.90m) in length, and of two-piece construction. This is not the most delicate trout rod, although it is beautifully made and is a highly sophisticated instrument. It is a strong rod, and I am often delighted that it is. There is hardly a season when I do not encounter salmon on my trout rod in Scotland, and as for sea trout, they form a regular part of the fishing of flowing water each summer and autumn.

However, a built cane rod of the sort I am keen on is a heavy rod compared with glass and carbon fibre, it is a slow rod compared with the crisp action of the synthetic fibres and it is now a much more expensive item of tackle than glass, but not yet so dear as carbon. Yet the weight in one's hand is useful. I like the slower unrolling of the loop in casting that you get with cane and I particularly like the progressive action of built cane. Some glass rods and carbon also bend and keep on bending into fish as if they would never stop. I regard over-bending of a rod when it is under strain as a serious weakness. It becomes most apparent when you suddenly find yourself hooked into a larger than average fish. I have had glass rods in the 8ft 6in (2.59m) class – delightful to handle, accurate, light and delicate – but in a good trout or sea trout they bend so easily into the fish that they allow the fish to play you rather than the reverse. These rods are also nice casters until you meet a good-going wind. You try to press them to punch the line into the wind and they cannot do it. However, they were never really built for this type of specific function, or to cover a wide range of functions. One should, if possible, tackle up with a rod which

Searching out lies with wet fly on the Gowna River, Connemara, Ireland (Michael Shepley)

has more than one function, and can travel with you from Grafham, where there are huge trout, to a Highland loch where there are quarter pounders, and give you sport. That rod will also handle the salmon which will rise to you in the Highland river or loch and it will do it without causing you anxiety.

I travel with two 9ft 6in (2.90m) rods in my car, a Pézon et Michel Sawyer *Stillwater* (now produced by Farlow-Sharpe) – a built cane rod of the highest quality, and a Webley *Grilse* which is a grand reservoir rod, better in my environment than the *Lake* which is 3in (8cm) shorter. The Webley is a glass rod with a spiggot ferrule and it does marvellous things for me in ordinary and in extreme conditions on the river.

I have avoided a very wide description of all the rods and types of design available today. Throughout the book I will refer, rather, to the rods in my hand. I hope this practical and non-technological approach will help readers new to fishing to choose their rods well. Clearly everybody will not want a Sawyer *Stillwater* – and they are both scarce and expensive today, but there are many two-piece cane rods, for example in the Sharpe's range of *Scottie* rods, which will come close to the Sawyer. There are multitudes of two-piece glass rods available, and in every tackle shop there are people to help you choose one. Choose nothing gimmicky, and be guided by someone who can cast competently and who knows his watercraft. Above all, choose something you can handle. Cane is heavy and may not suit someone with weak wrists, for example.

Reels again have several clear and essential functions. Reels store the fly line and its backing, they give off line to your hand when you pull line off for casting, or they give off line to fish when they run and take it. Thus your reel must have the capacity to hold a modern fly line and must have a check system which will allow the drum to be rotated quickly in giving line to a fish without over-running and causing a tangle. Reels also reel in, recovering line, say when a fish is being played. A reel which can recover quickly is a boon. Some reels on the market have a multiplying action – a geared up recovery – and I have several times found this to be very useful. But I have no doubt that I would start a new trout fisher on a single action reel, say 3½in (9cm) in diameter, carrying a No. 6 floating line with 70yd (64m) of braided terylene backing. The width of the drum will govern how much line can be carried and how quickly the recovery may be made. Beware of very narrow drums in these days of bulky floating lines. Beware of heavy reels – antiques from the brass and gunmetal days. Once again this is a topic I will return to again in the stillwater fishing section and elsewhere and these first specifications are intended to be introductory.

Lines for basic trout fishing are best restricted to one. Choose a double taper line, AFTM (Association of Fishing Tackle Manufacturers) No. 6, floating, any colour you care – the trout take just as well on a white or orange line, as on a sober brown one.

Nylon for making up fly casts and the various terminal tackles you may need in basic fly fishing is readily available and as far as I can see there are no outstandingly bad brands on the market. I have several times in this book mentioned that I have fished with Luxor *Kroic* for close on twenty years and I have no complaints to make. It is consistent in quality, is easily knotted, has a good breaking strain for diameter and, in brief, does everything I ask of it in a full gamefisher's year. Perhaps the best piece of advice on using nylon monofilament is to be profligate. Do not hesitate to scrap old tackle, especially leaders with wind knots in them or little kinks or whitish or silvery patches or roughness felt with the fingers. Nylon is cheap compared with the loss of a good trout or salmon.

In basic trout wet fly fishing we make up casts or leaders with three flies, or two. This means that when the nylon of the right weight has been selected – say 5lb (2.3kg) or even 6lb (2.7kg) strain

– a dropper must be added to the length. To do this, cut the nylon at the appropriate place, which, for me with a 3yd (3m) leader is 1yd (1m) below the attachment to the line, and tie a blood knot (*illustrated*), leaving the upper end of the nylon as a tail out of the middle of the knot. This tail is your dropper. Again I use the blood knot and have done so for all my fishing life. It holds fish well and is simple to tie. Master the knot once and it will serve you for a lifetime.

The cast can easily be attached to the fly line by a tucked sheet bend (*illustrated*) tied through a double overhand loop (*illustrated*). This is a slightly clumsy line-to-leader arrangement, and we will make other suggestions later, but for basic trout fishing for downstream wet fly work, it is thoroughly reliable and fishes well.

The choice of flies is more complicated, but let me, at this basic stage, cut through the vast array of flies and say that in rough-stream trouting you could fish all year with a Greenwell, a silver or gold bodied fly like the Dunkeld (gold) and a Black spider or a red spider for the bob. Give me a Greenwell No. 12 and a Black Spider No. 14, or be generous and give me these patterns in both 12 and 14 and I will fish right through the season with confidence on any stream in Britain, except the chalk streams of Hampshire and the south.

In this first discussion of tackle I have tried to be practical and down to earth. Interestingly, as I fish on and add yet more years of experience, I find myself narrowing the tackle I use, rather than expanding it. I do happily fish with a very limited range of flies, and I do actually find that I have one favourite rod and one back-up. Naturally there are circumstances in which I do use other tackle, but it is my view that the basic art and the basic tackle are capable of a whole range of sophisticated fishing uses. What the man adds to the tackle is critical, of course, and I hope this book adds cunning to every reader's hand.

The Basic Art

To fish wet fly well, you must think like a trout in a stream. The fish is poised, waiting for the stream to bring it down a variety of food. Tiny morsels like the nymph of an olive appear in the trout's field of vision – its 'window' – and present a kind of instant opportunity of the 'There it is; it's gone' variety. I liken it to playing tennis with a real hitter and getting up to the net. You can see some of the shots, but you can't react quickly enough. Trout must often miss food in this way and indeed, when you are fishing fast water you are often conscious of trout turning after missing your fly and having a second go at it.

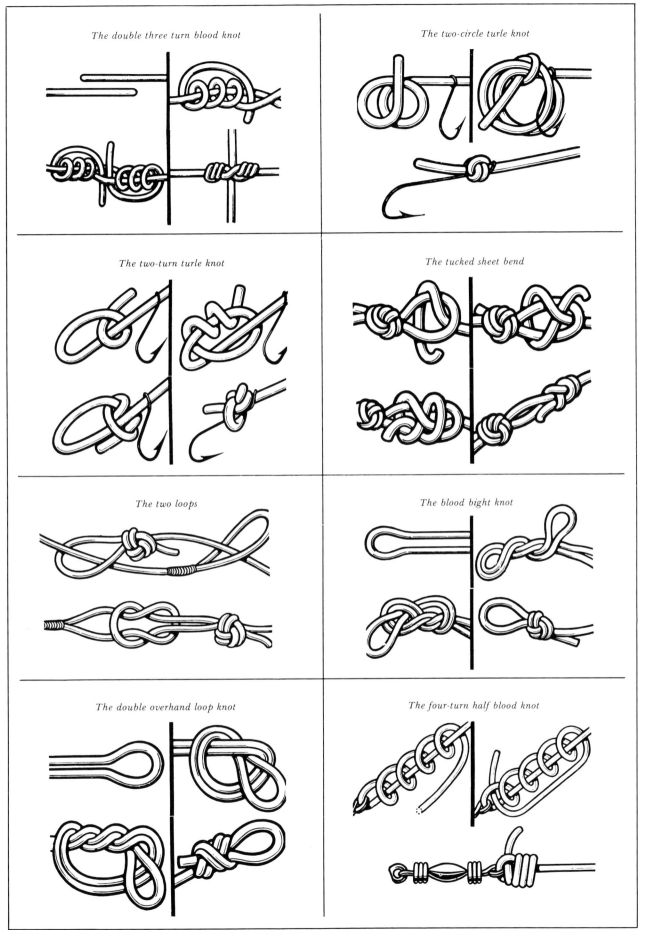

The double three turn blood knot

The two-circle turle knot

The two-turn turle knot

The tucked sheet bend

The two loops

The blood bight knot

The double overhand loop knot

The four-turn half blood knot

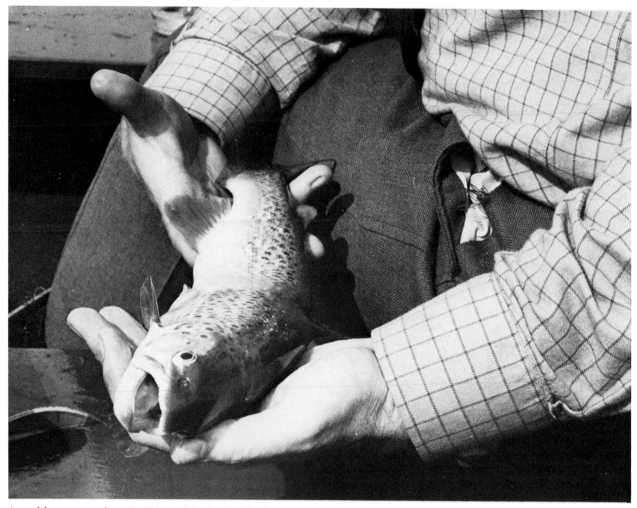

A good brown trout from Packington fisheries. Packington provide excellent stocked stillwater fishing, typical of the new pond and lake fisheries of central and southern England (Michael Shepley)

A trout in a stream does not have much time to see the details of the food borne down to it. It will sometimes rise to bits of debris, to seeds or flotsam and take them as food. I've watched this from trees above rivers and from bridges. I am always struck by the shortness of time between a take and an ejection, especially in fast water. In presenting a wet fly to a trout, I do not think pattern is as important as in dry fly fishing where the trout has plenty of time to inspect the fly. What is important is size, general colour and above all, the behaviour of the fly in the stream.

The basic art is to cover the likely water with your team of flies, swimming them down and across the water, and trying to get the hooks home when a trout rises to the flies as they pass. Clearly, downstream wet fly fishing is not a very demanding art. The water does much of the work for you. It conceals you; it straightens out your bad casts; it swings the flies over the trout. In some cases the force of the stream will hook the trout for you. My very first trout on fly, taken as a boy,

illustrated the ease of doing things right. My rod was adapted from a long garden cane, my line was attached to the rod top, my cast of three flies was thrown out over a fast stream and I let the stream swim the flies round as I kept in touch by raising my rod top. About half-way down the stream after several casts, I saw the most beautiful flash in the water and I raised my rod and was into what turned out to be a splendid trout of 1¼lb (0.6kg). It seemed so easy and so satisfying. I shall not tell you how long it was until I caught a trout of similar quality and sincerity!

The trout will teach you a lot about how to fish for them. For instance, you will find that trout in a stream will often take a great interest in the bob fly just as it is emerging from the water. Watch for this. Trout rising to the bob do so in a fast sudden arc of a rise and you have to be alert to hook them. It is a little easier to hook fish on a longer line when it is sweeping round in a stream. The fish which actually gets to your flies (some miss) may well pull or pluck hard at them, and you may find that merely raising the rod is all that is required to hook them well. Downstream wet fly fishing produces many splashes and plucks and tugs, which result in nothing more. But these offers do remind one to keep closely in contact with one's flies at all times. I am a great advocate of keeping the line running between your right forefinger and the rod butt and handlining with your left hand by pulling in a foot or a yard of line, as your recovery requires, as you fish. Try to feel the flies in the water and keep your rod top low enough for good line feel in the water. Then when a trout takes, you will feel it at once, and be able to react to the take by raising the rod and sending the hook home in a gentle, but positive and quick strike.

Reading water helps to locate fish, but it also helps you to fish your flies well. A fly which is dragged off course across a stream may excite splashes or plucks, but these are usually the smaller fish and are usually not hooked. The angle you present your flies at affects the speed of the fly across the stream. The angler who casts 'square' across a stream will get maximum drag on his flies and will probably hook least fish. The greater the angle downstream, the slower will your flies cross the lies. Clearly, the ability to cast out reasonable lengths of line affect how well you can cover lies and will affect how steadily and effectively you can control your flies over the fish. Equally, when you can control your line and prevent the force of the stream sweeping it and your flies away indiscriminately, you vastly increase your chances of covering fish well and hooking them when they rise to you.

There are two ways of slowing down the sweep of the line. The first is to hold your rod top up and keep the belly of the line off the fast water near you. This is simple, but is remarkably effective. I do it a lot in salmon fishing for much the same reason as I suggest it for trout fishing; to control the fly in a reasonably slow way over the trout. We want a slowish fly to try to give the trout the impression that it can get hold of the morsel. Yet the fly must swim over the trout. Flies which skate on the surface may sometimes be wildly attractive to trout, but are generally frightening to the fish. Flies which whip across streamy water will just not be seen. Trout in streamy water will often rise to flies which break the rules of the river. A natural fly is swept down with the current and follows the vagaries of the stream as it does so. Our cast of wet flies cannot do this effectively in downstream wet fly conditions. The line holds them back. Trout will often rise to flies hung in the stream over the fish, and even will come to flies moved upstream against the

Well hooked on the wet fly (Jens Ploug Hansen)

current by handlining, doing something no natural fly could ever do.

Clearly in wet fly fishing we are not indulging in a precise art. It is sometimes called chucking and chancing it, and there is no doubt that it is sometimes just that. It is a relatively easy and generous method of trouting in rough water and most anglers do it. The finer arts of wet fly fishing include upstream wet fly fishing. You might see an angler wading up through the streams fishing a short line and repeatedly casting and lifting the rod top and casting again. The action of casting and retrieving in fastish streams is almost one continuous movement, and some Tweed upstream trout fishers look as though they are stroking the water with flies as they wade. Upstream wet fly allows the flies to cover the fish in a manner much nearer to the natural presentation of food. The flies come over the trout at the speed of the current and the fish has to respond to the presentation as fast as it would have to respond in nature. If a trout has to be fast, in upstream wet fly fishing, so do we. It is really very difficult to hook fish which take the upstream fly. A longer rod helps. The old Tweed fishers used to use 10 and 11ft (3.05 and 3.35m) rods because they gave them water coverage, and by raising the top, gave them much better control, including hooking control. Fishing an 11ft greenheart rod must have been a wrist breaker. What is a definite possibility is fishing an 11ft light glass rod or a carbon fibre rod, which is the lightest rod length for length available. Carbon fibre is also the dearest rod material, length for length.

One of the problems of upstream wet fly fishing is that it is very difficult to see the take sometimes. In the north of England, a tradition of fishing a spider bob fly which will float is used. In this way the dry bob works as a take indicator; when the bob jerks, strike.

Wet fly fishing becomes finer still when you fish nymphs. The nymph which interests us most is at the stage immediately before surface hatching. Excellent patterns of nymphs covering the most common flies can be bought in tackle shops. Nymphs are wingless, or have wing buds only. Indeed, many of the spider dressings we have enjoyed for generations must fairly represent nymphs. I like fishing nymphs to trout which I have seen feeding in glides, and in pools, although the nymph will work like a downstream wet fly in runs also. A nymphing fish rises but tends either not to break the surface at all, thus giving a kind of bulge, or breaks the surface with the back and dorsal fin only. Presenting a single nymph to a fish like this is a considerable art. The nymph must be accurately cast and must be made to puncture the surface film. I do this by giving the rod tip a little check or even a small upward movement just as the cast is unrolling. This accelerates the unrolling and flips the nymph through the surface. But the presentation does not stop there. The nymph must be quickly held at the right depth and must be moved over the fish in a lifelike way. To do this, one must use the angle of the rod and a judicious amount of handlining. This can only be mastered with experience. A detailed description of this comes later (*see* p.39).

Trout like flies which are swum over them, rather than washed over them. Ordinary wet flies fish quite well merely by being led by the head, or pulled over the trout. Nymphs can be fished much more subtly and can be washed down slowly to within a short distance of the trout, then checked and made to twitch, or head up weakly. Natural nymphs do behave like this. They get to the underside of the surface film, especially in still reaches and they cannot get through the film.

They may get their heads out but are trapped in their shucks and have to struggle for some time to get clear. At this stage they are very vulnerable and trout scoop them up. In our presentation of nymphs we must try to imitate as many of these nymph-like twitches and jerks as possible.

The basic arts of wet fly fishing, then, are presentation of the flies downstream and upstream and in nymphing. Clearly, the basic arts quickly merge into much more skilful fishing, and no easy line can be drawn (or ought to be). Possibly the basic arts rely more on the ability to cast a consistent and fairly accurate line, on developing a feeling for what the flies are doing in the water. It is vital to learn to read the water and to keep in touch with your flies.

Nymph Fishing
Reading about nymph fishing, as some anglers describe it, you would be forgiven for thinking that it is an art half-way between wet and dry. This is a misleading idea. Nymph fishing is wet fly fishing with its scientific hat on. It is a more precise presentation of more accurately dressed imitations of flies as they hatch, but it is an underwater art. You might really argue that wet fly fishing should have two divisions: deep wet fly fishing, where the larvae of the flies is imitated, and nymph fishing, where the flies are presented much nearer the surface in imitation of the nymph as it is about to emerge from the water and take up its brief aerial life. Anglers have, however, classified wet fly

(Jens Ploug Hansen)

Top right: **Fly fishing for trout in Lapland. The Juutuanjoki River, Inari. This river carries a run of very large lake trout which may reach 20lb (9kg) in weight**

Right: **A 6lb (2.7kg) brown trout from the Juutuanjoki River, Lapland. Given the right environment, brown trout can grow rapidly to substantial weights**

fishing much more traditionally. They have, in effect, said that wet fly fishing is the older, more conventional form of fishing flies at, or comparatively near, the surface; that there is a branch of this – sunk line fishing where flies are fished well down in the water, possibly even on the bottom and, finally, that there is nymph fishing where the finest representations of the hatching fly are made and the last stages of underwater life are represented.

This representation is a tackle-based one. We have a very long tradition of fishing fly-type lures under the surface. There is evidence of it in medieval Scotland, and throughout the trout regions of Europe one has little difficulty in tracing references to catching trout on sunk fly right up to industrial times. The tackle used for fishing fly below the surface was – taking the nineteenth century as a convenient starting point – a plaited horsehair line and a horsehair cast, either single or double, and the flies were themselves tied on to the leader as eyeless hooks (or tapered hooks) still are. The coming of silkworm gut revolutionised the tackle and made it more reliable and finer on a diameter-per-breaking-strain basis. It was in this era of development, roughly the mid-nineteenth century, that the anglers of the Tweed and, almost in the same season, the gentlemen anglers of the Test and Itchen began floating their flies.

There are some excellent descriptions of upstream wet fly fishing from the Borders around this time. Thomas Tod Stoddart‡ describes his upstream wet fly fishing and his gentle and natural revolution to floating flies in the Tweed and Teviot around this time. W C Stewart** leaves us in no doubt about his technique – fine upstream wet fly fishing, with options into dry fly as the conditions demanded. One could go on, but it is very clear that as tackle refined, and as leisure developed, standard wet fly fishing with the lures sunk became transformed into dry fly fishing because it was technically possible.

My argument, therefore, is that nymph fishing, in the form of more and more refined upper water wet fly fishing, was soundly in existence in the traditions of Scottish and English fly fishing which we find in the nineteenth century. It is easy to see, then, that fly fishing was wet, including heavy and light, or deep and near-surface, and it might have remained so classified but for the debates of the chalk stream fishers. There, once dry fly fishing had been established by great anglers like Hal-

ford*, the tradition became form and the form, as it so often does, became crystallised, almost fossilised, into a set of taboos. It is as though someone descended from a chalk mountain with tablets on which the three main laws were written: firstly, thou shalt cast to individual fish seen feeding; secondly, thou shalt float the fly over the trout on the surface; and, thirdly, the fly shall be a direct imitation of natural fly life being taken by the trout.

It was not until the early years of the 20th-century that G E M Skues† described the art of nymph fishing. But he described it as a chalk stream angler would. He fished well-stocked waters with big fish and he was used to clear waters and gentle streams. He was a leisured gentleman angler who would happily spend lots of time establishing the precise form of nymph or surface fly being taken by trout and he found his satisfactions in imitating this precisely. Thus, his form of nymph fishing was closely related to his chalk stream conditions, and while it looked like a revolution in chalk stream terms, it was only a more precise formulation of an art which has a long and distinguished history in Scotland, the North of England and Ireland. One has only to look at the type of fly used in certain areas of clear water, thin streams and wary trout to see that wet fly fishing in the North and in Scotland was often a fairly sophisticated form of nymph fishing. The upstream fly fishers of the Yorkshire streams flowing east from the Pennines have a style of upstream fly fishing which uses small lightly-dressed spiders which I have seen fished with delicacy and great effect on the upper waters of the Aire and the Ure. In Scotland, the anglers of the Clyde, fishing a river of great clarity in the hills above Lamington and Abington, developed a tradition of very small flies fished in dressings which are the lightest I have seen anywhere in the fly fishing world.

Perhaps I am protesting too much. I think I can identify the reason. I would like to de-mythologise nymph fishing and bring it back into good wet fly fishing so that one could not really tell where wet fly ended and nymph fishing began. In practice, that is how nymph fishing on flowing water is. We cast flies to showing fish in streams, or we search out lies where trout are likely to be. Our flies are fished near the surface and are presented in imitation of drifting, weakly-struggling hatching nymphs borne down by the current. When the

---

‡Thomas Tod Stoddart, *The Art of Angling as practiced in Scotland* (1835).
**W C Stewart, *The Practical Angler* (1857).

*See F M Halford, *Dry Fly Fishing in Theory and Practice* (1889).
†G E M Skues, 'Minor Tactics of the chalk stream' in *The Way of a Trout with a Fly* (1910).

nymph reaches the underside of the surface film, it might stick there – although rough water helps the fly to emerge quickly – and while the nymph is stuck there, perhaps crawling out through the surface and leaving its final shuck stuck in the film, we can fish our flies so near the surface that it seems like fishing on the surface, but on the underside rather than the topside.

Nymph dressings have evolved more because of the conditions found in the south than in the home of nymphing, the Border and Northern English waters. Interestingly, many of the best dressings from England do not work well in Scotland, but there are some very welcome imports too. Nymphs are scantily dressed, in traditional terms. Traditional wet flies have a body, possibly with a rib and a tail, a hackle wound round the neck of the hook to look rather like legs, and wings tied on to look something like the wings of the mature fly. Nymphs do not look like this. In Nature, larvae are like small grubs with gill and legs. Several times during its growth, the nymph casts off its skin in stages called instars. In the final stages wing buds appear giving the nymph a kind of hunchback appearance. When the time comes for emergence, nymphs have bodies with tails like mature flies, legs, a head, gills and well-developed wing buds. The artificials which represent them – and most nymph development – are thus dressed with a body with appropriate tails, some kind of ruff round the throat and a bulging thorax which may even have wing buds built in to its design. Nymphs dressed in this style are extremely well observed and very logical wet flies. In English stillwaters they work very well indeed, as I learned when I lived in the south. In Scottish waters conventional nymph dressings such as I describe (because it is a new convention) often do not fish as well as local wet fly dressings. Well, why should they? My experience of nymph fishing, particularly on stillwaters in the south-east of England, was that the nymphs there were many times larger than our nymphs in Scotland. I have, on occasion, fished No. 8 Footballer nymphs with great success

Wet fly fishing for trout on a small, heavily treed water – the Water of Leith, Edinburgh. Fishing in such conditions requires great accuracy of casting (Christopher Shepley)

Left: A 7lb (3.1kg) brown trout from an English reservoir. Trout find many of the new reservoirs in England excellent habitats and fish of good weight and condition are common (Trevor Housby)

Top: Playing a trout in the River Ure near Tanfield, Yorkshire. The waters flowing east from the Pennines provide some of the best wild trout fisheries in England (Arthur Oglesby)

Above: A selection of stillwater trout nymphs (John Darling)

Right: A good brown trout is brought to the net on an English reservoir (Trevor Housby)

on a Suffolk reservoir, for example. This is a representation of a black chironomid, dressed with a sparse body of alternate black and white horsehair with a ruff of peacock herl at the head. There are no chironomid nymphs this size in the waters I fish in Scotland. There, the midge nymphs, black and bluish and white, are tiny and a No. 20 hook would be too big. I have seen Scottish trout rising to knots in the cast when they were nymphing. It is more like nymph soup in the north than a meat course.

Yet, on our faster Scottish waters, lochs like Coldingham and Fitty and Linlithgow, the Pheasant Tail nymph can be excellent. It is a bulkier dressing, of course, than some nymphs. By and large, Scottish fish like more hair, more body and more bulk in general. Let me cite a case. When the white *caenis* comes on to our Lothian reservoirs, many anglers give up in disgust. It is maximally frustrating. Trout move everywhere and take little or nothing we can show them. But there are two flies which go on taking trout right through this awful period of tiny nymphs – the Soldier Palmer and the Black and Peacock spider. Both are bulky flies and both take trout well. This is, of course, stillwater trouting with nymphs but it has its exact counterpart in river nymphing. I have tried on various occasions on Tay, Tweed and Spey to present a tiny nymph to obviously nymphing trout. I have a box of minute dressings, some of which are not much more than bare shanks with a turn or two of body and a minimal dubbing for a head. These nymphs do not do particularly well. Of course they take trout, but you are quite likely to find, in the Spey particularly, that the angler near you fishing a Greenwell, a Palmer and a Pennell will bring in a better bag.

I do a great deal of nymph fishing, despite this problem of only achieving spasmodic success. I like the upstream approach to fish seen bulging at nymphs and, indeed, I have come to the conclusion, as I have said elsewhere in this book (Dry Fly Section), that what we think of as surface rises in Scotland are often nymph rises in which the trout are taking food from the underside of the surface and not the topside. I like light tackle and I am delighted when I can get an accurately placed cast and a well-controlled drift of the nymph, assisted perhaps by a gentle lifting of the rod to give it life.

The rise to the nymph is excellent. Sometimes the cast just checks in the glide and I tighten and the fish is there. Sometimes the rise looks like a dry fly take – there is a breaking of the surface, a momentary glimpse of a trout, and a satisfying hooking of the offer. Once or twice with bigger trout, the cast suddenly tightens and moves of its own accord violently sideways through the water. I have often found this to be a really good fish or sea trout.

I once had a salmon come to my nymphs on the Doon. I was fishing for a couple of trout which were nymphing nicely in a little basin among the rocks at Auchendrane, when I saw a salmon clearly moving towards the light cast and the tiny flies. I pulled the flies away, well knowing what would have happened had the fish been hooked on that tackle in that rocky place. Without moving, I reached into my bag and quickly tied on an 8lb (3.6kg) cast with a small ½in (13mm) Parker tube, a Stoat's tail, in the end. I wet this and cast it out and I think it was the second cast when I had his offer. The fish rose again like a nymphing trout and took well and I played and landed it on the sandy beach beside me, 8lb (3.6kg) and a lovely fresh fish.

Frank Sawyer,* that great angler and pioneer of tackle and techniques, describes hooking salmon on nymphs, on the Avon in Wiltshire. A H E Wood,† in his earliest descriptions of how he thought his way into developing greased line salmon fishing, gives us a very clear picture of salmon taking natural nymphs. If you were to come with me on to the Aberdeenshire Dee in May, you would think I was nymphing too. The long floating line and the tiny lightly-dressed flies which are led in a gentle swimming arc over the salmon reminds one very strongly of nymphing. But don't let us be surprised at that. Every salmon was once a parr, nymphing in the glides and streams of the salmon river. Perhaps, if the homing theory is as finely gauged as some people think it is, we may be catching on the greased line the very fish which hung as a parr in the pool concerned. When it feels the warmer waters of the spring, it reverts to a behaviour pattern which is wholly connected with the river, the only place the salmon has known such temperatures. Who knows? But it would be nice to think that the Dee fish are nymphing salmon!

Nymphing can be practised upstream to showing fish or downstream to showing fish. Of the two, I much prefer downstream presentation. In it, if your watercraft is good, you can approach the fish from above and, with luck, either see the trout or, from rises, be able to work out exactly where it is lying. The downstream presentation of the nymph is a very advantageous and skilled way of fishing. The nymph can be finely controlled in

*F Sawyer, *Nymphs and the Trout* (ed. Wilson Stephens), Stanley Paul (1958).
†A H E Wood, 'Greased Line Fishing', in Taverner (ed.), *Salmon Fishing* (Seeley Service, London).

depth, and by checking the drift can be made to give little upward swimming movements which trout often find irresistable. My downstream fishing is nearly all done in conditions where the nymph is fished very near the surface, but the nymph can be fished very well indeed by letting it swim deeply over the fish. There are the copper wire bodied nymphs, leaded nymphs and nymphs dressed on double hooks. These are all devices for sinking the fly. It is in fact a great art to gauge the depth of a fly. I believe this can be most successful as a technique on the clearer streams of the south of England, however. In our rivers up north, trout which are really on the nymph are all found near the surface. There is a case for really deep nymphing on stillwaters, but I do not know of any serious exponents of really deep nymphing on, say, still pools of the Spey. Of course people fish sunk line and wet flies, but that is not the technique I am describing. What I call deep nymphing involves a floating line and a long leader with a heavy nymph on the tail. The line is cast out and, by carefully arranging the slack, the fly is allowed to sink well (often a most difficult thing to achieve). Detecting takes in deep nymphing is very hard. It is perhaps only a tiny twitch of the line, or a sensation in the fingers on the line which tell you that the fish has taken. Many fish are missed because the angler has no sense of having had an offer. I do find that it pays to check regularly by tightening to feel whether an offer has, in fact, happened. Good line communication is necessry of course, but so is checking. Some anglers strike at the end of every cast, just before they lift the line out. It is absolutely astonishing how often a fish is there.

Nymph fishing in flowing water is, as I hope I have conveyed, a most exciting and yet a most ambiguous art. I sometimes long for all my wet fly fishing to become nymphing, because sometimes I feel that nymphing has brought us from tradition to something guided by observation and science. We have been brought by modern nymphing from folklore into knowledge. To change the image and use one of Jerome Bruner's striking metaphors, traditional fly fishing is almost a skill of the left hand, nearly intuitive and guided by indefinable relationships which the countryman has with the river; nymphing is an art of the right hand, a calculated skill which makes much more use of thought and observation and technique. Modern tackle has made modern nymphing possible but what I would like to see, rather than have nymphing separated off into some kind of special category, is to have upper water wet fly fishing and nymphing blend into a whole system of

representing the hatching fly. In my more accomplished moments I think that is what I am doing in wet fly fishing and nymphing on flowing water.

Dry Fly Fishing
Basic Tackle
I fish dry fly with the same rod and the same line as I use for wet fly fishing. This is for convenience as much as anything. Much of my rough stream dry fly fishing in the north takes place on the same waters as wet fly and nymph fishing and on a day when you might walk and wade some miles up a watercourse, it would be a luxury to carry two rods. Dry fly fishing on waters where there is not a mixed sport of wet and dry before you for the day may make you choose special tackle. The rod, for example, should be crisper in its action than a wet fly one, partly to allow the fly and the line to be flicked clear of droplets of water in the false casts between presentations, and partly for accuracy. I like a light, crisp rod; there is so much casting to be done in dry fly work that half an ounce extra adds up to much extra work in the course of a long day's fishing. Purpose built cane rods were delightful things, but one hardly sees them by the water these days. There are excellent glass dry fly rods, crisp and clean in their action and as light as air. There are now incredibly light carbon fibre rods with all the right characteristics and, according to the riverside conditions you expect, you can choose anything from a 7ft (2.13m) wand up to rods of 9ft (2.74m).

Lines for dry fly fishing should, of course, match the rod. One of my favourite dry fly outfits is an 8ft 6in (2.59m) ABU Zoom rod with a No. 5 line. I underline that rod according to the maker's recommendations, but I have produced a light and accurate outfit which places the line gently on the water and causes the minimum of disturbance. Lines should be, of course, floaters. Floaters however, do not always live up to their name. Some float in the surface and some float on it. I like lines floating low in the surface for wet fly fishing and some types of nymph fishing, but for dry fly fishing and the most delicate of still-water nymphing, I like a high floater. I recommend rubbing a small amount of line floatant on the line to make it ride high. Modern plastic coated lines do not need much dressing to make them float high. In the days of silk I used to work hard at my greasing and I kept a spare line ready greased on a spare drum for my reel, because silk would lose its dressing, become wet and sink. Worse still, greased silk would pick up sand and grit and have to be cleaned off. I bless the day modern lines

BASIC TACKLE

This chart attempts to provide basic recommendations for the main branches of game fishing
Your local tackle dealer will help you further.

Fish	Style	Rod	Reel	Line	Leader weight (lb)	(kg)
Trout	Fly	9ft–9ft 6in* (2.74–2.89m) Fibreglass*. Built Cane or Carbon Fibre	3½in (9cm)	AFTM 6 F D/T	4–6	(1.8–2.7)
Sea Trout	Fly	9ft 6in (2.89m) As for trout	3½in (9cm)	AFTM 6 F AFTM 8 S D/T	6–8	(2.7–3.6)
Salmon	Fly	12ft 6in–14ft* (3.80–4.27m) Fibreglass * Built Cane Carbon Fibre (up to 16ft 6in (5.03m))	4–4½in (10–11.5cm)	AFTM 10 F AFTM 10 S D/T	9–18	(4.1–8.2)
Salmon	Spinning	9ft 6in*–10ft (2.89–3.05m) Fibreglass* Carbon Fibre	Fixed Spool or Multiplier	Nylon Monofil 12–18lb (5.4–8.2kg)		

*indicates simplest basic rod

came in to make dry fly fishing cleaner and easier and thereby more efficient, even though silk lines unroll in the cast with a grace which synthetic fibres cannot match. But the time saved and the tempers left unruffled make up for it. I recommend double taper air cel lines, or their equivalents, with a whisper of Mucilin on them to make them ride high.

Terminal tackle really means leaders and flies. I use tapered leaders and I am happy to experiment with my own steps on the taper and produce a 9ft (2.7m) leader (or cast) which tapers over its length from a yard of nylon of some 6lb (2.7kg) at the line to about 3½lb (1.6kg) at the point. Try various intermediate lengths and weights to get the taper right for your own casting. I am often quite happy to step the cast down from six to four and then to three in three equal lengths. A more precise cast keeps the point shorter than the lengths above it. As in my wet fly fishing, I like the leader knotted to a short length of heavy nylon which is whipped to the line, or attached to it by a needle knot. I am off lines knotted to loops on casts. The delicacy of entry of a whipped leader-to-line joint is sensitive and satisfying, entirely in keeping with the fine conditions in which dry fly is often used.

Pre-tapered casts, that is, single continuous tapers, are often used in dry fly fishing and in nymphing. These are excellent pieces of tackle even if on the expensive side. But each time you cut off a fly and knot on another – something you do a great many times a day – you are shortening the taper. What the continuous taper gives you is a near perfect unrolling of the leader, however, and a delicate placing of the fly on the surface. Cocking the fly nicely on the surface with a delicate fall is the essence of attractive dry fly fishing.

The flies themselves are legion, but like other legions, they fall into camps. The best dry flies are delicate imitations of the insect in nature. They

Top left: Fly fishing for trout on the River Nidd, Yorkshire. Waters like the Nidd are noted for their upstream wet fly fishing and for their accurate and sporting fast water dry fly fishing (Arthur Oglesby)

Left: Into a good fish on a chalk stream, the Lambourn. Chalk streams are the home of traditional and highly-skilled English dry fly fishing (E. Atkinson)

Downstream wet fly fishing is the ideal method for the young trout fisher (Michael Shepley)

look remarkably like Olive Duns or March Browns in nature. They fascinate me, but therein lies a problem. Does an imitation look right to the trout? I have in my own fishing tried to think my way through problems from the fish's angle. Flies darken in colour when they become wet. They ride differently when they are cast, especially if the neatly groomed wings split. Also, flies which are heavily hackled to help them to float, have too many 'legs' for nature. Basically then, perhaps the best direct imitation of a floating fly would not look very like a real insect in your hand, but on the water would create the right impression. I like spider flies, that is flies dressed with hackles only.

In the north of England and in the Borders of Scotland the spider reigns supreme. Obviously successful spiders are not imitations, but are attractive impressions of flies. It has always seemed to me that how a fly is presented, how it rides on the surface and how it reacts to the current is vital – far more important than shop-window perfection of dressing. I write this as a fisher of northern and Scottish rivers, of course, and from the point of view of chalk stream dry fly fishing I suspect my slip is showing. If I had £20 to invest in dry flies, I think I would spend at least £15 on spiders and only £5 on winged flies. To chalk stream fishers that must sound a little like heresy.

The Basic Art

In many ways, fishing a floating fly to a rising trout is the most obvious form of trout fly fishing. Ask any layman and you might find that it would seem to him that it was logical to float flies, and, indeed, he might be surprised that anglers bothered to do anything else. Artists who paint pictures which find their ways on to chocolate boxes show trout rising to surface flies, dimpling the gentle waters of a pool. The world and his wife, watching the river from bridges see trout ringing the surface. Surely trout anglers see it this way too?

They do, sometimes, but what they make of a river with rising trout may be far from the apparent solution that rings on the surface mean trout rising to floating flies. Let's start with the rise. In my opinion, after fishing for trout for a considerable number of years, the bulk of rings on the surface of a stream are not rises to surface flies. The largest proportion of rises are to nymphs. As we have already discussed, nymphs are flies at the stage of hatching in which they rise through the water in a kind of drifting and swimming fashion and reach the surface film. That is, they reach the underside of the surface film and, to most nymphs, this is a formidable barrier. Some nymphs stick their heads into the film and struggle out of their last shuck or nymphal skin, and emerge at the surface on the topside of the film by leaving behind the nymphal case. In the waters I fish, mainly the Scottish rivers, trout feed heartily on the hatching nymph and show surface rings as

they do so. These fish may be tempted to take a floating fly, since trout are so often opportunistic feeders, but lots of seeming surface rises will not produce trout willing to rise to the surface fly.

Sometimes I find trout behaving as if the fully-hatched surface fly was slightly frightening. I have certainly seen trout refusing sedges motorboating on the surface while going crazy on the nymphs of these flies. I have often seen a river pool dimpled with rises, yet a dark olive, looking as large as a ship will float down the gliding water past dozens of trout before it is taken. Sometimes a prominent fly like that will attract a very small fish which misses once or twice before it takes the fly in.

Having noted that trout take more food below the surface than on top of it, in the rivers I know best – Tweed, Tay, Spey and Don – there are excellent days in spring and summer when trout settle down to taking flies from the surface and provide us with some tremendous sport. The techniques involved in taking trout on dry fly bring to a peak the whole art of presenting and controlling an artificial fly and the man who can do it can confidently do almost anything else in fly fishing. I would go further; the man who can make the approach to a rising trout, observe the mode of feeding and the type of fly is as secure in his watercraft as he is in his casting and handling techniques. Dry fly fishing is an obvious sport; you can see it all happening and at times what you see is painful, because every mistake is clearly seen and the consequences of mis-casting or failing to

A remarkable shot of a brown trout about to take a dry fly. The fish in this case is approaching the fly at right angles to the lie of the leader (Jens Ploug Hansen)

compensate for drag, or striking badly are immediately and painfully seen.

The basic art of fishing dry fly on flowing water is best thought of as a sequence – observing, approaching, covering and hooking. I will leave to a separate discussion the question of fly selection (*see* p.51).

Observing

A dry fly fisher scans the surface of the river with pin-point vision looking upstream for signs of rising trout. It is often a combined art of eye and ear. You might see rings on the surface or, in a stream, see the wave pattern being distorted slightly, or you might merely see a floating fly suddenly disappear into a tiny whirlpool no larger than a five-penny piece. Rises are themselves fascinating and at times it is tempting to lay the rod down and get into a good viewing position – say on a highish point of the bank or even up a tree or on a footbridge – and just watch the way of the trout with the fly. In Scotland, in my boyhood, anglers did not fish club water on Sunday and I used to spend the afternoons just watching trout. It taught me a tremendous amount. Feeding trout can be seen hovering just below the surface and a kind of excitement dominates their movements. They seem to hang on their fins in the water and sustain their feeding positions with an eager attitude, sometimes moving quickly aside to inspect a floating fly or some other floating item. In their feeding mood, trout are very actively curious, but they are not indiscriminate. I can remember one large trout which I got to know well under a bridge on the River Ayr. I had no way of fishing it, because it was impossible to wade to it and there was no way of using a boat by which one could get into position below it to offer it a fly. But I was able to watch it carefully and to see what it would do to fly-like items dropped over the bridge to land on the water just above its lie. It almost always came to see what was dropped when it was poised for feeding. It would investigate everything and would reject it. If the fish were not feeding, you could present it with all kinds of attractive items and it would not budge. If one showed too much head over the bridge, the fish would go down. That merely meant it would drop a little lower in the water and would stop 'finning', that is, would stop holding a feeding attitude.

When you see a rise, it will be one of several types. A rise to a genuine surface fly and not a nymph is usually one in which the trout breaks the surface with its nose and takes the fly in. If you can get down to water level and look along the surface (looking upstream from a weir can be ideal

for this) you will see this happening. The fish make the rise with their heads. The result is a fairly regular ring with concentric ripples spreading out. If anything is the classical rise, that is it. Smallish trout are usually the most vigorous risers and they may even make the loudest 'plop' as they move. This is partly because they are more vigorous than larger fish, and are less cautious, but it is also a function of size. Large trout can suck flies down more efficiently than small trout. Thus, there is a kind of inverse rule; noisy and irregular rises are often small fish, while dimples and very regular quiet rises are often much larger trout.

The largest trout often hardly make a ripple at all. I have seen excellent trout just syphoning flies down and only making the tiniest rings on the gentlest glides under trees. Large trout also seem to be able to rise very effectively without turning on the fly. Small trout often twist as they take the fly down and this causes a mottled pattern inside the rise form itself. Real takers are often quiet feeders.

When trout show a back fin as they rise, you should expect the fish to be nymphing. Occasionally, trout will put their heads out of the water and drown flies by coming down on them with their chins. Sometimes you will foul hook fish under the chin as they do this. In my experience this is usually behaviour associated with sedges and is normally a still-water phenomenon. But river trout may do this to a slightly dragging fly. Sea trout will certainly do it to your dry fly and, as I have mentioned in the section on dry fly on the loch, rainbows and some big browns in still-water seem to prefer the fly to move a little when they have it presented to them.

Below: **Dry fly fishing requires thought, observation and careful planning. The angler on the Kalemouth bridge of the River Teviot has a vantage point for spotting rising fish of quality**

The selection of a dry-fly and tying it properly to the fine leader are vital to the success of the art (Jens Ploug Hansen)

Observing the water is very much a question of spotting rises. Knowing where to look is a great time saver. The obvious trout rises in the bodies and tails of pools need little or no mention. These rises are the first ones you will be conscious of, say during an evening rise. But I have often found these open water trout the hardest to tempt. I love the trout that rise close to the bank in deep glides under trees. These fish in the shaded water are often marvellous specimens. Trout like shade. The instinct to protect themselves from predation by birds or by animals above them leads them to look for water well shaded and well supplied with food. Water beneath trees has more than its fair share of terrestrial floating flies which drop down from foliage above.

In faster trout streams such as the Scottish waters, trout rising to floating flies are not so idyllically positioned in glides and gentle pools; they rise in the streams themselves and in the aprons of water beside the faster water. The rise itself is very different in fast water. The fish moves quickly, often making a little splash and an irregular pattern in the run as it takes down flies. Trout have only a fraction of a second to inspect and decide to take a fly in these circumstances. It would be easy to think that trout would be far less discriminating in these circumstances, and sometimes this is true. But I have often found that trout in fast water can become pre-occupied with one type of fly and, despite the shortness of time involved in rising, they will select, say, dark olives, and will not be tempted by other flies floated above them. Clearly, in rapid water the trout must judge on the general outline and presentation of the fly rather than on details. Many Scottish anglers do not use winged flies at all for their fishing, but use spider dressings, that is flies dressed with bodies and hackles only. These spiders are often very successful on streams and I myself have the greatest faith in them. It is the general shape of the spider and its mode of floating which tempts the fish to take it. Wings seem to me to be for the chalk stream angler with gentle streams and great clarity of water.

There are rises on a streamy river which you never see. Sometimes you will be wading up a stream and just hear something like a splash and, reading the water intelligently, you can sometimes float your fly on the right place and get an offer. Sometimes you will see flies floating down and disappearing. That is usually a sign of an excellent trout. Most Scottish anglers observe what they can and cover the rises they see wherever possible, but they also fish the water. In chalk stream fishing it is much more likely that you would not cast your fly out except to a trout observed rising to the floating fly. I believe this has something of a cachet about it on some chalk stream waters. Chancing it by trying likely places, or worse still, fishing the water generally, is not regarded as acceptable fishing.

Approaching Fish
More than half the success in dry fly fishing comes from being able to get close enough to a rising fish to cast a fly effectively to it. Approaching fish in a river requires a combination of skills and experience which reflect how qualified one is in water-craft. Rising trout must be approached from downstream and even then, must be approached with as low a profile as possible. Trout poised just below the surface can be put down by the sight of a head over the bankside cover. Even worse, rising fish can be put down by just letting the rod tip show. I would rank trout with wild geese for difficulty of approach. All this makes it seem impossible to approach rising trout in clear water, but luckily there are some factors in the angler's favour. The first is that trout vision is restricted to a kind of inverted cone of visibility upwards and forwards from the fish. If the trout is poised near the surface, its vision only covers a small area of the surface and, provided the angler keeps well down and casts accurately, it should be possible to cast from a position below the fish in which he and the rod are invisible and only the fly and the point of the cast enter the trout's 'window'.

Clearly it is essential to be able to cast reasonable distances and to place the fly with accuracy in the window. In fact, the target is smaller than that. To cover a fish well, one must be able to put the fly within 6in (15cm) of the centre of the last rise. To do this well, I much prefer to wade. Wading keeps one low in the sky and gives room to cast, usually. Further, in wading, if one is lucky with the depths, the most advantageous point to cast from can be selected. For example, the angler can decide whether it is better to approach the fish from directly below, or from an angle to the right or the left. This has obvious importance when wind is being taken into account, but it also has importance for the cast itself. When casting, the line unrolls to the right or to the left, according to whether the cast is made from the left or from the right, respectively. Think of it in terms of right-handed people. A cast made with a right hand and a wrist action which brings the rod forward from the right will project the line forward but will, with your skill and help, unroll in such a way that the fly will be rolled round from right to left and will form a kind of curve on the water with the fly

Using natural cover in the approach is a great art. Cover behind the angler cuts out his outline. River Annan, Hoddom Castle (Michael Shepley)

further left than the line. The opposite thing will happen when casting backhand. The fly should end up further right than the line. Given reasonable wind conditions, one might be able to cast so that the fish sees the fly before the cast. This really is a question of covering rather than approaching, but the position selected to fish from obviously determines the way the loop unrolls.

Another factor in the angler's favour in approaching rising trout is that streamy water is easier than gently flowing glides or virtually still water. Streams break up the surface of the river in such a way that the images in the trout's window are distorted. This is why Scottish fast-water dry fly is often much easier than chalk stream dry fly. In rough water fly fishing one can wade right up to a rod's length of rising trout in some streams and this has great advantages when it comes to eliminating drag. Drag is the name given to the drawing of the fly off its natural floating line when the weight of the current acts on the line and exerts a pull. Drag is a bugbear and a bore and a sport spoiler. One finds a nice rising fish and manages by stealth to get into position for covering it. Out goes the line and the loop turns nicely over and places the fly on the surface a foot or so above the point of the rise. Perfect, except that the fly has to float naturally down to the trout's lie. The fly rides nicely and begins the slow float, but in the meantime the line lying on the water is being pulled by the intervening stream and little or nothing can be done to stop the fly suddenly being drawn off course and thus behaving unnaturally. The trout goes down. Drag claims another victory.

When able to cover lies with most of the line between yourself and the fly held off the water, as in rough stream dry fly fishing, one has a much better chance of preventing drag. There are several ways of reducing drag effects, of course, and I have already mentioned one – raising the rod top and keeping all or most of the line off the water. This only works with short lines and longish rods. Possibly some of the new 11ft (3.35m) carbon fibre rods will help to make more of this, but at the moment my thinking is geared to 9ft (2.74m) and 9ft 6ins (2.90m) rods which really offer one little scope for lifting the line. I usually try to prevent drag in its simplest form by letting the rod top follow the line down in the direction of the intervening current, thus getting a second or so of grace before the tension mounts and drags the fly off line. You can contrive to cast with extra line on the intervening water – formerly called a zig-zag cast – and this gives the stream a bit more to bite on, as it were, and leaves the fly undragged for a few more vital inches. Or the line can be mended. This simply means rolling a loop of line upstream so that the effect of the intervening stream on the line is still further mitigated. I like to mend the line as soon as I cast, because it is extraordinarily difficult to roll the loop upstream after the line is on the water, without jerking the fly. Mending is an imprecise movement. Years of experience help, but even then, how do you gauge exactly the amount of roll required to compensate for a stream you can see in front of you? I mend a great deal in my salmon fishing and there one is dealing with longer lines, longer rods and altogether coarser tackle. The fish is coarser too, and is not likely to

be put down if the fly does jerk a bit. Indeed, the sudden movement of a fly might induce a take. In dry fly trout fishing, flies must seem to travel untrammelled; they must imitate nature.

Mending works in simple stream conditions where there is one intervening stream and the rising trout are on the opposite side of it. But what does one do when there are two intervening streams? I know of such a place on the Spey. Good trout rise tantalisingly within finite casting distance, but it is virtually impossible to cover them without the streams dragging your fly off. Some streams can be conquered by deep wading, but not this particular one, where an eddy on the right bank promises to engulf you in a great sandy hole. Frustration unlimited! Eddies are something I nearly always associate with frustration in dry fly fishing. They are deep places and are food traps and have often some tremendous trout in them, but they are extremely difficult, if not impossible, to cover. To begin with, the water in an eddy swirls round slowly. Thus, a trout beyond the main eddy rising in the stream has a backwater

Dry fly fishing on the Kalemouth Pool of the River Teviot in the Scottish Borders. This water has good trout, fine grayling and occasional sea trout as well as salmon

between it and you and that backwater turns the stream in the opposite direction. Good, one thinks, that compensates for drag. Think again. The side of the eddy nearest one flows upstream, as it were, but the eddy keeps on turning and the outer part of the backwater turns downstream again. This gives a slow current downstream running beside a faster current downstream. I give up. I have almost got to the stage now of passing eddies by and only fishing the tail of the stream where the swirl rejoins the main stream and sorts itself out.

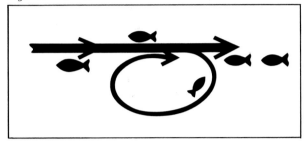

Diagram of an eddy

The ideal condition for covering rising trout is a fastish glide under the far bank. One wades out on shingle or sand on a gently shelving bed through water slower than the glide. The fly rides perfectly and there is no drag until the whole cast has covered the lie. The fly gets to the trout first and gives, for once, the advantage. I took eight trout out of such a glide one June day on a small Ayrshire river. Memorable stuff. Nearly as nice as wading up the gentle water between two moderate streams and casting to trout rising in the insides of them. This is marvellous fishing. In each case the fly travels faster than the line and there is no drag. One has rough water and does not readily disturb fish. To fail to take a brace or more from that approach, would be disappointing.

On summer evenings on the Border rivers, it is tremendous sport to wade upstream gently, casting the dry fly here behind a boulder, and there over a glide, covering likely water as well as a rising fish. On the Blackadder I spent a late April day doing just that; it was as varied a day as one could possibly imagine. I think I would use a shortish line in these circumstances and use a stealthy wading approach to get me to the fish. At times it is more like upstream wet fly, in which the angler seems more to stroke the water with the fly than let it ride down. The fly is on the water in such streamy conditions for only a second or so at a time. It is fast and accurate and challenging. Flies get soaked, and flies go out of sight. Sometimes one will lose sight of the fly and make to cast again, only to find a trout on. It is, of course, all too easy to smash your fine leader when you get secret takes like that.

There is obviously a scale involved in dry fly fishing. At one end is the rough stream fishing which looks like a version of nymphing upstream, where the fly may disappear or where the water may be fished at random. At the other end is the delicate art of stalking rising trout on chalk streams or on the clear glides of a limestone river where individual fish are noted, studied, stalked and covered, perhaps for fishing day after fishing day until someone gets the pattern and the range and the drag problem sorted out, and he is on. What satisfaction that gives! Between these extremes is the whole range of dry fly fishing, some of it inclining more to the accurate placing of a long line, and some of it more characterised by short line fishing and wading. Dry fly fishing is a single category of fly fishing in most books, but it is certainly not a single art in practice.

Casting a dry fly is different from casting a wet fly in two ways. Firstly, casting not only projects the fly forward to the fish; it dries the fly too. There is usually a false cast, or more than one, between each placing of the fly on the water. As I think of the casting I can feel it happening. The fly is riding down a glide in front of me with a good fifteen yards of line out. I gather line in with my left hand and, as I lift the rod for the backcast, I give the line a good haul with the left hand. This accelerates the line and plucks the fly off the surface. Get it off with a little plop, quick and easy; it will be less damp this way. The line sails out behind and, with a forward cast and a quick haul on the line with my left hand, I flick off moisture at the turn of the backcast. I repeat the process twice to dry the fly off. You can often see the little mist of drops flick off when you are watching someone do this. Then, lengthening or shortening line to cover a trout which has risen again in the glide, I use false casts until I get it right. Down goes the line and over rolls the fly. It rides well, this time giving me a little aerial crook on the leader which means that the fly is cocked on the surface without any nylon lying on the water immediately beside it. The fly rides down 6in (15cm) to the trout and he rises – a nice sucking, sincere take. I give the fish a hesitation of a pause to let it turn down with the fly and I tighten, using the left hand to pull line back through the forefinger of my rod hand and I raise the rod simultaneously. He's on. I'm into him – a nice fish. If only it always happened like that!

Striking

I have described one classic form of striking above. The fish rises, the angler gives it time to turn down with the fly, and he tightens into the fish.

This is as it should be. The pause to let the fish turn is more important in slow water. Indeed, in fast streams like the Whitadder and parts of the Tay and Spey I am not conscious of any great pause. The tradition of saying 'God Save the Queen' before tightening must have originated with the Houghton club on the Test where glides are glides and trout are large. On my home waters, glides are often fast, and trout are small and they move like lightning. I strike when I see the rise and am often too late. On one evening recently I found it just about impossible to get the hook into any of the trout I rose. I was gnashing my teeth until I suddenly lifted the rod to cast again and it coincided with a take and the fish was well hooked. On that evening the trout seemed to be incredibly fast in the take – or was I too slow? I think rise speed varies according to the size of the fish, the speed of the water (probably the main factor) and the type of fly.

The hardest dry fly fishing I have ever experienced is on the Spey in early summer when there are massive hatches of *caenis* especially towards evening. Trout go wild on them and you can count a score of trout rising steadily in one stream. I fish them hard, using all my skill in positioning and placing of the line. There are streams where I do not manage to get more than a couple of rises in all out of all the naturals and there I usually miss the offers because the trout seem to move very rapidly indeed on the small fly. I often wonder if it is a proper rise they make. They seem to be right on the surface and just vacuum the midges in. No wonder they call *caenis* the fisherman's curse.

I fish dry flies on a cast tapered to 3½lb (1.6kg) breaking strain and I not infrequently break in fish which take me unexpectedly. To fish heavier stuff seems counter-productive. One can fish far finer points than that, of course. On the Tarn in France I had to fish points of 1¾lb (0.8kg) strain and, astonishingly, I had some very nice fish on it, mainly grayling, which seemed to take more gently than the trout. But 2lb (0.9kg) strain is really too light, and 3½lb (1.6kg) is where I think the compromise between strain and diameter is made. Also, one can tie 3½lb (1.6kg) nylon, but finer stuff is incredibly hard to work with. When you are fishing 3½lb (1.6kg) points, it pays to remember that the 9ft (2.74m) rod and No. 5 or No. 6

Top Left: **A young angler into a trout on the Water of Leith, Edinburgh (Michael Shepley)**

Left: **Getting ready to fish wet fly on a Highland river – the River Tirry, near Lairg**

line are able to smash nylon twice as heavy as this without more than a twitch of the hand. A strike with tackle like this is a gentle tightening, and no more. I have a couple of light 8ft 6in (2.59m) glass spiggot rods which behave better with light leaders than my all round 9ft (2.74m) and 9ft 6in (2.90m) cane rods – which I realise are heavy and old fashioned now. I have fished only once with carbon fibre and a dry fly and what struck me after the incredible lightness and accuracy of the rod, was just how powerful such a rod was on the strike. Maybe it was that I thought the toothpick in my hand was so light that it must be weak and I applied too much power sometimes. Anyway, I felt that that carbon rod could have smashed my points. Glass seems sweeter and nicer for really light stuff.

Selection of a Fly
I am not bred in the school of entomological imitators who change their fly to match a change in temperature which darkens the olives' wings. I know most of my rough stream flies and I have half-a-dozen flies in my box which represent them well, allowing for variations in size of fly and in bushiness or sparseness of dressing, I feel that I can come close to most flies I meet on the rough stream in the course of a season. Broadly, the artificials which serve me well are these: Greenwell Spider No. 14 and No. 12; Black Spider No. 14 and No. 12; Tup's Indispensible, dressed parachute, No. 14; conventional winged Greenwell No. 12; Dark Olive No. 14 and No. 12 and possibly one or two nondescript Badger Spiders No. 14. That is it. Even then, I find that I fish either a Greenwell Spider or a Badger. You can see the rough logic of my situation. I do not find winged flies better than spiders so I go for the simpler dressing, namely the spiders. I have an olive range (including the Greenwell), a black range and a grey range. Indeed, it has been pointed out that the badger is a rather special pattern. Its points are clear and can be virtually invisible on the water. Thus what the fish sees is the darker roots of the hackle, and this makes for a very small fly outline indeed. Possibly, then, the Badger Spider is the ideal midge representation, since it is a visible fly of extremely small size in the middle of a manipulable and tieable fly of conventional size. I think I must represent something like a No. 20 fly in its No. 14 dressing.

This selection will not satisfy my friends in Hampshire and Wiltshire, I know. I hope they will forgive me. Chalk streams are exotic places for, like tropical climes, one enjoys them occasionally. My day to day trouting is over a wide range of water from the Tweed to the Don. I can assure you that the flies I have listed kill well there and, as far as I have tried them out, do well right down through Yorkshire and Derbyshire.

On Highland waters further north and west than the Spey one comes into the peaty waters where wind is normal and tree cover is non-existent. Further, many of them contain trout of considerable vigour and unsophistication. There I fish No. 12 dry flies, and I do not mind if the wind skids them about. There are sea trout there too, and I fish 5lb (2.3kg) points. I know this is fairly coarse tackle, but it is very practically defined for me. I would not risk fishing gossamer and small flies on waters where a rise might be either a wild snatch from a half-pound brownie or a real tug from a sea trout. Colours alter too when you think of dry fly up north. I like the black spiders, but I often undertie the black with another colour. Red below black is marvellous. Brown below black gives you a Kate McLaren. The Palmer-style flies fish well in the north-west too – Soldier Palmer fished dry, Black Pennell fished dry and all manner of bushy creation fished dry. I have seen quite small trout rise to a floating dap, many a time. On Loch Maree I have taken 6in (15cm) browns on a double dry fly cast with parachute flies dressed on No. 8 outpoints. Hungry and ambitious creatures!

Dry flies should be dressed with cock hackles which are more impervious to water absorption than hen hackles. Like many anglers, I am reluctant to use floating preparation on my dry flies if I can avoid doing so. Floating preparation coats the fly with an oil, perhaps impregnated with silicone. Usually, floating preparations are a wax or an oil in a solvent. The solvent evaporates off quickly and leaves the fly slightly coated with wax and ensures that the water will take longer to soak the fly and sink it. But I don't like doing it, so I would rather struggle with whisking and flicking my fly to dry it off, and regularly squeezing my fly on a piece of absorbent wool on my fishing waistcoat, or just pressing it against my pullover and blowing hard on it to take the droplets of water off. Natural feathers are far nicer than oiled feathers.

Equally, I am reluctant to treat a line to make it float. Luckily, modern floating lines do not need this, but there are sometimes advantages in making a modern line float higher in the water than its natural buoyancy would provide for. A high floating line is easier to mend and much simpler to cast than a line floating in the surface. In nymphing, I like the high line so much that I have sometimes greased line and cast to within a foot of the nymph. Then, using the high-riding line almost as a float is used in bait fishing, I let the nymph sink gently. Then a twitch can be given to the fly, just a simple twitch without moving much line. This can be deadly in calm reservoir fishing and in Suffolk ponds, and no doubt elsewhere too.

Some anglers find dry fly a world on its own and I know of several who really don't want to fish in any other way. I can see why they become exclusive. Dry fly is delicate, visual and effective. It makes some forms of wet fishing look like mindless flogging of the water. It is selective, picking the best fish and it is demanding in terms of tackle, knowledge and accuracy. Yes, it is seductive. But those of us who live in a land of wind and rushing streams have to fish in ways suited to a wider variety of conditions than the dry fly angler would be able to cope with. So I content myself with a range of floating techniques and a range of sinking techniques and, within that spectrum I love to use a dry fly in a wide variety of conditions and on different waters throughout the trout season, switching from wet to dry as I find it necessary.

The Art of Stillwater Fly Fishing

Introduction

A very large proportion of British trout are caught in stillwater. In the sixties and seventies, a large acreage of new stillwater was added to the trout fisheries of England with the opening of reservoirs, gravel pits and redeveloped lakes and natural waters. I have had some excellent sport in recent years in a high-quality trout fishery developed from a new irrigation reservoir in Suffolk, laid on a bed of polythene (12 acres), and in a lot of other new waters which include: an East Anglian water made by landlocking a brackish area on the mouth of a river and carefully controlling the salt content; several ponds formed in gravel pits; numerous small fisheries made by excavating water-holding hollows and, of course, on new reservoirs and old where trout fishing is of a high order. English trout fisheries have boomed since 1960 and many thousands of anglers have turned from other freshwater fishing to trout fishing. Stillwater trout fishing has a style of its own, and with very considerable rewards in terms of sport. Indeed, the term stillwater trout fishing, in the minds of many anglers, means the new leisure trout fisheries in waters such as I have described above, and not the traditional loch, lake and pond fisheries we have

On the Newport River, Ireland, where it leaves the loch (Michael Shepley)

enjoyed in the north of England, Wales, Scotland and Ireland for years.

The older stillwater trout fisheries of the UK are dominated by the huge loch fishing resources of Scotland and Ireland. Of course, in the north of England and in Scotland there has also been an increase in the trout fishing waters available. Again new reservoirs have been formed, and old lochs, given over to pike and perch through neglect, have been restored and restocked and brought back into our angling resources as good trout fisheries. But there is still a division in our minds between waters in Scotland where trout are wild and breed naturally in the feeder streams, and the reservoir and pond fisheries of England where trout are stocked in carefully calculated quantities and are fished for as a return on investment. I hope I am not putting too radical a division on our sport to say that the put-and-take fisheries of the midlands and south of England are examples of the nurture man can bring to developing and managing resources, while the lochs of the Highlands of Scotland are often excellent examples of what nature itself can offer the angler. The nurture/nature argument is, like other regularly used categories, apt to be misleading. Between the ultimate put-and-take rainbow fishery in a mill pond in Sussex with 10lb (4.72kg) fish and the hill loch in Sutherland which has no trout management at all for its small and numerous brown trout, lies a whole graduation of waters and conditions, and associated angling approaches and attitudes. Anglers might not immediately want to classify their local stillwater fishery into the nurture and nature categories I suggest. But it is true that the angling techniques of Scottish traditional fly fishing attract what I have sometimes thought of as child-of-nature techniques of a traditional and sometimes rather mindless sort. In this section of the book we shall try to tease apart the main types of stillwater fishing and show their distinctive characteristics and, I hope, also finally show that trout fly fishing is a seamless robe of sport, rather than a divided one.

Loch Fishing

I would like to introduce the art of fly fishing for trout on stillwater by beginning with loch fishing, my home, bred-in-the-bones Scottish sport. It seems to me to have the fundamentals of the art clearly traced on its practices. I started and developed there and, at one stage of my career, moved from the Scottish scene to live in the south-east of England, where, for two years, I translated my basic loch fishing into the idiom of the English stocked reservoir. Starting with Scottish lochs, then, is also, for me, an autobiographical way in.

Reading a river is a great art, but it is at least assisted by the way the river flows. Reading a loch is a little more mysterious. One is faced with trout dispersed, apparently, over a great area of water. There is no flow. The wind ripples and waves the surface and you would be a strange angler indeed who did not feel perplexed by the problem of locating trout in these great reaches of rippled water. Trout in a loch move usually in feeding routes, and usually upwind. Trout which you see ringing the surface of a loch with rises, then, are giving invaluable clues on where to drift your boat or where to wade and cast if you are bank fishing. How far trout move about a loch is not known. During a rise, I have the impression that trout remain located within fairly short beats, say within a given bay, or up and down a submerged ridge. At least, when I drift familiar lochs I know very often where to expect rises. Trout always seem to be around these places, although in feeding they may move possibly fifty yards or so upwind, before turning and repeating their feeding route.

What I am describing as feeding activity, is, of course, only one type of feeding activity – the mid and upper water feeding which constitutes a rise. Notice the use of the word 'rise'; it is used to describe the individual feeding mark on the surface or near it when a trout takes a fly, but it is also used to indicate that a time of general feeding in the upper water is taking place. We refer to an evening rise, a rise to this or that fly, or just a sustained period of activity. Trout in a loch do 'come on to the rise' at certain periods and then seem to go off again or 'go down' and you might be forgiven for thinking that the fish were no longer feeding. This is often not the case. Trout feed far more on bottom food than on surface food in stillwater. They forage for snails and pea mussels and bottom fly larvae before it makes its

nymphal journey to the surface. Trout may take a whole range of bottom food which anglers either do not imitate or find difficult. They take snails and other crustacea, which I have mentioned, and shrimps and water fleas, large insects like dragon fly larvae and every other form of worm, wriggler, small fish or even tadpole or newt they can get. When a trout goes down, it is quite likely that the fish is feeding on bottom food. When a trout rises it does so usually because there is a concentration of hatching flies at the surface. Anglers are therefore faced with not only a horizontal pattern of movement of trout as they feed near the surface, but a kind of vertical pattern of movement also when trout move from the bottom to the surface to feed.

Anglers, therefore, use techniques which reflect whether the fish is feeding in the upper water or is on the bottom and lower water. Most Scottish loch fishing concentrates on the mid and upper water. It presents the trout with sunk flies, fished through the ripple and the wave in such a way that the flies represent the typical hatching nymphs of the time, or appeal to the trout in some broadly similar way. On lochs we use floating lines for this form of trout fishing, or lines which sink only a little way into the loch. The old Kingfisher silk lines, for example, were really slow-sink lines and fished flies just below the surface when they were cast moderate distances. We all tend to cast further nowadays on lochs and these same silk lines would have sunk well, fishing, as they did, longer rods with weaker casting power than ours. But our grandfathers were highly successful in their loch fishing, using short lines, and working flies on or near the surface just off the gunwale of the boat. I sometimes think we have a great deal to learn from them still.

The most basic form of wet fly fishing a loch is to fish the flies from a boat which is made to drift down the food-bearing water. Two anglers usually fish from a boat and a third may act as boatman. On some Highland waters and some club waters you will have the luxury of a boatman. Most of us now fish without boatmen, and judge our own drifts, using drogues or our own skill in prodding a trailing oar as we drift and fish at the same time. In Scotland it is rare to anchor a boat and in this it is in complete contrast to many English reservoirs where boats are often anchored and the anglers wait for trout to move past them. This style of fishing, where trout come to the angler, is typical of waters with a considerably higher density of trout than we enjoy on most Scottish lochs.

The flies selected for Scottish loch fishing are usually mounted in a team of two, three or even

Left: **In flowing or in stillwater the trout can provide incredible fights on the right tackle (Jens Ploug Hansen)**

four on a 9ft (3m) leader. There is a fly on the point of the cast and one or two on droppers, that is tails of nylon left out of the knots to carry a fly. These droppers are usually about 4in (10cm) long and the top one is normally called the bob. Bob flies are often astonishingly successful and they very often provide the best sport of the day. Recently I was out on a lowland Scottish loch for an evening's fishing and I found conditions very difficult indeed. Trout would rise to naturals, and would ignore all my best presentations or would 'come short', that is bulge or swirl at the fly or just pluck it and fail to find the hook. This is infuriating fishing. I bore it for a couple of hours, hoping for a change in the conditions which would bring more sport. Then I decided to fish in grandfather's style, casting a very short line only and working the bob fly well through the wave with the main line held off the water. I had an excellent trout almost at once, a fish which came out of the water in an arc and crashed down on the Soldier Palmer on the bob, taking the fly deeply into its mouth. Number one in the bag. Then a smaller fish came, splashing like a monster and was played and returned to the loch. Another followed and several others had a go. Darkness descended and the rise stopped. It was an evening saved by the bob fly.

Usually we cast flies out on a drift and work them back in towards the boat. If the boat is drifting hard, you have to gather in handfuls of line with the left hand, drawing the line in over your right index finger on the rod hand, to give the flies attractive motion. In gentler conditions you might decide to give the flies little or no handlining, but to impart movement by raising the rod as the boat moves slowly forward. I am a great believer in lots of motion in the fly, and I would advise newcomers to the loch to err on the fast side when making their flies work through the water. Often trout will come to a fly which is stripped in at high speed. Do not think that trout cannot get to fast flies. I have caught trout while trailing a trout cast behind a boat with the outboard going flat out taking us from one drift to another. Trout can get the fly if they want it. Natural flies move very, very slowly through the water, and almost immobile imitations which just twitch from time to time would be the nearest to the naturals. My experience is that trout in a wave will take flies fished quickly, and, as the wave diminishes and gradually becomes calm, the flies should be worked with less and less speed. In nymphing on calm lochs, for example, we are fishing a lightly-dressed imitation of the fly as it reaches the surface and makes its last effort to puncture the surface and

emerge. In imitating nymphs, I strongly advocate long lines and minimal movement. The best technique then is a very natural one of twitch and rest, imitating what I have sometimes called a tired nymph. But in normal ripples and drifting conditions you should work your flies well, and expect the trout to take the flies vigorously. Judging the right speed is one of the delights of the sport.

The flies you select will probably divide themselves into two classes; those which seem to represent natural flies, or be very similar in colouring and style to the naturals, and those which we call fancy flies. These fancy flies are similar to other trout flies in shape, but are dressed with gold or silver wire ribbing and other exotic tyings. In the fly box you might feel absolutely confident that this was a natural fly and that was a fancy fly, but after many years of trout fishing I am fairly sure that many so-called fancy flies have a most natural appearance in the water. For instance, air or gas bubbles can shine like silver on a nymph. Remember, too, that trout look up to the flies they take and therefore tinsel bodies may be seen merely as slim black shapes. Following this further, flies with red tails are often good imitations of flies which hatch and struggle out of the water trailing their reddish final shuck behind them. The Blae and Black is a good example of this; so is the Silver Butcher. But many fancy flies are just what the name implies; they are so and so's fancy. They have been invented to please the designer.

Apart from silver and gold bodies, and red tails, I shun gaudy flies. I do not like bright reds or yellows or greens. They seem to me to be a kind of offence against nature. I like loch flies to be broadly representative of the fly life of the loch, and therefore my favourite cast might be a Greenwell on the tail, a Hardy's Gold Butcher or a similar bright-bodied fly on the middle dropper, if I am fishing three flies, and either a Black Pennell or a Soldier Palmer on the bob. In really rough conditions on Highland lochs I often use a Worm Fly on the tail, which is a tandem dressed fly like a couple of Red Tags (brown hackles, peacock herl bodies and red tufted wool tails). 'Worming' is an old word for copulating, and a worm fly is a representation of the common phenomenon of coupled flies on and in the water.

Top right: **On a Sutherland loch, Loch Fionn. Sutherland has thousands of natural trout lochs in unspoiled Highland settings**

Right: **An excellent bag of brown trout from a stillwater fishery (Trevor Housby)**

Where to Drift

In boat fishing, the main problem is always where to drift. Sometimes, on new waters especially, it can be rather difficult to work out drifts. The best drifts are over shallow water, that is, water under 10ft (3m) deep. Trout are more likely to be feeding in mid and upper water there because fly life on a loch largely concentrates in water where there is a fly bearing bottom and reasonable light penetration. By a fly-bearing bottom I mean silt or shingle or weeds where the eggs, laid at the surface, can drift down and find an environment in which the larvae can grow and find shelter. There are midge larvae in deep lochs, but in general you should use the 10ft (3m) rule in determining drifts. An oar is a good depth gauge.

What I do on a strange loch is firstly study the shore. The configuration of the bank gives you a very good clue to the shape of the loch bed. Broad shallow bays are usually backed by gently rising fertile shores and the curve of the bay itself gives you a very reliable clue to where the water shallows. Where burns or rivers come into the loch, there is often a big deposit of silt off the mouth and, where rivers leave lochs there is often a natural rim before the run out and this is a good area for feeding trout. Sometimes, if you study a good contour map of the whole area you can get some idea of the broader pattern of depths on the loch. But there are one or two pitfalls in all this. For example, moorland lochs over peat in the Highlands of Scotland or Ireland have sudden holes in the peaty bottom in which the bottom falls away. 'That's bottomless in there', says the gillie. Yet these deep holes are often backed by gently rising moor. Beware. Deep holes are not good places for fishing the fly.

The wind is another very important factor in reading a loch. Wind writes its story on the surface. You can get dusking of the surface as a light wind marks it – not good for wet fly fishing. The wind might darkle the existing ripple, smudging the even pattern of it. Ripples might rise to be waves and these waves can have secondary ripples on them. If wind gusts hard on the surface of a loch which is already well rippled and waved, and produces that blackening scud we so often see when nor'westers are blowing, fishing is often unproductive. By far the best wind and overhead conditions for loch fishing are a well-clouded sky giving the loch below a grey appearance. I do not

Top left: **Into a trout on a Scottish loch. The oar is being shipped to allow clear water for the fight**

Left: **A small artificially made trout loch in a beautiful setting in the Ochil Hills, Perthshire. The angler is drifting over a productive reach of water close to the reedy shore**

like blue lochs. A steady wind of moderately warm temperature should be blowing, giving long straight drifts. Changes in direction of ripples and swirls and gusting on top of ripple are not any good for fly fishing.

Where the wind laps the waves over promontories or rocks are often excellent food harbouring areas and trout love them. Of great fishing value, too, are the slicks which the wind forms on the surface giving oily-looking roads down the waved surface of the loch. In these slicks the glassy water is often very difficult for nymphs to pierce through and the water is rich with struggling and highly-vulnerable flies which the trout often cruise up and down taking. The best place for a take beside a slick, however, is just where the rough water meets the glassy middle road of the slick. Trout like the security of the rough water and the proximity of abundance of food.

Where the wind strikes the water, just off the windward shore (the sheltered shore) in the lee of the bank is a marvellous place for trout to congregate. There, flies borne by the wind from the land behind are deposited on the water. There the winged ants fall, and the sedges gather and there the heather beetles collect and the moths get bogged down and taken by waiting trout. The trout again, seem to like the rough water for security, like having a corrugated roof over their heads. I like fishing this water not from a boat but from the bank, casting a long line to it and raising fish in the edge of the rippled water.

Handling the Boat

A considerable part of good loch trout fishing is in positioning and controlling the boat during the drift. Boats drift according to their design and materials. Clinker built boats, for example, are heavy and usually have a good keel and they are, in my estimation, the best drifters. Fibreglass boats are lighter and drift much too quickly. Boats with high freeboard are naturally more susceptible to the effects of the wind than those with low sides. I find that a most important part of my equipment for loch fishing is a drogue or drift anchor. This is simply a specially-shaped bag or sheet which is opened out in the water behind the boat and causes a drag which slows the boat down. My drogue is a purpose-designed one with a shaped polythene bag on the end and coralex ropes. Others I have used have been more like parachutes in their design and they may be made of strong nylon or canvas. Impromptu drogues which work well include sacking cut to give a shallow umbrella shape and attached with four cords like a parachute to a rope. We have one in our club boathouse

which I use if I forget my patent drogue and, I must say, it works very well, even if it is a bit soggy to bring back on board. An old bucket on a rope will slow you down, or a plastic bin with a hole cut in the bottom to let some of the thrust water out. I have also used a birch branch with its leaves on and that gave a great surface area which stopped the drift effectively on a windy day on a Highland loch when we had nothing else. Boats can also be made to drag a boulder over a fairly clean bottom. It is astonishing what a boat will move in a wind, even an anchor.

The drogue should be carefully attached to a strong part of the boat. I like to bring my rope in through a fairlead and attach it to a seat or to the ring at the bows. You can damage a boat badly with a strong drogue or an anchor. Sides can be ripped and that could lead to disaster. Treat anchors and drogue ropes with great respect and always try to anticipate the effects of a jammed drogue and a fast-drifting boat.

Where you attach the line changes the angle and the drift of the boat. Obvious examples are attaching the drift anchor to the stern, which will cause the boat to drift bow first down the loch. I have sometimes done this when I have been alone in the boat, but it is only to be recommended when the wind is so strong that it is not effective to drift across the blast. Drogues can be attached to angle boats, to cause them to head in or out over a drift, to steady them and, most obviously, to slow them down.

One of the most valuable services a drogue offers is correcting drifts of boats with tendencies to make by the stern or by the bows (making by the stern is the usual curse). You row to the head of the drift and you turn the boat and it starts reasonably but soon begins to cross the drift stern first, cutting a line at a shallow angle to the intended drift. One club boat I fish does this so effectively that it leaves a wake at its bows and it ruins drifts. Further, the bow angler is always fishing the water just covered by his colleague in the stern. The cure is simple; fit the drogue to the forward rear fairlead or lead the rope out round the forward oar pin, or otherwise fasten the drogue roughly where the side of the boat curves in to make the bow. This will hold the boat back by the bows and you will find that the drogue will set itself out at an angle behind the boat and will correct the drift.

I once had a fearful time on Loch Brora with a club boat made of fibreglass. It was a rotten drifter and I was, at that time, fishing salmon. It was May and the fish were present in some numbers on the sandbank at the head of the loch waiting to

Close up of a trophy. A 7lb (3.1kg) brown trout from a reservoir. Note the excellent condition of the fish, with its high shoulder and clear markings (Trevor Housby)

run up the upper river. I knew that the boat had to be drifted with considerable accuracy or it would drift on to the shallow lies and frighten the fish. Well, the worst happened. Nothing I could do with the rear oar could keep the boat from skidding over the fish and I had the teeth-gnashing sight of salmon fleeing before the boat like sheep. I touched and caught nothing. A drogue that day would have been worth its weight in salmon, I reckon.

Trout are not afraid of boats. They will rise to flies fished right under the gunwale. But trout are afraid of silhouettes of anglers in boats. Anglers standing in boats do frighten feeding trout. I have seen them rising steadily until the feeding route comes beside the boat, then, with a splash of disturbance, the fish go down. Similarly, line falling in heaps on the water can put down trout instantly. I would go so far as to say that line in the air over a calm loch puts trout down. As the ripple gets less, the tactics must grow finer. But boats themselves are innocent.

Dry Fly

Many loch fishers regard dry fly on lochs as a technique associated with disaster. They run to it

when the wind fails, or when thunder threatens and when the trout are preoccupied with surface food which no wet fly can imitate. I admit to being partly of that mind, but I also admit to being wrong. All our loch fly fishing relates to the hatching cycle of the aquatic fly. The larvae progress through stages of development and shed their skins as they grow. They make the hazardous journey to the surface either by swimming or drifting upwards or crawling out via a reed stem. Trout feed heavily on the ascending nymphs and it is this stage of the fly's life which lies behind wet fly sport on lochs. Most of us fish wet fly on the floating line and we concentrate on representing flies just before they break through the surface and shed their last nymphal skin. But why are we so shy about imitating the flies on the surface after this has happened?

There are several answers to that question of reluctance to fish in a logical and obvious way for feeding trout. One answer must relate to prejudices; dry fly fishing is thought of as something exclusive – something rather up-stage and special. After all, it was the great dry fly cult of the chalk streams which marked out the gentleman angler of the nineteenth and early-twentieth centuries. Books abound praising the high sportsmanship of the dry fly fisher. Dark tales exist of the man who dared to sink his fly on the Test and was blackballed. Much of this is little more than cult mythology, but there is a truth in it. Dry fly fishing is thought of in any context as something fine in tackle and fine in sportsmanship and I know many Scottish loch fishers, for example, who would regard the fishing of the floating fly as not for them. They are wrong.

A second reason for not fishing dry fly on lochs is that it is usually associated with the kind of day when the standard wet fly methods will not work well. Scottish lochs hate calm water. Such days are frustrating, because you see lots of trout, obviously feeding and you either fail to tempt them to take, or have poor offers to the wet fly. Quite often a switch to the dry fly in such circumstances does not do very well either. Fish turn away from the fly, or rise to it and give you no contact at all on the strike, or the smallest touch as if the fish had just picked at the fly with the very tip of its mouth. What is happening in most of these cases is that dry fly is being fished on the loch in conditions which are very difficult in themselves. A switch to dry fly proves that conditions are difficult for the dry fly as well. I am reminded of the remark made

Right: **A memorable catch on wet fly from a Scottish loch. The brown trout came from Loch Fitty, near Dunfermline and weighed 5lb 12oz (2.6kg) (Michael Shepley)**

by G P R Balfour Kinnear, that great authority on salmon fishing, when he was dealing with a question of the testing of new flies. He said that anglers tended to try out new flies when old ones would not work. A new fly should be tested when the old ones are working, he said. Isn't dry fly on the loch like that? It is turned to when nothing will work, and it doesn't work either. The reputation of the dry fly, then, becomes one of a method which is difficult, frustrating and often unproductive when everything else would be too.

I had a very interesting evening recently on Gladhouse Reservoir, near Edinburgh – one of my home waters which I see in all its moods. I took one trout on wet fly very easily in a nice ripple as soon as we started the first drift, but although trout were rising well all round us in a nice drift, they were not interested in our wet flies. I changed to a cast with a dry fly on the tail and a small nymph on the bob – a combination I recommend for summer loch fishing. I seemed to hit the right method for the next hour or so. I had three fish on the dry fly on the tip – a small parachute Tup's Indispensible, which I use whenever I get loch trout apparently midging. The fun was excellent. One of the fish, a nice pounder, typifies it. I cast out the flies and saw them plopping neatly into the gentle wave, and I just had a glimpse of the dry fly riding over a small ripple and then I lost sight of it. A Tup's is a very hard fly to see in certain lights. I saw a small rise in the area of my flies and was suddenly conscious of the cast and the line suddenly zipping through the wave to the right. I had no time to strike and luckily had no time to raise my rod quickly or I would certainly have broken the fine leader (3½lb) (1.6kg). But I needn't have worried, because the fish had hooked itself beautifully in its take and sudden wild dash. An excellent fish it was – most encouraging in an evening of some frustration. I went on to take two others before the wind dropped away and gave us a calm. In that calm the fish would not look at the dry fly at all. They bulged at it, turned away from it and generally left me in no doubt at all that they did not like what they were seeing. I switched back in the dusk to a cast of two nymphs, and continued to take fish. There was a case of the dry fly working well in conditions which looked ideal for wet fly work, yet failing in conditions of calm water where most anglers would have turned to the dry fly and would have found it poor. In the calm water the nymph far outstripped the floating fly.

It is not always like that, but the principle is something I would like to pursue. Dry fly is an entertaining and productive way of fishing a rippled loch. In the mood of G P R Balfour Kinnear I advocate using the floating fly when the trout are active and are obviously on the feed in the ripple. Sometimes the dry fly will take far better than conventional flies fished wet; as my Gladhouse evening showed. There are good reasons for this. A rippled loch offers matching flies an easier passage through the surface film than they have during light ripple or calm. When a loch is calm the surface film is a formidable barrier for the nymph, and trout make the most of this by feeding heartily on the nymphs which are stuck in the surface. Of course, during that calm, it appears to anglers that the trout are rising to surface insects. It is much better to assume that in calm water they are rising to nymphs in the surface, rather than flies on the surface.

On lochs I like fishing two flies and, from time to time, I fish two dry flies. But recently I have turned to hedging my bets and fishing one dry fly on the tail and, on a dropper about two metres above that, a nymph. A mixed cast of this sort is not unusual. Yorkshire trout anglers on the fine streams of the Pennines often fish a cast of wet flies with a dry fly on the bob. Some say this is only for a bite indicator, but I disagree. It does indicate twitches and tiny takes effectively, and I have used it for this, but it also takes fish. Reversing this order and fishing a dry fly with a nymph above has manifest advantages. One of them is that you can move the cast during the fishing and this allows the bob nymph to emerge from the surface like a successfully hatching fly. That often takes trout well.

I strongly advocate moving the dry fly on lochs. I mean by that, twitching it or gently skidding it for short distances over the surface before letting it rest again and float steadily. Drag may be anathema to river fishers (is it always?) but it is not a disadvantage on lochs. The trout which rises near the dry fly and seems to ignore it can often be made to take the floater well if you move the fly in the right way. That does not mean that you work the fly back into the boat like a wet fly. Far from it. You give the fly that amount of life you would expect from a newly-hatched fly struggling to dry out its wings and flap them about and struggle off the surface. Loch flies will demonstrate this to you themselves. They cause minor disturbances on the surface as they emerge and dry off.

One of the best stillwater trout I have ever taken fell victim to a dry fly. It was a rainbow and I was fishing a largish pond at Torrington in Suffolk. On that water there were rafts which one could pull out on a rope and fish from, very effectively – an idea other fisheries should consider. I was out on the raft, fishing out into the pond where trout were cruising and rising, when I heard a 'plop' behind me. There, within a foot of the edge of the pond and right beside my raft rope a trout was cruising and sucking down flies. I had a small No. 14 spider tied with a black hackle over a red hackle – someone called it a Bloody Butcher spider, if such a fly exists. I flipped the fly in front of the rising trout and it ignored it, and cruised past the raft rope and on along the margin of the pond between my raft and the bank. I cast again, and this time just after the fly landed, I gave it a slight pull and it darted an inch or two and then stopped. The trout sucked it in perfectly and I was into a fish which tore out into the open water and fought very hard. It was the best rainbow I ever had on that splendid water – 4lb 9oz (2.07kg) – and on the tackle it was an absolutely tremendous fish to take. That trout fell to the moved dry fly, after previously ignoring a static dry fly.

Part of the reluctance to change over from wet fly to dry on a loch relates to the tackle people use, or rather to the tradition which is associated with that tackle. Floating lines have been with us for over twenty years and now every angler has one or several on his reels. These lines float low in the water, floating in rather than on the surface. They can be greased to make them ride high, but I can see no particular reason for this in the kind of fishing I am describing here. The modern trout fisher does not need to change any more than his leader to fish dry fly and, indeed, I have on occasion merely changed the fly on the tail – but I would advocate separate tackle. The traditional fisher had a problem. His oiled silk line was in fact a slow sinker and had to be specially dried and dressed with one of the proprietary floating substances like Mucilin to make it float at all. It was a great bore in the old days to have to keep spare drums for your reels with ready greased lines on them, and I always had a dry one ready too, because as sure as guns I would find the trout rising splendidly on the river or loch just as my line got waterlogged and sank. Another great problem was grit. If you got a greased line covered with sand, which I often did, it was a menace. It had to be cleaned off and dried and re-greased. It was no wonder that anglers became rather set against the bother of switching to dry fly. In the boat on a loch there is no room, and no facilities for all this tackle changing. Enthusiasts like me took out several rods and I once went out on to Loch Leven with three rods – two already mounted – one wet and one dry – and, for some reason, a spare. The dragon of a woman who used to run the office at the pier heard that I had several rods

and she immediately suspected some breach of the regulations and protested when I weighed my bag of trout. There was, of course, absolutely no irregularity, but it does point to the inconvenience of having, in those days, to carry several reels or several rods.

One of my loch fishing companions, an accomplished trout fisher, still carries his dry fly rod separately on to the loch. He has a splendid Pézon et Michel Ritz rod (we are both addicts of this tackle house) and he has adapted a metal rod tube to take the dry fly rod in its two pieces, but ready with the reel on and the line and leader attached. It is the work of seconds to set the rod up and fish it. I am cruder in my tackle handling. I take one rod and one line, and just change the leader. It works well, but I recognise that my Sawyer *Stillwater* (Pézon et Michel) 9ft 6in (2.90m) rod is not the ideal dry fly rod. It is too strong. I have to watch how I set the hook, or I can smash my light leader in a fish. If I do carry two rods, the one I select for dry fly is normally a 9ft (2.74m) glass rod and a favourite is the Webley *Lake* which is 9ft 3in (2.82m) and is gentle on the strike. Of course, rods in themselves are not gentle; it is myself and my own right hand which decides the power of the strike. Nevertheless, a right hand which is used to set the hooks in sea trout, where the leader is usually an 8lb (3.6kg) strain, and to get the hooks into fast brown trout on the loch where 5 or 6lb (2.3 or 2.7kg) leaders are common, may make mistakes when it is suddenly changed into a dry fly hand with a 3lb (1.4kg) leader.

Dry fly is used extensively for reservoir trout in the midlands and south of England. The principles are much the same as those I have described above taking a biggish rainbow on a small dry fly in Suffolk. I took many trout, both browns and rainbows, like this when I lived in that area, but by far the best dry fly tactic I found on these still waters was the skidding dry fly on the bob. This is a sedge tactic – that is, it is most useful when the trout are crashing down on scuttering sedges. At that time of the year – June and July are the best months – trout rise to surface flies in this characteristic way. If you are in a boat and can look right down the wind you will see, during the rise, trout seeming to reach up out of the water and splash down on the surface, almost like dolphins at play. These trout are usually drowning sedges. In such conditions I like to fish a big sedge nymph on the tail, or an outsize Pheasant Tail, say No. 10, and on the bob above on a 9ft (3m) leader I like to attach a largish parachute fly, again No. 12 or No. 10 and I try to skid this fly through the wave like a scuttering sedge. This is

A good trout taken on the sedge on Portmore, near Edinburgh
(Michael Shepley)

marvellous sport. Trout show wildly in the tackle and you have to be very alert and controlled to get the hooks in well. Since fish are trying to drown the sedge they may well crash at the fly and not take it, or turn immediately after the splash and take it. The idea of fishing a sedge nymph below is obvious. The fish are likely to take either form of the fly. Indeed, I have often seen trout shunning the surface sedge despite its surface motorboating, especially in the evenings when things are beginning to get still, and preferring to go for the nymph. Several dressings of this nymph which I have are very bulky, and the nymph can easily be made to furrow the surface, especially with a dry fly on the bob above. Fishing both is an insurance policy, but well worth investing in.

Left: **Fly fishing at sunset on an English stillwater fishery. The hour around sunset often produces the best fly hatches of the day and can offer the angler the best chance of taking trout of above average size for the water (John Darling)**

Lots of random windborne fly life gets on to the surface of stillwater during the season. Let me mention three forms of surface insects which make a considerable contribution to our summer sport. The first is ants. Swarms of ants will suddenly develop wings and take off, following a queen and being blown out over the loch in great numbers to make trout go wild and rise determinedly and steadily to them These are difficult flies to imitate. One dressing, however, which I have found effective in ant blows is the Partridge and Orange. It is actually a wet fly, but you can float it. The partridge hackle, however, is soft and straggly and it does not stand much wetting. Nevertheless, fish it dry and, as it gets damp and sinks a bit, don't worry. Trout seem just as keen to take the spider when it is getting waterlogged as when it is riding high. It is essential to fish this fly at the right time and in the right place, especially on a Scottish loch or on a reservoir. Go to the windward side of the loch, which is, for all colleagues who are not used to sailing terms, the side from which the wind is blowing. It is the side of the loch with the sheltered patch under the bank. Typically this is marked by a glassy, unrippled band of water inshore and where the wind strikes the water the corrugations begin. This precise point is the place to concentrate on. Wind which carries flies out, deposits them here and trout congregate just where the ripple starts, or very shortly thereafter, and they cruise up and down, waiting for the wind to bring its bounty. The technique for fishing ants is similar to the settle and twitch approach I described earlier. Let the fly rest and it may be taken at once. If the wind blows the fly about, let it, because this is very natural and a killing movement. But if the fly is resting on the surface immobile for, say ten seconds, without any interest, give it a little skid and let it settle for a second or two longer before trying a further twitch and possibly a re-cast at that point. Trout love natural movement on dry flies, and they shun coarse and unnatural movement, like river drag. Wind drag is fine, and small skidding or twitching is excellent. They represent the blow and the struggle respectively. These are in tune with the natural circumstances of the fishing, and, in our sport, that is the way to operate.

I was up at a small loch in the Borders a short while ago and I found the wind dying during a fine summer day. Trout were showing all over the water as hatches of a very yellow olive came off the surface. It was interesting to watch the hatch. A fly would pop up and would flutter on the surface and the wind would catch it and skid it a foot or two, then the fly would seem to grip the surface and hold on, while it dried off. Fluttering and skidding would go on for many yards as the fly made the most hazardous journey of its life across the bay. It seemed, at the height of the rise, that hardly any flies reached safety either in the air or by reaching reeds and getting off the water. Some flew off right away, of course, neatly illustrating one of the principles of natural selection, survival of the fittest. I fished my dry fly in imitation of these rolling and fluttering olives, and not having a precise imitation with me I just used my old favourite Tups. It did well enough. I allowed it to blow out over the feeding trout, as far as the wind would oblige. Trout seemed to like this and four of them took it in a very short space of time, before the rise weakened, or, possibly before I had reduced the rising population by four! I think I also disturbed the fish by my fishing. It is inevitable. I was thinking about this book when I was fishing on that loch and I tried to pinpoint

one or two principles which might help to guide another angler facing the same circumstances. I think one must be matching the movements of the natural fly, and letting the wind be your guide in part of this.

The second principle relates to tackle handling. Casting a longish line, close to twenty yards, if you can contrive to lay the line on the water with a straight cast but a slightly snaked line, to give you the slack you need to use the wind drift, you are likely to reflect the movements of the natural fly better. This has one disadvantage. Trout sometimes take the fly as soon as it lands. To hook this fish, you have to be in contact with the fly as soon as it lands, and obviously, if you have snaked the line on the surface, say by dropping your rod point just at the end of the cast, you might not manage to make it. I can only advise that you cast in the way I describe, but remain ready for the immediate take and haul the line in with the left hand, almost as if for a new cast, when you are striking. This is sometimes rather difficult to do effectively. Here is a case where a decision has to be made, whether to emphasise the natural, free motion of the fly or to keep maximally in touch with the trout. The decision you take will dictate how you present the fly to the trout. In my case, on that small Borders loch, the rise was so obviously to rollers and skidders that the decision was easy. On Gladhouse the previous week the signs were different; trout fed in cruise lines up slicks and in the rippled water beside them. In that case, I cast a straight line and kept maximally in touch with the flies.

Another windborne food which makes one want to use dry fly is the Jenny longlegs (the cranefly, often also called the Daddy) which blows on to our Highland and Hebridean lochs in great numbers in high summer and represents a marvellous way to fish for brown trout and sea trout. The big Jenny rolls and blows over the loch, or gets stuck in the surface and struggles about in a spectacular manner. Mating Jennies struggle on the wave and form a very succulent mouthful for waiting trout. The obvious way to imitate the Jenny is to fish the live insect and dap it on a long rod with a floss silk or nylon line to carry it out. This is excellent sport and I have seen it done well for browns and sea trout. I have sometimes found however, that I do not have dapping tackle to hand when a blow of Jennies comes on. In these cases I have tried various tyings of dry fly and, strangely enough, have not found the dry fly to be as good as the wet. I have in my box one or two long hackled size 10 Partridge and Orange flies and I find these marvellous for this sport. I fish them in the calm beside the reeds where the trout are lying waiting

A selection of flies and lures for trout fishing on English reservoirs. All these flies were created by Richard Walker (Arthur Oglesby)

for the Jennies and the trout seem to regard the straggly, sinking fly as a better take than a big surface fly. Ah, they say, one has sunk, let's take it. Have you noticed this happening in sedge fishing too? Trout will seem to shun the most obvious surface 'motorboater' when the sedges hatch in still evenings, and will readily take the nymph or the waterlogged fly. Too much surface movement frightens trout. This principle does not hold for sea trout.

Dapping itself is an interesting way to take brown trout although it is not really a dry fly art in the way we usually think of dry fly. In dapping you do not cast the fly. You allow the floss silk line to carry it out with the wind. You do not use your normal trout rod, but you get a very long

light rod which will exploit the wind and get a long belly of silk to blow out in front of the boat and dance and roll the big dapping flies, or the natural flies, and tempt trout. I have covered the tackle and techniques in the sea trout section, but it is worth saying that on many of the lochs I fish, dapping seems to do well for short periods only. Often lochs which look ideal for it do not produce anything more than abortive rises. Trout will splash wildly at the dapped fly and often miss it, as sea trout do. The early season is best for trout dapping, and June is possibly the best month. Dapping takes big trout and some of our larger Highland lochs can have a marvellous period of sport in June with dapped flies, and thereafter revert to being best fished with wet flies.

Ponds, Lakes and Reservoirs

When thinking about stillwater fly fishing typical waters are often divided into two – lochs and other natural waters on one hand and reservoirs, ponds and lakes on the other. Clearly, this is one of those divisions which quickly adds confusion to our thinking. It is the sort of definition in which the extremes are clear, but all the grades in between are not. At one end of the scale lie the natural lochs of Scotland, the tarns of Cumbria, the natural lakes of Wales and the lakes and loughs of Ireland. These stillwaters are quite likely to be found today to be more or less as Nature formed them. They are filled with water drawn from the hills and the countryside in a natural drainage area, and this water reflects the natural chemistry of each region. Their waters rise and fall according to rainfall. Their banks have been carved by millions of wave years and their food regimes have reflected the natural forces of the environment. Their trout co-exist with other fish, or are the sole inhabitants according to Nature and their breeding efficiency is controlled by availability of suitable spawning streams. Their average size of trout is fixed by the balance which exists between population and available natural food.

On the other hand, we have waters created by man – water supply reservoirs for drinking, industry, irrigation, or lakes and ponds sculpted for ornament in the landscape of estates. Some man-made waters are formed almost at random – gravel pits fill with spring water or rain, for example. These waters may be linked with old, natural ponds or lakes in the past, but today's lake or pond is radically different in size, shape, ecology and function. For example, when Ardleigh reservoir was formed, near Colchester, in the sixties, a shallow fertile valley was made into a reservoir of not quite 200 acres. In that valley there had been several natural streams and small ponds in which trout lived. This is typical of many artificial waters. They are logically positioned where water drains to naturally.

The picture becomes less clearly focused when we think that many of the large natural lochs of Scotland have been raised in level for water supply purposes, or for hydro-electric generation. Equally, many of the natural waters have been managed in some way, either by stocking, limitation of stock to manipulate natural size, the elimination of pike, etc. I wonder sometimes whether there is a true wilderness loch left in the

Right: **Fishing one of the lakes at Packington, near Rugby (Michael Shepley)**

Bank fishing an English stillwater fishery in excellent conditions of ripple and light (John Darling)

UK. The blend also takes place, to some extent in stock, with Scottish fish being planted elsewhere, although it is obviously ludicrous to think of nationality in Nature.

Many of the fishing techniques I have described as being successful on lochs are also excellently suited to ponds and reservoirs in England. For example, if you drift a boat over a rippled bay in Grafham or Hanningfield or Ardleigh and fish a team of three size twelve flies over the trout, say a Greenwell, a Dunkeld and a Black Pennell, you would take trout. I have done this many times and I have, on occasion, found that this simple – some would say simple-minded – technique can work really extremely well. The day visitor from Scotland on a water like Ardleigh might find that conditions were right for fishing the reservoir as if it were a loch. Why, he might say, are all these Englishmen fishing large lures down on the bottom, or large nymphs, and why do they anchor their boats? It would be easy to pick a day like this and feel that some present-day fly fishing techniques on English reservoirs were a hang-over from pike fishing, or a faulty understanding of the simple techniques of loch fly fishing. That judgement would be wrong. Fertile reservoirs on clay beds, or gravel make quite different demands on the fly fisher from those typical of Scottish hill lochs. But I do not see these different techniques as in opposition to each other; they are part of the seamless robe of fly fishing, and if the English have learned any fly fishing techniques from the Scots in making the most of their excellent new stillwater trout fishing, I can show many ways in which the Scots have learned, or are learning from the tackle and techniques developed for the new stillwaters in the south.

I lived for two years more or less on the banks of Ardleigh reservoir and I fished most of the ponds and reservoirs in that area during my stay. This is a low-lying clay area with waters which are neutral to slightly alkaline in chemistry. This means that we have waters which are greenish in appearance, are given to algae blooms, grow weeds in profusion and provide the most amazing abundance of trout food I have ever seen. In Ardleigh I saw freshwater snails as big as whelks and even larger, shrimps were big and scaly, the nymphs of the aquatic flies were massive compared with Scottish lochs, there were masses of coarse fish fry and a variety and abundance of windblown food to top the diet. The result was that trout introduced to Ardleigh in the right numbers showed a growth rate and a body quality which reminded me of Scottish sea trout rather than browns. The rainbows of waters in this area of England showed astonishing growth and I have quoted elsewhere the achievement of putting on 2oz (57g) a month in these habitats (see p.19).

I found, in fly fishing Ardleigh, that I could increase wet fly size quite radically and do well. I used sea trout flies at first, size 8 and found that these, fished two to a cast, on a floating line did well in the wave. When the wind dropped, I found that Ardleigh behaved in a way quite different from most Scottish lochs. In Scotland, a calm loch is usually unproductive; in England, a calm loch is often magnificently productive to nymph fishers, to dry fly and above all, to those who fish lures and carefully chosen large nymphs very deeply, either on the bed of the water or close to it. I think each of these areas is worth looking at more closely.

Wet fly fishing from a drifting boat is practised on most of the midland and southern reservoirs in England, but in my opinion drifting is principally a way of covering as many fish as possible in water where trout density is low. On a Scottish loch you might have twenty or thirty trout to the acre; on a good English lake you might have ten times as many. Fishing from anchored boats is quite acceptable in England, whereas, if you anchored your boat in the middle of a popular bay in some waters in Scotland, people would tend to look sideways at you. Since coming back from England I have felt less self-conscious about anchoring than formerly. But one must always remember that the tradition up north is drifting and people expect you to do it. In the same way, bank fishing in Scotland would usually imply moving round the margins of a bay, but on the reservoirs and ponds of England, it is likely that the angler will stake his claim to a given reach and fish it for long periods. This was something I found curious when I first fished English reservoirs. I was amused to find anglers wading out into the reservoir and sticking their large landing nets into the bed of the reservoir, as if marking out territory. Some would stay in the same place all day. I am, by nature and tradition, a mover, but I do not find it necessary to move quite so much on well-stocked English ponds and reservoirs.

Let me divide this form of stillwater fishing into three departments: fishing on the surface, fishing nymphs just below the surface, and fishing nymphs and other lures near the bottom.

Right: **Fishing wet fly down the margins of Ardleigh reservoir, near Colchester, Essex. The ripple is almost at right angles to the bank, giving the angler ideal conditions for covering the bank shallows with wet fly fished on a long line at about 45° to the bank (John Tarlton)**

Pond and Reservoir Nymphs

We have discussed the basic arts of nymph fishing elsewhere in this section (*see* p.32), but a special word ought to be said about the range of nymphs and nymph fishing on the reservoirs and ponds of England. As a northerner living down south I was astonished by the size of the nymphs. I have seen nymphs ½in (13mm) or ¾in (19mm) in length in many trout gullets. On Ardleigh, we had chironomids (midges) which were well represented by No. 10 or even No. 8 dressings. Similarly the sedge nymphs, the silverhorns, and the great red sedges were astonishing mouthfuls. We used to imitate sedge nymphs using a Woolly Bear nymph dressed locally in Essex and its main characteristic was a fat woolly body overwound with hackles which I would not at first use because of its size

and bulk; but I learned better. I have a couple still in my box and I cannot get Scottish trout to take them. My advice on nymphs for local reservoirs is two-fold. Take local advice and trust the local patterns, and, secondly, study the gullet contents of the trout you take. This will give you the size required. Broadly, I would select size 12 and 10 as standard, but the smaller nymphs also do well and one cannot do without them in the box. English ponds and reservoirs do not eliminate the small nymphs; they merely add a whole range of large ones to our existing range. The largest nymph I have fished was a size 8 Footballer (chironomid) and the trout of Torrington reservoir in Suffolk tore it to bits in their enthusiasm for it.

In really still conditions on English ponds – and ornamental ponds always seem to be sheltered and

Close up of a good brown trout taken on nymph in stillwater. The hook hold on the point of the lower jaw is not the best one for security, but the fish came safely to the net (Trevor Housby)

A pattern tied to represent a sedge fly. Sedge fishing on English rivers and on English and Scottish stillwaters offers tremendous sport from mid-summer onwards. The fly is fished on the surface to imitate a 'scuttering' sedge (John Darling)

to lack wind – it is advisable to fish a long tapered leader with your nymph, say 3½ metres, and grease at least two metres of the leader. This will give you control of the nymph fished just under the surface. It will help you to see small takes, and it will greatly assist in striking. I experimented with greased floating lines as well, and I found that the high surface floater and the greased leader were safer for striking, more accurate for casting and were, all round, far more delicate to handle, resulting in fewer breakages than normal floating lines and ungreased leaders. Leader points may be less than 3lb (1.4kg) breaking strain in the finest nymphing and dry fly fishing, but I do not really trust myself with these very light points and I am happy to use 4lb (1.8kg) or even 5lb (2.3kg) points, especially where there are heavy fish about.

Getting the nymph through the still surface film if often difficult. When you cast, try to accelerate the entry of the fly by raising the rod tip quickly just before the line finishes unrolling in the cast. This will flip the nymph over and will punch it through the surface film. Nymphs, of course, are of various profiles in their dressing and of different weights. Woolly Bears are hard to get through the surface in calm water, but big, sparsely dressed chironomids, which are little more than hooks with thin bodies, are easy to punch through. Also, many nymph dressings are weighted, either with lead in their dressings or copper wire or other weighting. These dressings are really intended for mid and lower water nymphing, but do not rule them out for use on a floating line. I saw a magnificent

demonstration of this once. A visiting angler on my reservoir fished a floating line, a 12ft (3½m) leader and a weighted nymph and took fish after fish from water where my high water nymphs were only of limited success. There is nothing wrong with a nymph fishing several feet below a floating line; indeed, there is everything right about it. But it is probably no longer sub-surface nymphing in the sense in which I use the word. It is nearer deep nymphing which we will go on to discuss.

Nymphs hatch on the bed of the reservoir or on vegetation growing there; they live and feed there and grow through their various stages there. Some spend months and some spend years there. Some make the journey to the surface when they are a few millimetres long and other varieties when they are several centimetres in length. Thus, the array of bottom food in a rich reservoir is wide. A whole new science of trout fishing has grown up around this range of bottom food. In the north, where we have far less food available and where food size is smaller, we have, in the past, tended to write off bottom food as outside the scope of fly fishing. When trout become bottom feeders, we more or less say they are uncatchable. English reservoir and pond fishers, however, have shown us that not only can the deep nymph be fished effectively on trout rods, but that it will usually produce far heavier trout than the floating line and nymphs fished just under the surface. The nymphs which are fished deeply are usually heavy and may be large. They may well be dressed to represent one of the larger bottom nymphs such as the May Fly or even the large Dragon Fly, the *corixa* or Water Boatman or some other largish form of bottom life.

Getting deep down to the feeding fish is an art in itself. There are two main ways of going about it. One is to sink the line and let it take the nymphs with it. I have done this a lot in Scotland, where there may be less weed and bottom vegetation, but I do not like it as a technique. The sinking line is usually thin, cuts the finger tips when you handline a lot, gives you a sense of heaviness and loss of delicate control and is rather like fishing bait off the pier rather than outwitting the best of fish. By all means try sunk line. It fishes best from a boat and is a menace from the bank. From a boat the line is at least off the bottom immediately in front of you, but on the bank the line grounds and trails through weeds and mud and dead leaves. I much prefer the deep sinking techniques possible with a floating line and a heavy nymph, or with a sink-tip line, where the fly line is in control on the top of the water but allows the heavy nymph to search out the bottom-feeding fish. In this form of fishing you can strike when the line moves, and you are in a position to get in touch with your fish quickly by taking up slack line. A deep line may be pulled down by the fish and as the trout runs to the side, may foul all sorts of weeds. The worst thing in fly fishing is seeing your fish showing at the surface while your line is still dredging around among the weeds. It usually leads to a break.

Trout will take your deep nymph when it is going down, when it is hanging or resting near the bottom, when it is twitched or jerked as if it were starting out on its journey to the surface, or on pulls upwards when the drift up is simulated. In angling terms, we cast out, allow the nymph to sink and watch carefully as it goes down for a tell-tale movement of the line to indicate a sinking take. We have least control over these takes, but I have sometimes found them to be the best cases of hooking I have had all day. One may stop the nymph in mid-water voluntarily, or may find that one cannot get the nymph right down to the bottom. The nymph is stopped by raising the rod tip and also, if required, by handlining until direct contact is made with the fly. Further handlining will raise the nymph. It is surprising how much movement is imparted to the nymph by a seemingly small movement of the rod or line. When I have fished the technique of the tired nymph, where the nymph is allowed to lie unmoved for long seconds and then is gently twitched as if tired activity was being resumed, the fly can be moved attractively by the merest stopping of the rod, or the merest change of rod tip height.

At its most extreme, deep nymphing can lay the nymph on the bed of the reservoir and it can either be moved minimally there to attract trout, or it can be left lying, to be moved by the trout as it forages. This technique of legering a nymph for trout is slightly controversial. Does a trout take a static fly? My view, after trying various forms of this type of fishing for trout and sea trout is that first of all it is very hard to prevent movement of the fly; the tiniest change of rod position can move

(Jens Ploug Hansen)

A magnificent fish in perfect condition (Jens Ploug Hansen)

A fish well hooked in the scissors. This is by far the best hold of all (Jens Ploug Hansen)

the nymph. Secondly, there is no doubt that foraging trout, especially big rainbows, create a considerable degree of bottom disturbance – presumably directed towards dislodging and revealing natural nymphs. There is no reason why artificials, dislodged in this way, should not be maximally attractive to foraging trout.

Lures, Streamers and Other Deep 'Flies'

In stillwaters, there is a great range of food available to trout in addition to flies and their nymphs. There are shrimp, crayfish, minnows, coarse fish fry and other items such as tadpoles. These are hardly flies, but even under fly-only regulations, various fly-like lures can be fished effectively in imitation of non-fly life. I say 'fly-like' but, more carefully examined, that really means lures tied in the manner of fishing flies. Lures tied with tinsel bodies, hair wings, and hackles and at least some of the appearance of flies are widely fished. Some waters draw the line and have a size regulation, which eliminates the grosser fish representations. Some other waters restrict the number of hook points which may be used, thus cutting out lures with double or treble hooks on them. Many reservoirs do not legislate at all, and whatever can be cast out like a fly on a fly rod and line is accepted as a fly within the rules. Check up before fishing on any new water.

Let us discuss these deep lures in three simple categories: the big nymphs; the fry; and the exotic. Large nymphs such as the dragon fly larvae have already been mentioned. These can be 3cm long, larger than some reservoir minnows. But there are also the freshwater shrimps and crayfish, which are not flies but can be represented by nymphing tactics. I am sure our most traditional wet flies are often taken for shrimps, for example the fancy flies

contain several dressings which are claimed to be shrimp imitators and these include the Peter Ross. Some patterns of shrimp imitations set out specifically to imitate shrimps and nothing else – all within fly fishing.

I fish a lot with streamer lures and I am not really sure whether these are taken as nymphs or as fish fry. I suspect the latter. Recently, fishing Inverawe Lily Pond, I decided to fish a small bay between the lilies with a streamer, and after a dozen casts I had not moved a rainbow. I cast back to where I had started and this time stripped my hair wing streamer as fast as I could move it. I had a great take and landed a splendid rainbow of just under 3lb (1.4kg). That fish had, presumably, spurned my streamer fished as a gently moving nymph and had taken with vigour when I fished it as an escaping prey. This is hardly fly fishing in the natural sense, but it is exciting fishing with a fly rod. Incidentally, I am a great believer in the pursuit principle. Fish which are reluctant to take a small fly will go vigorously for it if it seems to be fleeing. To heighten this effect I sometimes put a large sea trout fly on the tail of the cast and make it appear that the tail fly is pursuing the dropper fly. This works well on English reservoirs when the fly is tripped in fairly quickly. Do not slacken the pace of the retrieve if a fish swirls and misses. Keep up the illusion of a hot pursuit and you may find you get a second or even a third take from the following fish. Also, one following fish may attract others.

Some of our fly-cast lures are obviously fish imitators. The famous Polystickle is a single hook fish lure with a specially shaped wing tied in to make a fish shape and tail. The Muddler Minnow range, dressed on single hooks with hair wings and a great ruff round the throat, are clearly fish

Two good rainbows from the Lily Pond, Inverawe. These fish took in heavy rain as the light faded towards evening. Rainbows of this size and quality are typical of the put-and-take fisheries which have grown up recently in England and Scotland (Michael Shepley)

imitators. I have tied up several perch fry imitators with streaming hackle points and they can be very effective when big trout are marauding the newly-hatched perch, 'or other coarse fish. My sea trout box, with its demons and tandem dressed flies proved a boon when I was first faced with an English reservoir on which rainbows and browns seemed to prefer the bottom diet to hatching flies. With these obvious fish imitators, I am keen on long casts and a stripping technique. It is interesting to see the most amazing lures taking trout in this way, not only deep down, but on or near the surface. I was fishing one evening on Ardleigh with a local fly tying expert and we were not doing well. Fish were moving in the slicks and were making fools of us by refusing everything we cared to offer. My colleague decided on shock tactics and took out a white lure, tied with white cock hackles and mounted in big tandem style. He had several fish right away, and they seemed to want this lure whether it was sinking, being retrieved, brought up from the depths or – I think I am right – left lying in the surface. It was incredible. It was like nothing on or in the water.

I have one or two dressings I sometimes use similarly. I have a very realistic tadpole which worked well once, and has never worked since. I have a Yellow Muddler, which likewise had one day of glory. I have the most realistic creepy-crawly three centimetres long, and some day it will save me from a blank I am sure. These are exotics, and are as far from fly fishing as legering a worm, but they are cast out on a fly rod and line. Where should all this stop? Our reservoirs are fly fisheries. Should we allow plastic American bass wigglers (I have seen one working well) or should we allow fly fishers to cast out plastic fish on fly hooks, of which there are many available? If we allow that, would it be permissible to cast out a fly with a tiny little spinning flasher at its head? Such flies exist. How big should the spinner be? I could, if you asked me to, cast out a Mepps spoon on my fly rod, or if my own fly rod is too precious to misuse, I have a black stick of a thing which would cast out a very respectably-sized devon minnow. Clearly, we will have personal limits to what we would fish as 'fly'. To help further, most waters have quite clear regulations limiting the size and style of flies which may be fished. Personally, I cannot be bothered with deep fishing unless the pond or lake is unresponsive to surface or mid-water fly fishing. I think I would rather take nothing than revert to forms of fly fishing which remind me of mackerel feathers and are fished with a significant lack of finesse. This is personal, but I do preach it to newcomers to the sport. The delights of fly fishing are in fishing the fly, and not really in fishing large lures and baits masquerading as a fly of sorts. Logically, my approach can be attacked, but I am enough of a hedonist to want to please myself in my fishing above all, and I would be being false to myself if I said that deep line fishing excited me. This may be one reason my name is not often on the lists of killers of record trout.

Dry Fly on Ponds
In many ways this is the most obvious sport; when a trout is firmly on surface food it shows itself clearly in its feeding and it is not too difficult to detect the fly it is taking most consistently. Dry fly fishing works on stillwaters occasionally, and I do not propose to spend very much time on it, since we have discussed some of the basic techniques in relation to loch fishing. I have had some marvellous sport with both rainbows and browns on the dry fly, but I think browns are more consistent in taking the floater. This is true in two ways. The browns take up steadier feeding lines and I find that I can predict where a brown trout is moving

and how best to present my fly more easily than I can with rainbows. When I was fishing a rather special pond in Scotland at Inverawe – the Lily Pond – where the owner has formed a stocked rainbow fishery of very high quality. I watched rainbows as they rose and it was really impossible to put a pattern on to their movement. One large fish, which I succeeded in rising but not hooking, moved along a gentle curve and without any apparent reason, suddenly did two U-turns and rose vigorously along a fast S-shaped course. On one of these turns it saw my nymph and bulged hard at it, without taking. A dry fly might have been absolutely right for that fish. Rainbows also have some peculiar feeding patterns which browns do not share. You will find little shoals of rainbows cruising along just under the surface 'vacuuming' as they go. They make tiny rises as they swim, sometimes giving off a sucking or plopping noise which reminds me of shoals of roach on summer evenings. Not only in this way, but in ordinary

The fascination of taking trout at evening on smaller lakes and ponds gives some Scottish areas great appeal. This pond was the ornamental lake of a Scottish estate and was stocked and managed by a group of enthusiastic Edinburgh anglers. Notice the trout rising to the right of the angler's cast

rising, rainbows can sometimes produce extremely tiny surface rings. On the Lake of Menteith I found one August evening that the rainbows were making the tiniest vortices on the surface and that it was a test of eyesight to detect them. But if you could, a well placed fly would tempt them. Rainbows, for me, are fitful surface feeders, and are inconsistent in their lines of feeding and in their reaction to flies presented to them.

What stillwater trout take from the surface will be best answered by the angler observing the rises and the flies actually on the water. I do not carry a chalk-stream collection of dry flies when I go out on to stillwater. I have a range of three or four flies, all broadly representative of flies likely to be encountered and I find that this degree of representation is enough. In my box are Black Spiders, Greenwell in spider and winged form, Tup's Indispensible and Badger Spiders. I very much favour the 'Parachute' dressings which Dickson of Edinburgh and Martin of Glasgow carry. These dressings carry the hackle wound round a vertical spike on the back of the fly, rather than wound round the throat of the fly. The result is to give a fly which has a tiny raft of hackles to support it in the surface. They float extremely well and are excellent hookers. My view is that I have two darkish flies and two lightish flies in the patterns listed above. I fish these in size 12 and 14. In addition to these basic patterns I have one or two larger winged dry flies, either dressed as parachutes or normally, and these larger flies, say size 10, are used as dragging flies or skidding sedges on a good wave. I found the English reservoir browns very keen on this, especially in high summer.

Rainbows have a characteristic which every dry fly fisher should remember. Small rises may conceal big trout. Rainbows taking a dry fly down may, in the very act of taking, speed down from the surface and smash fine tackle. Browns, in my experience, take more slowly and react more slowly to the strike. I have lost some lovely rainbows on stillwater because they took and dived and smashed me in the strike. How can one guard against that? Well, it is certainly easier to hook well on a short line, and it is better to use a softer rod for the fishing. I am notoriously bad on both points. I am continually being tempted to fish long lines on stillwater and when a rainbow dives on the take, it smashes me. Equally, I have grown to like rods which have some power in the hand, and that does not mix well with fine floating tackle and big stillwater fish.

Dry fly fishing makes up only a small part of reservoir fishing, however, and while it is a face-saver on a day when nymphs and lures will not work, the floating fly should be thought of as an occasional technique, and not likely to be used often in normal fishing conditions.

Basic Tackle for Stillwater Fishing

When trout fishing lochs I often carry two rods, one with a lighter line and, usually a dry fly attached, and one with a No. 6 line – my regular line – which I use for wet fly fishing and nymphing. But the lighter tackle can equally fish wet fly or nymph and sometimes delicacy can pay off. Normally, in good ripple, I stick to my 9ft 6in (2.90m) cane rod, the Sawyer *Stillwater*, a Ritz parabolic rod originally built by Pézon et Michel, Amboise, but now available built in Aberdeen (Farlow-Sharpe). I love this rod for Scottish loch fishing and make no apology for singing its praises. This rod is a powerful piece of equipment – 9ft 6in (2.90m), two-piece, ferruled. It is equal to anything a loch can produce and those who know Scotland will realise that this can mean the occasional big trout, or, more likely, the taking of sea trout and salmon during trout fishing. I have had several salmon in this way on my *Stillwater* and I have the utmost faith in it.

I had a *Stillwater* first in 1960 and I fished it hard through the sixties, including taking it to Lapland. It became my favourite all-round rod and I was mortally grieved when someone stole it one night when I was fishing the Border Esk. I had it replaced and have fished since then with the replacement. In 1979 I chanced to stay in a hotel in Grantown on my way home from the Findhorn and, among other collected tackle which the proprietor showed me was a mint Pézon *Stillwater*. It was in superb condition, used only once, I was told. I managed to buy it, and I have already taken on it a 4lb (1.8kg) sea trout and a host of smaller sea trout and trout.

The tackle most people fish on a loch in Scotland these days would probably be like my other loch outfit, a 9ft 6in (2.90m) fibreglass rod with a No. 6 AFTM double taper line, fishing a leader of 5 or 6lb (2.3 or 2.7kg) breaking strain and No. 12 or No. 14 flies. I once wrote a paragraph like that and was soundly taken to task for fishing coarsely. Let me defend the tackle at once. Of course one can go lighter for smaller flies or for finer fishing. I often do. But in the main, on good ripples, I strongly advocate modern 6lb nylon. To begin with it is not thick, it casts and straightens well, it is thick enough to knot well (and thin nylon does not knot well) and it is thick enough to get the wind knots out of when you inevitably cast them in it. Wind knots are those little half hitches that appear

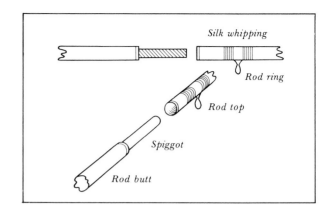

out of nowhere and, if tightened, can weaken the cast seriously. Another advantage of 6lb stuff, of course, is that it is still strong enough to fish effectively with a wind knot in it. After all one does not *always* know if one has one.

A 9ft 6in (2.90m) fibreglass rod, two-piece, with a spigot fitting, preferably, is a delightfully simple yet sweet piece of fishing tackle. I use a delightful rod which I believe to be misnamed, the Webley *Grilse*. Its smaller neighbour is the 9ft 3in (2.82m) *Lake*. Again, this is a delightful rod, typical of many you will see on lochs. My preference is for the slightly longer rod, since it has just that little bit more control of the bob fly coming out of the water. That is critical. A short rod casts nicely and really does well, but it lacks bob fly control. It also lacks rolling power. A good 9ft 6in (2.90m) loch rod should be able to roll line out of the water easily. This is invaluable if you suddenly spot a rise to your right, say, and you are fishing your line out in front. With the longer rod you can roll the flies off the water and flick them to the right and often get a chance at feeding fish which would not be accessible to you if you had to lift the line, change direction in the air and try to place the cast at right angles to the last one. You will probably also foul your companion's line and that can fray tempers.

The traditional rod for loch fishing in Scotland was often longer than I have advised. I have fished rods of 10ft 6in (3.20m). A traditional rod was soft and gentle and heavy. Today there are rods of 11ft (3.35m) and even 12ft (3.66m) available in carbon fibre, so light that the longer rod can be fished single-handed with no bother at all. I have used one of these carbon eleven footers and it is extremely competent in working the bob fly. I don't think I need the vast overhead casting capacity it has, but the power is there if you need it. What worries me a little about the longer fibre rod is that you might find that, like its brothers in the carbon fibre salmon range, rolling and rapid changes of direction will break it. Carbon fibre is an astonishing material, fast and crisp and powerful and expensive but it does not react well to roll or spey casting and sudden shocks can shatter it. This has happened to me during salmon fishing, and it has slightly altered my thinking as far as carbon fibre is concerned. It is too expensive and rare a material to be used for only part of the multiple job a trout rod must do. Cane and glass both do everything I ask of them, with cane doing better than glass on roll casting and, in longer rods, in spey casting.

There is a great tendency to over-line rods. Manufacturers are not quite so extreme as they used to be. Often on rods one would find the Association of Fishing Tackle Manufacturers (AFTM) number, usually shown with a little sign like a musical sharp followed by a number. I have trout rods with recommended numbers like 7 and 8 on them. These lines are far too heavy for decent trouting. They may flatter the caster by making the rod bend well, but fishing is not just casting. I think the over-lining of rods is a hangover from the days of enthusiastic competition casting. I would ask every new trout angler to fish 9ft 6in (2.90m) rods and No. 6 lines, choosing a floater in the double taper style.

Double tapered lines merely mean that the line has a level centre and some yards from the end, each end, the line begins to reduce its diameters to provide a 'rat's tail' which gives the line nice casting and water entry characteristics. It keeps the business end of the line thin and the idea of the double taper is that you can reverse the line when you shorten the taper at one end, through time, by cutting off the knot. Be careful of this. Try not to cut the knot off if you can avoid it. Indeed, many anglers would scoff at a knot between line and leader anyway, much preferring to attach the leader by a blood knot to a tail of heavy nylon whipped to the end of the line or attached by a nail knot. I have also done it in some cases by using one of those little eyes supplied by the line manufacturers where the metal eye had a barbed shaft which would be thrust up the hollow core of the line and would grip well. I always felt

Three excellent brown trout taken on wet fly (Jens Ploug Hansen)

Above and right: **Fishing a stillwater (Ardleigh Reservoir, Essex) in the late evening is magnificent sport. The ripple dies and the fish move into a good evening rise. This fish was a well-shaped rainbow which took a nymph at last light (John Tarlton)**

that such an arrangement was insecure. The nail knot or the fine whipped splice is best. Then the fly cast can be knotted on or fitted by intertwining two loops of nylon, one on the cast and one on the line leader above. But the old style of knotting the line to the loop of the cast by something like a tucked figure of eight knot is perfectly adequate. I use it regularly (see p.29).

Distance casting is not usually necessary for Scottish loch fishing, although distance helps when you are bank fishing and the trout are rising in slicks tantalisingly far out. Thus, the tackle I have recommended, while competent for longish casting, is not intended as distance casting equipment. I can cast roughly twenty five yards of No. 6 double taper floating line with my *Stillwater,* or possibly, if lucky, a whisker more. In general this is far too much line for normal loch fishing. When I am fishing certain kinds of river for sea trout, I sometimes put on a No. 6 weight forward line, that is, a line which has a tapered end, a thick portion of body behind it, (about 20 yards), and a long running line behind for shooting in the cast. I can put the whole of this line out (thirty yards)

in clear overhead conditions, and this can be useful where distance is absolutely essential. On Scottish lochs, especially in boat fishing, it is, in my view not necessary to cast such long lines. In salmon fishing on the great glides of the Dee and, indeed, on the major rivers everywhere, long casts are necessary, but that is quite a different set of conditions and tackle. Weight forward lines have disadvantages in normal fishing. They do not roll well, because they do not have the length of body to do so. There is one excellent design, however, called a longbelly which gives you 18yds (16½m) of body in front of the shooting line. I like this design of line very much and I believe it is very popular on English reservoirs. Garcia make a range of floaters in this style.

On English reservoirs, where distance casting is often very important in bank fishing, especially where deep lures are fished, you will often find anglers using a shooting head rig. This is something you might make up yourself. It consists of the forward half of a double tapered No. 6 line (or even heavier), spliced to a nylon monofilament shooting line behind. The shooting line has very

low friction and, with a couple of false casts and judicious acceleration of the line by left hand line hauls, you can project the shooting head forward and take multiple yards of the monofilament line behind to get huge distances. I have tried this in both England and Scotland and, although I see the line going out miraculously, I have never quite got used to the fishing feel of nylon in my hand when I have been working the flies back in. I hate the feeling of a lump forward. There is a secondary problem too. Fishing nylon through wet fingers for hours on end cuts the flesh. I even get this with sunk lines where the diameters of line for weight are less than in floating lines. One does however get distance and you could use tape on your finger or a finger stall. Both tricks would lose you sensitivity, but if distance is the object, you have to make some sacrifices. And as for rolling a shooting head out of the water – forget it. It has to be retrieved until the backing is all in and then lifted cleanly from the water and accelerated in the air before projecting the lump of line out again. I am certainly rather against it.

The lesson we learn again and again is that tackle is a statement of what kind of fishing one does, how it is done and what typical conditions one meets. I have described, clearly I hope, my most regular stillwater conditions, namely wind-swept Scottish lochs or reservoirs, and fishing done mainly from boats. When I lived in the south-east of England, however I was faced with quite different conditions.

On Ardleigh, near Colchester, I had a bank fishing season on a fascinating and well run brown and rainbow fishery in a clay bottomed, fertile reservoir. I waded its margins and covered fish in that way and I also fished it from a drifting or anchored boat. I had two seasons there and I got to know its ways fairly well. Like many reservoirs, Ardleigh offers sport in different categories. Fish do rise well to flies fished on the floating line, and some of the evening rises I have had there have been memorable. But it also fished with deeply-sunk flies and lures and produced some of the best browns I have ever seen. Deep lure fishing requires distance casting, and that indicates either the use of a shooting head or a weight forward line. I used both there and on neighbouring reservoirs and ponds and had some great sport, but it was sport in an idiom which has never worked consistently for me in Scottish waters. My cane rods were not really right for this kind of fishing and I used a Milbro 9ft 6in (2.90m) ferrule glass rod, two-piece, and a WF (weight forward) AFTM 6 line. I also fished a shooting head and the rod I used to like for that was an ABU Zoom 8ft 6in (2.59m), two piece rod which had great powers of projection of shooting heads. I think there is a critical length in glass for distance casting, and in my view it is around 8ft 9in (2.67m). Rods of this length often give superb handling and casting characteristics but they are usually too short for the kind of fishing I like doing. They do not work the bob well, and they are distressing rods to roll-cast with. But when you are bank fishing a reservoir you may not want any of these things. The longer glass rods often lose something of their sweetness as they are built for maximum projecting power in casting. They become rather too pole-like for good fishing characteristics, but they again throw marvellous lines. Fishing sweetness in a rod implies sensitivity and delicacy in response which is so easily lost in building a rod to outcast other rods. I am delighted to say that in the last few years, a census of English reservoir fishers would reveal more 9ft 6in (2.90m) rods than 8ft 6in (2.59m) ones, fewer shooting heads and more weight forward and longbelly lines (and a growing number of double tapers), and rods which have settled down to being a good compromise between casting and fishing. The Hardy Jet range has some excellent rods in it and they are popular on reservoirs. Geoffrey Bucknall rods which you can make from kits are much in evidence and can be tailored to suit your own requirements. There is a fruitful and ongoing revolution taking place on reservoirs in England and all sorts of fresh and good ideas are emerging, perhaps because the anglers on English reservoirs might be turning to trout fishing as an alternative or a supplement to ordinary freshwater fishing. Some of the best Ardleigh trout fishers were also excellent pike fishers. Where there is no trout tradition, the chances are that you get some very clear analysis of the needs of the new trout fishery and tackle is developed to suit.

A particularly interesting idea developed first in USA, but well adapted to reservoir fly fishing, is the line tray. When you cast long lines and fish in by handlining, you soon find that coils of line are lying dangerously round your feet. I have lived with coils round my feet in boats and rivers and loch banks all my life and it can be dangerous and can lose you fish if it snags. A line tray is simply a flat tray buckled to an angler's waist into which he drops the coils of line as he retrieves his flies. Casting is thus made easier. Instead of having to haul line up out of the water at your feet and aerialise it by multiple false casting, the line is more or less safely in the tray. If you are using nylon monofilament backing on a shooting head, this can be a boon, since coils of nylon round waders and reeds and who knows what, is a menace. Nylon in loose coils is a menace anywhere, of course, and it has the delightful habit of kinking and twisting round itself, even in a line tray. The new flat nylons are better, but not yet as safe as braided line with dressing. Line trays have considerable advantages for bank fishers seeking distance.

Other tackle advances associated with reservoirs reflect techniques of fishing and I have discussed these in a previous section of the book when I dealt with basic techniques for reservoirs and ponds in the south, but let me just recap a little bit by saying that the southern reservoir fishers have shown us that trout are remarkable bottom feeders with well developed predatory habits. The deep lures developed within fly fishing clearly represent tadpoles, newts, sticklebacks, perch fry, roach fry and minnows, large larvae like dragonflies, and even crayfish. To fish 'flies' like these well, one has to think one's way through trout feeding habits which are very different from those in Scotland, where much of this food is not present or is thinly distributed. To fish these flies, one also has to mount tackle and rigs which will do the job. This is why a whole new dimension has entered trout fishing since the English reservoir and pond revolution has arrived, and it has vastly benefited all, and has re-educated many traditional trout loch fishers. Of course some of the techniques are unrewarding in Scotland, but the process of education is that we have at least thought our way to this discovery by trying new tackle and new lures. But some of the approaches do work well and some of the tackle is of universal application – witness my delight in the Webley rods which have reservoirs in mind.

I have said very little about reels. I recommend the Shakespeare *Beaulite* range for good design, reliability and function and modest price for the marque. The Hardy *Marquis* reels are superb, better engineered than the *Beaulite* and a little better to look at, but much dearer. I have both in my tackle cupboard and both have done me excellent service in trout, sea trout and salmon fishing. The *Beaulite* and the *Marquis* ranges are similar in that they have an external rim of the drum exposed to your finger for line control during the fight. I use this a great deal in salmon and sea trout. Both designs have adjustable ratchet checks and this is essential in my fishing world. Ratchets are not designed to tire fish out during the fight, they are designed to stop reels over-running when sudden demands are made to give line. These demands are not necessarily during playing fish. Quite the reverse; they are typically made during casting when you tear line off the reel during false casting to feed it to the line in the air, often in enthusiastic lengths as you try to get enough line out to reach a particularly attractive rise.

I like wide drums because my own angling career has been full of surprises like hooking salmon in the dusk on my trout rod and having to deal with a shrieking, long running fish while trying to get the boot of my car open to get the big net out! (*see* p.163). Most fish in my experience do not run far, even large salmon and sea trout, but they often do run very fast and it is there that the reel must be absolutely trustworthy, giving line at speed and not over-running. At real speed a trout reel shrieks as if it were about to disintegrate. It is in extreme conditions like this that it is important to know that the pawls of the ratchet and the clip holding the drum on the spindle are reliable and well maintained. It is also at times like these that the extra capacity of the wide drum is comforting. I have never seen more than sixty yards off any fly reel, yet, but sixty yards is a fearful length off any reel.

Finally, on the subject of reels may I make a plea for line guards. My old reels had excellent line guards, preventing the line falling back during casting and fishing and cutting into the front of the lower cross piece of the reel frame. Line guards are not of much importance for playing fish or for re-winding line on to the drum. That usually comes through the fingers anyway to provide tension and level wind. But if manufacturers would just provide a simple hard face for the bottom cross member of the reel frame or would again produce something as simple as the old Beaudex wire guard which just clipped on to the reel, anglers would be much cheered.

In terminal tackle, my advice is to buy your favourite nylon in lengthy spools and tie up all your own casts and rigs. I think it is hopeless to rely on tackle-shop-ready leaders. Fishing is not like that. One is always adapting, repairing, retying and making up tackles to suit the conditions. I treasure a patent nylon spool carrier which I bought a couple of years ago which carries four 25-metre spools of *Kroic* nylon which I can pull nylon off at will, leaving a tail out of the spool for the next demand. The box is made of hard transparent plastic and is oblong. Top and bottom on the long sides have tight-fitting lids and inside the box is fitted with compartments which neatly fit a *Kroic* 25-metre spool allowing it to turn when nylon is pulled off. The tail of each spool is fed out through a slot in the end of the box, giving four tails – top and bottom front and top and bottom back. Rubber friction guides are provided in each slot and this holds the tail of the nylon firmly and allows controlled pulling off of any required amount for making up casts, etc. The weights of nylon can be read off through the transparent lid of the box, and I have one box for trout weights and another for salmon. This box has sorted out what was, for me at least, a real problem area in tackle storage and handling. I used to have reels of nylon on a tube so that I could draw off lengths of whatever weight I needed. The ends were held by rubber bands on the reels, but these would come off or break and the resulting spillage of nylon was a hazard causing tangles and mess. Every so often I used to take my scissors and give the whole collection a kind of haircut, losing lots of nylon in the process. The *Kroic* box is certainly a breakthrough.

The market is well supplied with excellent brands of nylon. I have already mentioned *Kroic* which I have used consistently since its introduction to this country some twenty years ago. This nylon is greyish in colour and is said to be dichroic, ie it takes on the colour of its surroundings during fishing. I use it because it is reliable, pliant, strong, knots well and has been extremely kind to me in my fishing. It does not kink readily, has good resistance to sudden pulls, is flexible, even soft in casting and gives the fly a natural look in the water. I am not keen on very brittle nylons which tend to hold out the fly in too stiff a way and be difficult to knot safely. Such a lot of habit comes into recommending nylon – my colleagues fish other brands and do as well as I. But their feelings are probably as firm on their brands as mine are on Farlow's *Kroic*. The diameters of nylon I use are included in the table.

Diameter of Nylon	mm	Breaking Strain
Dry Fly Fishing:	16/100	3¾lb (1.7kg)
Wet Fly Fishing:		
Trout	21/100	5½lb (2.5kg)
Trout	22/100	6lb (2.7kg)
Trout or sea trout	24/100	7lb (3.2kg)
Sea trout	20/100	8lb (3.6kg)
Salmon Fly Fishing:	30/100	10¾lb (4.9kg)
	34/100	14lb (6.4kg)
	38/100	16½lb (6.5kg)
	40/100	18½lb (8.4kg)

The diameters of a given breaking strain have altered a great deal in the past few years. I have, in some cases, been able to increase the breaking strain by up to 2lb (0.9kg) for the same diameter as formerly. A good case in point is salmon fishing where heavy autumn and spring leader was 16½lb (7.5kg) strain up to about 1974 when I stepped up to 18½lb (8.4kg) for the same diameter (40/150).

Nylon monofilament should be without roughness or blemish or kinks or bright spots. These are all indications that the nylon has been damaged and may fail you. I run my fingers down my casts regularly during fishing to feel for abrasions and knots. When you get a wind knot, for example, and you manage to get it out, perhaps by using a pin or a hook point to help, you may find that the nylon had a sharp little point of light inside it where the knot was. This can be a sign of strain and potential failure. I usually satisfy myself that the nylon is still strong enough by hand testing it, but even then it can be misleading, since the worst strain nylon can get is a sudden snatch or tug which sends a shock wave suddenly along it and can break at blemishes which stood a steady strain without trouble. I would rather cut a wind knot out and tie the ends together with a blood knot (see p.29) or a grinner rather than risk a snap when a fish takes.

I lost a much valued fly and a very good sea trout partly because I was in the middle of a superb rise of fish and was doing well and was very excited. I had taken three, one of which was 5lb (2.3kg) in weight, fishing my trout rod at night. On the tail of my cast I had the most miraculous Dark Mackerel tied on a tiny Waddington shank with a small treble hook at the end. What a fly! I was fishing from the tip of an island on Spey and had taken the boat over to reach the vantage point. Each time I netted a sea trout I put it in the boat and with a 3¾ pounder (1.7kg), I had the problem of a fish which slipped through my hands and walloped on the bottom boards of the boat while still hooked. I seized the fish and eventually gave it the necessary knock on the head, not by using my priest, but by banging the fish's head on the boat seat. This must have damaged the cast. It felt all right and in the dark I thought it was sound and it responded well to a hand test. The next cast brought a walloper to the fly which may in fact have been a salmon, because it ran and broke me. A repaired cast would have saved that fish and saved that fly, my only pattern tied up specially for me in Dickson's of Edinburgh. Still, it had done well. But always look to your nylon and scrap those leaders which are in any way damaged.

Carrying casts or leaders ready made up can be difficult; but by far the best way is to use cardboard castholders (they are now also available in plastic) on which the tail fly is hooked in to the central hole and the leader is wound round the 'cogs' on the rim of the card. As a dropper is reached, the fly is taken in to be secured in the middle of the card. I carry these cast cards in a Farlows cast holder with clear plastic pockets and I can thus flip through my casts in each wallet and draw out the card I want to use without fouling or snagging other tackle. Gone are the days when I used to carry spare cast, carefully wound, inside my cap. Sometimes I forgot them and took my cap off in the fishing hut or in the car or even, in some cases, in my estate car just before turning in to my sleeping bag after night fishing for sea trout. Casts turned up everywhere, tangled in my socks, attached to a favourite jersey and even inside my waders. I had to come out of the river and take the waders off to get the cast out – waste of good fishing time. The moral is straightforward; use cards, be systematic and tuck the cards away as soon as you have changed. A great advantage of cards of course is that you merely attach the line to the cast loop and pull the leader off, flies and all. It works well in light or dark and it is undoubtedly the simplest way of dealing with cast changes. Indeed, it is such a simple way of changing tackle, that one of my closest friends, a most accomplished salmon fisher, now never changes a fly, but carries a whole range of flies ready tied up to the leaders and runs them off cards, changing the whole cast rather than cutting off a fly and knotting a new one on. I don't go to these lengths of enthusiasm for cards, but I do keenly advocate them for storage and ease.

Defining the Ideal Day

An ideal day for trout fishing is something usually defined in retrospect; one finds that, for a change, one can do no wrong and trout rise sincerely to our flies. Looking back one may also decide that one felt well, that casting and striking technique was better, that tackle was showing its true quality and indeed the sky was bluer than it ever had been . . .tra la la. What I am saying is that an ideal day is usually defined by its results and our own state

Right: **In a remarkable action picture, the whole spirit of the art is caught. The trout leaps wildly in an attempt to throw the hook (Jens Ploug Hansen)**

of mind as much as by any combination of the weather or water. There really is not much point in protesting that it is an ideal day for wind and water, but for some perverse reason the trout are not aware of it. Nevertheless, if one looks at one or two days when things were at least thought to be 'fair to middling' and asks oneself whether the weather on these days had elements in common, one might come up with a pattern worth thinking about.

It is extremely hard to select a series of days on which the fishing was of even, high quality. For instance, I had a splendid day on the little River Eye between Eyemouth (its estuary) and Ayton, a few miles inland. It was a day in early May and it had a warmth and softness which I will long remember. Yet, after a slow start, and an hour or so in mid-day when trout were distinctly unwilling to rise to wet or to dry fly, the afternoon produced a film of high cloud and, as the light slowly diminished, trout rose and rose as if they were famished and had never seen a fly before. That is, it was not an ideal day for twelve hours. It became ideal and produced three or four hours of steady good fishing which brought twelve trout to the creel and produced many more which one wanted to return that day but which would have been most acceptable on almost any other day of the year.

In complete contrast to the Eye, which yielded a day of walking, wading and all the variety of wet fly fishing in a clear Border stream, I had an evening on a reservoir in Suffolk which went so well that for two hours or more it seemed that every wave of the water held a rainbow close to 2lb (0.9kg) in weight. The day had been rather poor, and one of the club members had met us at the stile with a long face. He had seen fish, but all far out and absolutely uncatchable. He felt that it was probably not worth waiting until the evening because that would only bring calm weather and even more frustration. We were only arriving at seven and we commiserated with him and said we would try our luck anyway.

It was a May evening after a rather hard and bright May day with white clouds against a blue sky. In terms of weather it was a day of steady high pressure and a constant breeze which, even on that sheltered little lake caused the whole surface to ripple except for the usual strip in the lee of the western bank. When we arrived at about half-past seven the wave diminished and it seemed that the calms of a May evening were about to

Left: **A fine four pounder from one of the Packington ponds, near Rugby (Michael Shepley)**

take over, but in fact the calm seemed to announce more than that; it brought a slight change in the atmosphere. The air became moist, as is usual in the evening, but instead of the sky clearing as the wind fell, it skimmed over with high cloud and a little puff of evening wind darkened the surface of the water. It was a new kind of weather altogether. The barometer fell and a much more westerly feeling took over. When I say westerly, I suppose it is a way of saying that much of my fishing has been done in Scotland where the westerly winds bring softness and gentleness to evening trouting and the northwesterly or easterly winds all bring hardness to the air and spoil the sport. 'Westerly' is my way of saying that I felt hopeful that the evening was going to be soft and steady and kind.

It was. The water instead of lying mirror-like in calm or rippling with hard black and silver lines on the wave, presented us with a matt grey prospect with a uniform ripple running right down one of the most accessible banks. In this matt gentle drift of water, trout had already begun to rise.

As the light changed, trout rising became more general and fish appeared closer to the shore. I fished a black chironomid and had a good trout of nearly 2lb (0.9kg) in a few minutes and another which I returned shortly after. There was hardly any need to move about. Trout were roving about everywhere and the choice of the dark midge nymph seemed to be perfect. My companion and I decided to take two trout each from the water and to return all other fish and I had a personal ambition to make my brace top 4lb (1.8kg) in all. I already had nearly 2lb (0.9kg) in the bag and with luck I would connect, on a fine evening like this, with a fish in the 2½ to 3lb (1.1 to 1.4kg) class. I was thus getting into trout of a 1½lb (0.7kg), a 1¾lb (0.8kg), etc and releasing them in the net. At one point I released a cock rainbow of about 2¼lb (1kg) because it looked slightly out of condition, as many cock fish do in May. My second trout was just over 2lb (0.9kg) and it made up the bag, but I reckoned I had released eleven other fish of good quality, and in the course of the evening may have had hold of 19 such trout. My tail fly, the chironomid, was stripped of its dressing, and to try out a pet theory of mine I changed from an all black nymph to an all white one and took two trout on it! I do not think colour meant anything to these evening feeding fish. Presentation and depth meant something; they were all feeding through the wave and showing well at the surface.

One could go on like this *ad nauseam* – recounting days on specific waters and trying to sketch in the precise quality of weather and water which seemed to contribute to the conditions. Certain things would be held in common of course, as they are in fishing, and for river fishing in the Borders of Lowland Scotland, I would tentatively list them as these:

Water
Water height above minimum but not in any sense in flood.
Water colour clear or clearing after being coloured (perhaps by rain).
Water level constant or very slowly falling.
Wind
Westerly or Southerly, gentle, steady or falling.
Sky
Half covered to fully covered with high grey thin cloud.
Barometer
Steady or slowly falling around 30in (76cm).
Temperature (Air)
Not lower than 55°F (13°C) and preferably 60 to 65°F (15 to 18°C).
Humidity
High. A distinct moistness in the air, with dew on summer evenings.

For stillwater I would ask for slightly stronger winds than for a river, which, after all, has streams to help the presentation of the fly. I also like skies fully covered with cloud, and it need not be high and fine as for river fishing. Lower clouds, for instance the grey clouds after rain, are excellent for Scottish lochs. More fertile waters such as artificial reservoirs and lakes seem to flourish on finer conditions, although this may merely be a function of where these ponds are usually found – in the midlands and south of England. Perhaps the most important feature of wind is its steadiness and its temperature. Winds below 50°F (10°C) seem to me to load the dice against good fishing, although I have caught trout in even cooler conditions.

There is a danger in thinking about the ideal, however. In one sense it cannot exist, because it is an amalgam of bits of *good* fishing days. Further, a good fishing day may well be one in which the conditions suddenly changed and turned hopelessness into delight. Then there is the angler himself. Who can settle to fish well if his tackle is misbehaving or, put another way, who can make his tackle behave well if he is unsettled or agitated or angry? Clearly the weather is not one's psychology, but it is a known fact that the weather and our state of mind are closely linked. All these caveats! But that is typical; I feel more and more as I go fishing that the most important words for a fishing discussion are 'nevertheless', 'however', 'yet' and 'but'. In the case of weather for the ideal day the need for these words is clear. You can find conditions far from ideal, yet the trout, nevertheless, find something in the day you cannot rationalise. But if you are alert and can adapt your fishing, you may take an ideal bag, weather or no weather, and behind all our discussions about weather, tackle, and water height it is this ideal which we are most concerned with.

Section Three
The Quest for Sea Trout

Thinking about Sea Trout

You can think of sea trout in two quite different ways. The fish can be seen as a migratory game fish, closely linked with salmon, or it can be seen as a bigger and gamier brother of the resident brown trout, a kind of bonus trout which comes back to the river or loch like an uncle returning from fat living abroad. Anglers who think of the sea trout as some kind of component of the salmon fishing on a river or loch are likely to look down slightly on the fish. Like woodcock on a pheasant drive, they are regarded as 'etc'. I know well how this feels. You may be fishing very seriously for salmon with a 14ft (4.27m) rod, fish are showing in the main lies, and your hopes are high. The greased line comes slowly round over the likely tail lie in a named pool and you get a draw. 'Into him', you think, but there is something wrong. The fish pulses and pulls in a dynamic and strong way, but obviously the fish you have hooked is not 10lb (4½kg) in weight – probably nearer 2lb (0.9kg). On salmon tackle, the fish gives a rather poor performance. It is brought in quickly, and instead of the highest praise, one gets the comment, 'Only a sea trout'. You might even go further and express the hope that the sea trout has not disturbed the salmon lie.

It is not easy to fish well for salmon and sea trout at the same time. Your salmon tackle is likely to be a 14ft fly rod or a 9ft 6in (2.90m) spinning rod, and the line you throw on your fly rod, for instance, will most likely be an AFTM No. 10. Hooking sea trout on that tackle is so far removed from the real sport of sea trout fishing that it should be regarded as a travesty.

But think of the other side. Suppose you are fishing for trout on a June evening on Spey. You are fishing with your favourite 9ft 6in trout rod; it might be a cane one or a two-piece glass or carbon fibre. A No. 6 line with a 5 or 6lb (2.3 or 2.7kg) strain leader is being cast out delicately and you are fishing a wet cast of two flies, say No. 12 in size. As you keep your profile low and wade down a glide, casting over the seductive, mysterious water under the bushes on the other side, you see the water bulge powerfully, and you are suddenly into a fish which takes, runs and leaps in one wild movement – a fish which makes the brown trout of the river seem pale. You have your hands full with a wild fresh, hard fish on the end. Now that is certainly exhilarating sport. This is the other end of the scale, seeing a sea trout as a big brother of the browns, and taking it on tackle and flies intended for the residents.

In between lies the art of fishing exclusively for sea trout. But it is an art of trout fishing, not one derived from salmon tactics. It is a single-handed rod approach, and, if you are like me, apart from the choice of fly and a cautious increase of strength

of the leader, the rod, reel, line and tactics are those of trout fishing. In these circumstances, sea trout are magnificent, memorable and quite without parallel in game fishing.

There is, of course, a slight confliction between the sea trout as a migratory game fish and as a better quality brown. The law firmly identifies sea trout with salmon. Estates let the salmon and sea trout fishing together in many cases. In places, like Scotland, where the laws relating to brown trout fishing are lax, and protection and care of the fish is difficult, there is a strange anomaly. The salmon fishers leave the pools, probably, at five or six in the evening. Local trout fishers may have permission to fish for brown trout, but are certainly likely to catch see trout. The result on some beats is interesting. Sea trout fishing is given to local trout fishers on a strict permission basis. In this way, sea trout regulate brown trout fishing to some degree. But the fact remains that a trout fisher on water with no permit, and getting into a sea trout, must either return the fish or face prosecution for taking a migratory fish without appropriate permission.

Sea trout may of course run big. The largest I have caught in river fishing to date weighed 9½lb (4.3kg), but I have had my share of fish from 6 to 9lb (2.7 to 4kg) in weight. The largest I have ever seen caught was Oliver Williams's 13-pounder, taken at dusk on Endrick when we were fishing together one August evening. I shall never forget my first sight of that fish as I went into the water to net it, with a small torch to help. I saw a great back, but it was the breadth of it that amazed me. It was an enormous fish, and I was immensely relieved to see it safely in the net – so was Oliver. That was an exceptional sea trout. Not the largest ever or anything like that – Bill Brown of Strathpeffer had a sixteen pounder from the Ewe in Wester Ross one evening about the same date. The Endrick fish was memorable, however, and a case of a sea trout on the bank looking as big as a salmon, but taken on a trout rod.

On Tweed, sea trout run very late and I finished my salmon season on that water with a seven pounder on my salmon tackle in November 1978. That was not an unworthy fish. It outpaced a 7lb (3.2kg) salmon all the way and it gave a splendid acccount of itself on the double-handed rod. But what a fight it would have given in summer on my

Sawyer *Stillwater* trout rod! Yet, on Tweed, sea trout seem not to respond very well to being treated as trout. It is the big salmon tube flies that they take, usually long after trout fishers have disappeared from the water – October and November. Strange fish, these Tweed sea trout. They seem not to be the same race as the Spey sea trout, or the West Highland fish we catch in summer.

At the other end of the sea trout scale is the grilse of the sea trout race, the finnock, sometimes called whitling. This little fish is normally ½lb (0.2kg) or a little more in weight and it may come into our sea trout rivers and lochs in quantity from about mid-July onwards. As a boy I loved finnock. They were in the streams and pools of the Doon, near my home, and in a summer evening, or in the run off from an autumn flood, I could take them on my trout rod and have the time of my life. When my fishings moved north and east in Scotland, I met the finnock again, but this time as a spring fish, as an overwintered fish which spends the close season in Highland lochs and is to be caught in rivers like the Spey in good numbers in late March and April.

The finnock is, however, the growing sea trout and it is sad to report that in the 1970s numbers of the fish have been declining seriously. One sees finnock now in penny numbers, one or two at a time. But in the late fifties I knew two local finnock murderers (who thought themselves great anglers) who took 60 finnock one morning in an hour. To give the act its true character, I should tell you that it was on a Sunday morning during church. Who said the wicked did not flourish like the green bay tree? In Scotland it is illegal to take migratory fish on Sundays.

Killing finnock is foolish, because you are killing the young sea trout which have reached the sea as smolts, have fed in the estuaries for some months and have returned to the river on a kind of mock spawning run, but have remained virgin over the winter and, when caught in spring, are returning to the sea again, to put on more weight and possibly to return the same summer as pounders or better. Anyone who has thrilled to the pull of a fresh sea trout in the Spey in the still of the night, and who has fought a thick silvery five pounder in the Shiel would never take a half pounder when it has the very real chance of growing into the mature fish. Of course I thrilled over catching finnock when I was a boy, but there were vast numbers of them in the rivers and lochs. Sea trout are clearly a decade of eclipse in the seventies – and I hope it is only for a decade – and to kill immature fish is folly, defeating the whole purpose of conserving fish stocks to produce quality

Left: **Wet fly fishing for sea trout. The fish is almost beaten and is nearing the net. But beware, sea trout have a reputation for sudden, furious resistance just when you think they are beaten, and many escape at the rim of the net (Jens Ploug Hansen)**

angling. My catches for 1979, however, have given me hope that a resurgence is on the way.

The sea trout, then, is a splendid anglers' fish, offering sport on wet fly and sometimes on dry. It offers superb sport on the dapped fly on lochs. Light spinning for sea trout is good fun in certain conditions. It is a fish which brightens up day loch fishing in the Scottish Highlands and produces memorable long dusk sport from late May onwards. It tests the angler, since it is a very timid fish, and it tests our tackle since a good sized sea trout on trout tackle puts considerable strain on the outfit and clearly sorts out the inadequate items. A fish with these facets is an asset well worth conserving and well worth studying and fishing for in its own right.

Where and when Sea Trout Run

I know Scottish sea trout best, and there the fish run most clean streams which have easy access to the sea. I have taken them in small burns in Wester Ross, where the water was, you would have sworn, too thin for fish larger than a minnow. I remember once taking two good sized finnock from a small pool just above the tide in a Wester Ross burn which had falls immediately above that

point which sea trout could not have passed over. The distribution is interesting in Scotland. Sea trout in their best qualities and quantities favour water systems which have a short, well fed river joining large lochs to the sea. Think of them: Loch Maree has the short River Ewe below it; Hope has its own short river; Assynt has the Inver; Shiel has the river of the same name. Many others abound. One would almost assume that the loch ought to be north-west facing, as the major sea trout lochs are. Loch Lomond has the north-west orientation, but its river, the Leven, is southerly in direction, but short, like the others.

These are all west coast systems which I have mentioned. Sea trout also run the waters on the east coast, but I have often found myself thinking that they were rather different fish from those of the west. The fish is not fond of the Thurso or Wick rivers, but the Brora, Conon and Beauly rivers draw in good stocks. There are numbers of sea trout running the Ness into the great Loch Ness system above. Notice again the short river and large loch characteristics. Fish run all the rivers of the north-east, and are especially noted in the Spey. This is a splendid sea trout river taking fish of some size, three and four pounders, right

Fishing a long line down the glides under the trees on the far bank of the Hoddom Castle stretch of the Annan in Dumfriesshire

up into Loch Insh and beyond. The Aberdeen Dee has some of the earliest sea trout I know, coming well to the fly on May evenings. Dee fish are not usually big. My experience of them indicates that they are usually around 1½ to 2½lb (0.7 to 1.1kg) in size and only exceptionally larger. Spey fish average over 2lb (0.9kg) and often this river will show fish of 6 and 7lb (2.7 or 3.2kg) in an evening's fly fishing.

The Tay system also brings in sea trout, but these fish, although often 3lb (1.4kg) or over, are not fish of the build and quality of west coast fish. In recent years, and certainly since the mid-sixties, Tay sea trout have seriously declined in numbers and quality. I hope this is temporary, since the great haughs of Delvine and the glides of Stenton and Murthly provide splendid sea trout fishing water.

Further south again, we find that Tweed sea trout are a strange race unto themselves. The finnock there are often large, and the main runs of sea trout carry very big fish. But they run late. You will see some sea trout in the dusk in summer evenings, and you may or may not catch them. But large fish run the river from September onwards, and fresh fish are still moving in right up to the end of November, when the salmon and sea trout season ends. It is the last river to close in Scotland and, as I have mentioned, I have often taken sea trout during my salmon fishing in the cold waters of November, when winter has already started. Tweed sea trout are not as well shaped as Highland fish, offering a slimmer profile than their northern brothers. They are often 'heady' and rather coarse in finish with tails and fins which somehow seem too large for their bodies. On Tweed, they sometimes call them sea dogs, and lots of salmon anglers look down their noses at the run of sea trout. In Till, an English tributary of Tweed, there is a reputation of pools filling with large sea trout which will not move by day or night to any lure.

The earliest sea trout are often the largest of the year. On some systems they are known as a fishable separate run, but on many waters the numbers of very early fish are small and they do not attract anglers. For instance, in western Inverness-shire I have heard local gillies refer to 'the trout of March' in Gaelic, meaning the earliest and often the largest of the year. During the sixties, when sea trout numbers were high, one keeper on Loch Eilt, fishing in early April, landed several sea trout in the teens of pounds at a time when no tenant would have bothered to try for the fish. On the Inver system further north, in Wester Sutherland, I have heard C C McLaren declare

that by April a small but important number of very heavy sea trout would be in the river – as opposed to the loch above. I know that the earliest sea trout fishers on Loch Maree, and those who fish fly for spring salmon there are often taken aback by hooking a large sea trout, clearly a fish of the current season, but as dark as peat, indicating that the fish must have entered the Maree system in early spring.

We often get small numbers of fresh new fish in April on various rivers and at the same time of year we take unspawned, that is virgin, fish which seem, like finnock, to have overwintered in the river or loch. But serious fly fishing for sea trout, in my experience, does not begin before May. I take some salmon fishings on the Dee near Aboyne in mid-May and, by that time, the book always has a few sea trout in it, say four or five, and, by the end of our week, given reasonable weather – which May usually produces – I have added as many fish again to the total, since this coincides with the first real evening fishing on the river.

The Spey fish show in April, good strong big sea trout, and one sees them while fishing for salmon, but remarkably few are caught. Maybe this is because in the evenings, we are usually trying for salmon. May brings good sea trout to the Spey and early June marks the best run of the year. I think the Spey run is getting earlier. I noticed in 1978 that the best catches for quality were taken in the earlier summer and the rest of the year, despite reasonable water, yielded only modest returns. This sort of thing, on any river system, of course, might indicate the absence of a generation. If the earliest fish are usually larger than the high summer ones, you might get a year when spawning is poor, or when the smolts of a given spawning were decimated in a drought or were diseased. That would lead to a profile of the generations of sea trout with the older fish, returning earlier in reasonable numbers, since they are multiple returners, and the new generation of pounders being absent.

We must always bear in mind that sea trout do return to fresh water again and again. Their survival rate is much higher than that of salmon. Sea trout feed to some extent in freshwater and they appear to be able to sustain themselves well. Scale readings of large fish will give a history of five, six or even ten returns to freshwater. Sea trout of great age have been reported, often into the teens of years in exceptional cases. Since the whole profile of the stock in a river system includes old, large fish at one end and finnock at the other, it takes many years for the stock to reach its full strength. Losses of individual hatchings, or smolt

The taking of a sea trout. In this remarkable sequence taken in Norway two anglers were fishing side by side and both hooked sea trout simultaneously on fly. Both fish can be seen above. *Below:* The larger fish runs downstream and then up and ends the run in a leap. The line is slightly 'drowned' as a result, but the hooks hold

The fish tires and is netted – a fine fresh sea trout taken on sporting trout tackle

runs, is serious in that it knocks out a generation of the fish. But general disasters like UDN killing the older and larger fish have very serious effects on stocks. On many west coast fisheries in Scotland stocks took a serious knock in the early seventies when UDN wiped out old and young fish alike. True, many of the fish seemed to have spawned successfully before the disease killed them, but this has only produced the first elements of a replacement. These fish in turn must produce each year the basis of the finnock runs of two years later and the multiple returners which will have the heavier fish in their numbers. Of course, some sea trout may opt to remain in the sea for more than one feeding year. Some of the scales of my own fish have shown this to be a common characteristic of larger sea trout. This would ensure that a small number of mature fish would be available to fill a few of the gaps in the grid of generations returning to a river or loch system after a general disaster in a given year.

It may be impossible to characterise the pattern of sea trout runs, but my own angling experience suggests the following. Small numbers of large fish run north and west coast Scottish rivers in March and April; better numbers of fish, including a diminishing number of heavy sea trout, come into western waters in late May. East coast waters bring in good numbers of medium-sized fish from mid May onwards. On both west and east coasts the bulk of the smaller fish – in the under 2lb (0.9kg) class – appear in late June and run with floods until the end of August. In late summer the Tweed brings in a run of large or very large sea trout which is preceded by a run of more moderately-sized fish, but the bulk of the heavier sea trout are autumn runners. Finnock are to be found in all systems from July onwards, peaking in late August. Winter finnock typify certain east coast waters of Scotland, offering sport with downstream migrating fish from late March to about the end of April.

Where Sea Trout Lie

High Water Lies

When the river is in flood at any time from late spring onwards, sea trout will run upstream from the estuary and will populate the pools and streams of the river. During the spate, they will be seen splashing in certain places such as the tails of pools, in broad flats and in the gentler wells of deep pools, and you might be forgiven for thinking that these were the lies to look for the fish in. But this would be misleading. These showing fish are

on the move. They can be caught during the run, but they will tend to take bait, or if the water is clear enough, fly in sheltered lies such as vees behind boulders, eddies under banks, shelter below weirs or between double dams and in obvious sheltered lies such as these.

It is at times like these, with a spate running and water brown with silt that the coarse worming brigade make hay. You will see them fishing town weirs or certain pools on the club water where the locals know sea trout lie in spates. Lines of worm fishers wielding heavy tackle will be seen, and when they hook a fish, it is more likely that they will lift it straight out of the water and swing it in an arc on to the rocks behind or even on to the public roadway! I cannot hide the fact that I dislike this form of worm fishing and that I feel sea trout caught like this represent a terrible waste of sporting material. I do not grudge the old-age pensioners their fish, nor the truant schoolboys

theirs, but I feel that this kind of worming is absolutely unworthy of the sport of angling for sea trout, which means quite different things to me.

Low Water Lies

When the water falls and clears after a spate and the river returns to normal, a very different pattern emerges. Sea trout will populate pools and secure glides. They love glides which are heavily overhung with trees and they will lie along the sides of moderately fast streams. Where sea trout lie in the river alters with the time of day. They are timid fish, and during the day they will hold to the main pools or lie in deep glides. On the Border Esk, for instance, when the light is right, you can see the stock of sea trout in main pools lying on the gravel bottom. When the evening comes, however, the fish distribute themselves in the headstreams, often in the very thinnest rushes; they will move up and

Left: **Wet fly fishing for sea trout on the River Nith at Thornhill, Dumfriesshire. The Nith brings in substantial runs of fish from late May onwards (E. Atkinson)**

Below: **A brace of fresh run sea trout from the Hebrides, Loch Voshimid, North Harris (Arthur Oglesby)**

down certain aprons of gentle water at the sides of the pools, often, again, in very shallow water. But most of all, fish will lie in the glides at the tails of pools. The part of the pool we call the tail includes the shallowing water below the main well of the pool, and the so-called hang of the pool immediately before the water plunges into the stream below. In glides, as dusk deepens, sea trout will rove about, distributing themselves up and down the evenly flowing water.

You will catch sea trout on fly by day, even when there is no spate to colour the water. I have waded deeply into the big glides of the Shiel, for example, fishing a long floating line with a trout cast on, and have had some excellent fish over 3lb (1.4kg) for my trouble. It is harder to catch sea trout in bright light. Indeed, they shrink from it. Think of it from the sea trout's angle; the fish has only recently left the estuary which has wide waters to flee to and has the sea itself behind. Once in the river the fish is in a restricted, vulnerable environment. It is little wonder they hide during the day and appear in the evening.

I am often baffled by sea trout lies. In 1978 I was fishing the Spey for salmon during the day in bright June weather. I thought I could see, with the help of my polaroids, every stone on the bottom of a favourite sea trout pot of mine. There were no fish showing in it. That evening my attention was caught while I was fishing the tail of the large pool above by a splash in the pot I mentioned. I moved down to it and hooked a splendid fish which alas, threw the hooks after a strong fight. A chance fish, I thought. Later in the evening, in fact after midnight, I saw two fish moving again in that pot, but I did not manage to hook one. Now, these fish may have moved up into the pot after dark; sea trout run mainly at night in non-flood conditions – but I am positive that they were residents there which I just didn't see. Sea trout distribute themselves in completely different places after dark. They take up roving beats or glide lies where they are eminently fishable.

Sea trout moving at night may not in fact be runners. I have mentioned sea trout roving and I shall write more of this later. On calm summer evenings you will see the surface of the water in the tails of pools veed with roving fish. On some gentle pools such as Craigbel on the Endrick (a small dam) you can see fish moving all the way down the pool, splashing here or there, and veeing the surface when they come into shallow water. This is tremendously exciting, because these fish are on a kind of predation beat. I liken it to the exciting ranging which sea trout carry out in estuaries. There, you will see them 'veeing' the surface among the tangle, often turning and bulging as they feed in very shallow water. The salmon is a non feeder in freshwater, but the sea trout, used to foraging in the brackish waters of the estuary, does feed in the river, albeit to a limited extent. Fishing for a feeding fish, or one which is programmed to range after food, is a help to angling. It helps us to be logical about the fish. With salmon, in comparison, you are fishing for a fish which may have residual feeding behaviour but which in fact does not feed. Taking a salmon on fly or bait, then, is like trying keys in a door. One might work, and presumably work again. With sea trout we are tempting a feeding fish to take a fly which appeals to an active feeding urge; we tempt salmon to take a fly which triggers off a feeding urge in a fish no longer able to feed actively

My approach to sea trout varies with the clock, or, rather, with the light. Much of my fishing is done from early evening onwards and into the night, often right through to the dawn. I begin the evening by creeping around and trying a trout cast over streamy places. This often produces a fish and it keeps one occupied until the light really dwindles. Even then, when the dusk is deepening, I usually keep my head well down and try streams. It is a great mistake to approach the tails of pools and other still places until the light has almost gone. Wind helps you to get to the tails of pools a little earlier, of course, but always consider the possibility that you will scare the fish rather than tempt them in fine, light conditions on glassy glides.

When the light goes, try to get your fly over the shaded water under the overhanging trees on the far bank. You will, very likely, be fishing a floating line with a two-fly cast on. Most of your sea trout will take the bob fly, but, in an Irish way, a bob fly without a tail fly does not fish well. The tail fly straightens the cast and holds it out in the water, allowing the bob to work near and in the surface – note that I say 'in' the surface – and it is there that the fly has maximum tempting power. I will describe in some detail the techniques in a later section.

Wet Fly for Sea Trout – Rivers

One of the two main arts of sea trout fishing is taking the fish on wet fly in rivers. The other is fishing wet fly or dap for the fish in lochs. Fishing rivers with wet fly is, in many ways, the fundamental art and, for me, comes to grips with one of the essential characteristics of sea trout – their shyness. Most wet fly fishing for sea trout is done in the evening – fishing in the dusk and into the dark. Sea trout are caught during the day in flowing water, of course, especially after a flood. Indeed, in highish water, day wet fly fishing may outclass night fishing. But when the water drops back, forming summer pools and glides and flats, day fishing might prove somewhat unproductive. In glides and flats your ally during the day might be wind. Some stretches which will not yield fish normally by day will produce fish after fish when the wind troubles the surface. In night fishing, wind will be your enemy. Stillness and sweetness characterise good dusk and dark fishing.

The basic art of sea trout fly fishing is similar to that of trout downstream wet fly fishing. I don't think I can remember ever taking a sea trout on wet fly fishing upstream. The fish like a fly cast on a longish line and swum round through the stream over their lies. Or, at times they go wild over a fly presented almost square over their lies and drawn off their lie either by the force of the stream or by raising the rod and dragging the fly off. I know a stream on the Border Esk at Irvine House – the Island Stream – and it is possible to creep down the grassy bank at the head of the run and cover a series of lies behind stones in the rush at the neck. Fish lie there in shelter and dash at flies presented to them across their noses on a short line. It is usually a biggish dropper fly they seize in these circumstances, something like a size 8 Black Pennell or Dark Mackerel. I often think that sea trout rising suddenly and very rapidly like this are induced to rise by the sudden appearance of the fly in a take-it-or-lose-it moment. These splashy takes are in contrast with the nice turning pulls sea trout give you on the longer line swung downstream. Sometimes sea trout seem to like the fly on the dangle and one of my best Border Esk fish took me with a very hard pull in this way, and fought very hard before being netted – 4½lb (2kg). I think I was lucky with that sea trout. It had seized my Peter Ross on the tail of the cast and had firmly hooked itself in the point of the lower jaw. Most successful takes are hooked in the scissors or along the top jaw. A dangle take is, as my experience with the Esk fish proved, a snatch or a pluck.

The outstanding characteristic of sea trout is their shyness. If you are lucky enough to be able to observe sea trout in pools you will see them restlessly moving about the pools by day, flashing over the gravel and sidling out of the deeps to glide warily past your observation point. To catch sea trout by day I believe you need to find them

settled, either resting in lies during a run, or undisturbed in secure streams and glides. At night sea trout which have been in the pools during the day change their behaviour and rove to the pool tails. There they swing round and hover and are at their most temptable. I like, in my day fishing, to fish a long line, to wade well (in larger rivers) and to try to cover fish from such a distance that one is fishing sea trout undisturbed by anglers, and I include myself in that. In the dusk one uses different tactics. Wading is only used to get to vantage points and once there you should fish carefully and persistently and let the sea trout come to you as they rove. Shyness goes with the light.

The tackle for sea trout fishing, to give the best sport, is all similar to that used in trout fishing. In Scotland, I fill all my trout reels with plenty of backing knowing that I will use them for sea trout and will encounter the occasional salmon on them. Indeed, my two or three favourite 9ft 6in (2.90m) trout rods, all two-piece rods, are excellent for river and loch trout fishing, are old and trusted friends for sea trout in light or dark, and each has several salmon to its credit also. I think it is a mistake to change over to a longer or heavier rod for sea trout fishing, just because the fish are larger and stronger than the brown trout you are used to. The familiarity of the trout rod is important in sea trout fishing, especially in the dark, and the kind of trout rod I describe is not likely to be strained by hooking and playing sea trout. Avoid weak, floppy rods for sea trout fishing, just as you would avoid them for trout fishing. The reels are the same and the lines are similar. The floating lines I use for normal day and dusk wet fly fishing for sea trout are all AFTM No. 6; indeed they are my regular trout lines. The only special lines I use are two slow sink lines which are marvellous takers of sea trout in conditions where the fish do not want to come to the surface, or near it, for the flies or streamers I use. Sinking lines similar in diameter to your floating ones are two sizes heavier – AFTM 8 is the weight of my slow sinkers. Clearly, rods without a certain backbone to them will not readily handle lines of AFTM 8, but most trout loch or reservoir rods today are built for lines up to this weight.

I like to mount two rods for dusk and dark fishing. One might be my Sawyer *Stillwater* (a Ritz Parabolic rod) 9ft 6in (2.90m) in length – a

Overleaf: When the light fades on river and loch, sea trout change their character. They come into thin water and can be tempted on wet fly in the dusk and dark much more easily than they can by day (Trevor Housby)

two-piece built cane rod on which I fish a No. 6 double tapered floating line. I have sometimes tried weight forward lines on this rod and, while they shoot further than double tapers, they do not give one the feel of the line on and in the water which the D/T gives. You cannot 'mend' a weight-forward line – that is, correct the lie of the line on the stream to compensate for drag – and when it comes to re-casting, you have to handline in until the correct amount of the casting head of the weight-forward line is outside the rod tip before you can lift the line and aerialise it for the next cast. With a D/T you can roll the line off the water and place it where you want to without much trouble. I would trade the extra yard or so of casting distance for the flexibility of handling which a double tapered line gives.

On the *Stillwater* with its D/T No. 6 line (floater) I would normally fish a leader – sometimes also called a cast – of about 9ft (3m) in length presenting two flies to the sea trout. The breaking strain of a sea trout cast is a matter for personal taste and the conditions you are fishing in. I would not recommend lighter leaders than 6lb (2.7kg) strain and with modern fine diameters, I would probably feel that 7lb (3.1kg) nylon was the lightest I would use. In the dusk I change to 8lb (3.6kg) nylon for my general night work on a floating line, but on the sinking line, where there are greater pressures on the leader both during the take and in the subsequent fight, I would fish 9lb (4kg) strain.

The flies would be chosen from the usual range of Scottish sea trout patterns, many of which are scaled up trout flies like Dunkeld, Grouse and Claret, Invicta, etc. Sea trout like a large fly in the dusk and dark, and indeed, there is good evidence that sea trout prefer a large fly in most conditions. Err on the generous side. Size 8 is usually regarded as 'sea trout size' in Scotland and Ireland, but experienced sea trout anglers will quite happily fish demons, streamers, tandem dressed flies and tubes for sea trout and these lures are well above size 8. Hugh Falkus, who is a great authority on sea trout, advocates large demon-type lures in both floating and sunk line fishing. It is logical, after all, to assume that a fish which has fed on all the flashing, darting food of the estuary and which, unlike salmon, does not give up feeding when it enters fresh water, should want to pursue these lures.

Lots of sea trout take trout flies, especially in daylight. My normal practice is to start fishing the streamy water, the necks of runs and well rippled water elsewhere, with a trout cast fished in the dwindling light of evening. Keep out of sight, of course and leave the more exposed water until the light goes. Trout flies of No. 12 or No. 10 are excellent for this, and again fish two flies to the leader. Sea trout love the bob fly in river and in loch and it is this fly which I pay most attention to. It should have bulk, should cut the surface of the water well when the cast is being fished out and should be a good hooker. It is odd that, even when flies are fished deep, sea trout very much prefer the bob fly on the cast. I often get round to the Irishism that if I had to fish a single-fly cast for sea trout, I would cut off the tail fly and fish only the bob. I cannot wholly account for this, but it seems to me that in addition to its attractiveness in emerging from the water as the cast is fished back in towards the rod, the bob fly rises and falls on its dropper as it is worked through the water. Added to this attractive whole-fly motion is the fact that bob flies are usually well hackled and bulky and this gives them good hackle movement as they work. Interestingly, a good bob fly like a Black Pennell or a Dark Mackerel or an Invicta transferred to the tail does not perform nearly as well as it does on the dropper.

The second rod I carry ready mounted at night carries my slow sinking line. Sometimes I use my spare *Stillwater* or my 9ft 6in (2.90m) Sharpe's *Scottie*, but recently I have taken to using my Webley *Grilse*, which I have mentioned elsewhere in this book. It is a two-piece glass rod with a powerful but sensitive action. It is a rod capable of handling a salmon or a really hefty sea trout on a sunk line. The makers supply a small extension butt for it and when a salmon is encountered, this 6in (15cm) extension keeps the reel off the angler's coat and gives one much greater control in the fight. I have extension butts for several of my rods, including one of my *Stillwaters*. The Webley rod handles an AFTM 8 slow sinking line beautifully, again a double taper, and it provides me with a splendid second rod which can come to the rescue if my cane rod or its tackle runs into trouble in the dark.

A final item of tackle which I must mention for sea trout fishing is the landing net. Much of your best sea trout fishing will be in the dusk or darkness and it is essential that you have a net which will carry easily, will deal with big fish in the dark, including salmon, and which will hold the netted fish safely once it is in. Often in my Spey fishing I am well out in the river, up to my middle in a glide when I hook my fish. If the fish is a sea trout of up to about 5lb (2.3kg), I net it out there, and if I can, transfer the fish to a fish pocket in my fishing jacket. Big fish often bring me ashore. With sea trout I prefer to net them and come ashore with the fish netted. With salmon, after subduing the fish a bit I wade in and walk the fish back with me towards the shore where I can, with luck, find a quiet backwater to net it safely, or beach it.

The net I have used for some fifteen years of sea trout fishing is the 18in *Gye* made by Farlows. I have a 24in *Gye* for salmon. These are wonderful nets. They have a duralumin ring strongly fitted to a sliding block which moves on a squared duralumin net shaft. In its collapsed form the net hangs on one's back in a sling, and when a fish is ready for netting one pulls a release tail on the harness, the net slips down and the head locates in position on a swollen stop on the shaft end. For night fishing I sometimes fish with the net ready extended and stuck into my belt. This is a strong very competent net in which I have had salmon up to 18lb (8.2kg) – of necessity – and the 18in ring is perfect for safe netting of fish at night. The salmon size takes fish up to 25lb (11.3kg) without much difficulty.

Dusk Fishing

One would want to begin sea trout fishing at dusk by trying a fly down the streamy water. I usually begin with a trout cast, say of 5lb (2.3kg) strain, carrying two flies. The tail fly might be a No. 12 or possibly a No. 10 trout pattern such as a Dunkeld or a Blae and Black or, indeed a Greenwell. The bob fly, however, which is the real taker, should be a Black Pennell, a Soldier Palmer or that killer of killers, a Dark Mackerel. The approach is really that of trout fishing. You keep out of sight, as far as you can, search streams and the margins beyond, since you will probably have frightened the fish on the side you are wading on. Work the flies quickly, keeping them on the move by control of rod angle and, above all, drawing in line by hand – perhaps not quite stripping, since you have a stream to help you keep the flies on the move, but always keeping the flies in action.

Do not be tempted to go down on to gentler water, such as glides, or pool tails until the dusk is really deep. It is difficult to give advice on when to start on these places, but let me say that in a Scottish June evening, one is seldom finished the streams by 11p.m. and often not on to the pool tails until nearly midnight. If it is cloudy and heavy, and if there is a wind, you can advance the fishing of the gentler water by some time. If you go on to the tails in daylight, you will get nothing, and you may well disturb the water a lot. What will probably happen is that you will raise nothing and will lose patience and wade out again, causing more disturbance. Even in the deep dusk, if my

first half-an-hour of fishing the tail produces nothing, I would always wait and fish on. Sea trout move about and they will come to your pool tail eventually. If you see sea trout, but move none, and if there is no obvious reason for this such as a change in water height or a change in the cloud cover (sea trout hate clear skies), it is always well worth waiting for the other half-hour to see what eventually comes down into your casting range. However, one can be impatient and decide that it would be better trying two pools further down. Doing this at least lets the pool settle and lets the light fade, and one may well return from the lower pool to find that one only has to cover the tail with a cast to get immediate interest.

Sea trout run at night and it is fascinating to watch them crossing a weir or 'veeing' up through shallows in the dark. Often one will hear them without being able to see them. On Craigbel, on the Endrick, where the main pool is a small dam, we often hear the clattering and splattering of a good fish as it tries to run the dam face. These fish often seem to prefer to try the apron of the weir rather than seek out the pass cut into the middle. It is almost as if sea trout prefer edging their way upstream in the shallows, rather than in the gushes. It may also be that the configuration of the bed below a dam may have channels which draw sea trout away from the main fish pass. I don't know, but fish do run shallows in the dark and it is thrilling to hear them or see them.

The nice thing is that you can and often do catch runners in a different way from taking salmon from a run of fish. I was once fishing the long stages of the Garrison Pool on the Shiel and I saw the splash of a good fish below me well down, beyond our normal fishing range. There was a pause and a fish splashed just below me and I was sure it was the same sea trout, which I covered as well as I could with my floating line – cast well out over the gliding water. Nothing happened. I then thought I saw the fish above me a little way and I turned and walked upstream along the wooden stages and covered the water I judged the fish would then be in. I had a take at once and was into a very fresh, high-backed sea trout of 5¼lb (2.4kg). I firmly believe I killed a very fresh runner that late June evening, and a beautiful fish it was. Runners *will* take.

On sea pools of course, one is killing runners all the time. Again on the Shiel on the sea pool I have, as many other anglers have elsewhere, taken fresh sea trout straight off the tide. It is even possible there to note a run coming through, and follow it up to Columba's, the pool above, where with luck you may encounter it again. Following fish up like this is typical of beats with very good bank access. On many of the other waters I fish, one is either waist deep in a glide or in a pool tail and one tries hard not to disturb the water by moving, sometimes getting pins and needles by just standing still so that sea trout will not be frightened by wading. Whether I exaggerate this or not I am not sure. Certainly when you get into a good fish and you play it and net it you disturb the water a good deal. So often your next few casts produce another take. Was that fish not frightened? I agree that there are cases where it would seem that the sea trout has abandoned all its timorousness, but there are so many other cases where one false move or the sight of an angler walking down the bank sends fish off, that it is better to leave the cases in which sea trout seem bold as exceptions, and play safe, treating the fish at all times as excessively shy.

Phases of the Night

There are at least four phases of a sea trout night. There is the evening, when the daylight has not yet drained away. During this time we fish streams. Then follows the deepening dusk, when fish begin to move about the pools and take up feeding positions or make feeding tours to the tails of the pools and glides. This is often followed by a quiet, dark, still period, – the *howdumdeid of the nicht* as Scots poets call it – and fish appear to go off at this time. Finally, the night turns and the feeling of dawn comes into the air. The night wind stirs, even on a calm night, and the earth almost seems to be wakening up. Then begins the dawn rise, which can be as productive as the dusk rise, or more so.

In terms of fish movement, the evening begins with a good brown trout rise as the light goes, followed by a sea trout and brown trout rise, during which the browns often go down. Then follows a period with little surface activity, except for the odd crashing fish, in the dark. The dawn rise brings a confident, steady sea trout rise soon to be mixed with a brown trout rise which can continue well into the still monochrome daylight of the morning.

How we fish the various phases can be judged from the advice I have given in this section. Clearly, floating line techniques suit the evening and dusk rises and again come into their own in the dawn rise. But the dark still night period is the time for the sunk line.

Floating Line Tactics

I am a long line man. I like casting at least twenty yards of line over a glide and working the flies from the moment they touch the water. I am referring to tactics with a floating line, of course. To me, movement is of extreme importance. A typical case would be casting a long line over to the gloom under the trees on the opposite bank, or under the shadow of a rocky bluff or high bank. I suppose you would describe this as fishing from the shallows into the deeps. In fact it is more fishing the deeps back into the shallows. The fly should be cast out so that it presents a straight leader and a straight line and, as soon as the cast lands, your left hand should hook the line over your right index finger – your rod hand – and the left should draw in at once a yard of line in a steady draw. So often a sea trout will take the fly the moment it lands. A fly which lands and moves in one uninterrupted sequence is deadly. The flies should then be moved in a series of hand pulls and some rod movement so that they fish fairly quickly over the pool tail concerned. Sea trout will follow and seize the flies, sometimes taking well below you. It is easy to assume that the fish are lying below you – and they may be – but it is probably better to believe that the fish have followed the flies round and take only when the cast changes direction below you, in the dangle position – just as salmon do to our chagrin. Sea trout usually get a better hold than salmon in the dangle take, however. They nearly always take the bob fly and they are usually well hooked on it.

As I write, I can vividly remember one or two places where these tactics seem to work well. On some of the pools of the Border Esk, near Canonbie, sea trout lie over under the trees or under the grasses of the far bank. There I have often found that it was the first yard or so of draw which took the fish after dark. In the earlier evening, fish in the tails could be taken on a scuttering bob fly, that is a bob fly made to break the surface and furrow as it moves, 'veeing' the glide surface. Very fresh fish go wild over this, but the slightly more timid fish often take without previously betraying their presence.

The floating line, fished as I describe, is best on the most lively glides. Where your main pools are slower, as, say, on a dam or a naturally slow pool, the floater seems to lose some of its charm and there the slow sinker takes over. I shall devote a page or two to sunk line fishing later, but it is interesting to note that two things characterise floating line fishing of glides and pool tails. The fish one takes are often the freshest stock and they are usually medium-sized fish, very sprightly and very wild. This is an over-generalisation, of course, but it is an impression. I have had my best hour of sport ever with sea trout on floating line on the

Part of a memorable catch made by the author on the River Shiel, Argyll, in one hour on a June night. The best was 8½lb (3.8kg), and the two next fish weighed over 6 and 5lb (2.7 and 2.3kg) respectively. A fourth fish of around 2lb (0.9kg) followed before the fish went off the rise

Shiel, fishing a line over to the shade of a bluff from the stages below Grassy Point. That marvellous hour brought in an 8½ pounder (3.8kg) and three fish which together with the big one totalled 22½lb (10.2kg). I have also taken a nine pounder on a loch on the floating line and many other respectable fish running up towards that mark. But my strong impression is that floating line does not always move the heaviest fish, although it may provide the nicest, most visual, and liveliest sport of the evening.

Sea trout taking the floater do so in a variety of ways. I have already mentioned the instant take, when your fly touches the water and is seized as soon as it moves. Fish which see the fall and either miss it or are not well positioned to take it may pursue it and take it at any point across the pool, or, as we mentioned above, may take it on the dangle, as soon as the cross-pool movement stops and the fly changes direction and begins to be worked upstream. On the bottom cast of one pool I know well in the West Highlands where the water begins to become hazardous and weedy, the long line cast over the tail may well yield a fish in

the main stream, but equally, has a chance every time it passes over a basin between walls of weed. I had some lovely fish in the 3 and 4lb (1.4 and 1.8kg) class from such little pots there and it always amazes me that these small patches hold such good fish. I would wade the water during the day and marvel that it could hold such fish. Sea trout lies are often like this. Either you are covering fish which are slipping upstream, or you have wandering fish which tenant little holts like this all over the pool tail. In these cases, whether you fish floating line or sinker might be dictated by the weed, or the depth of the water.

In fishing a wet fly on a floating line I like to make my cast at right angles across the glide or nearly so. In this way the fly can be made to move quickly and provocatively through the glide. In my experience, sea trout like a fly moved positively, and will spurn a sluggish fly or will take it poorly. Of course, altering the angle downstream gives you a whole range of speeds. It allows you to use your left-hand pulls to make the speed, rather than allowing the drag of the current to do much of the working of the fly. It is probably impossible to define exactly how you should fish your fly round, but there are one or two guides. The first is something I have noticed developing in my own fishing over the years. I do not look for visual signs of speed; I concentrate on feel. Once or twice I have resorted to shutting my eyes to get the right feel of the fly as it comes round. I remember fishing a river in the Pindus in Greece, for trout, and coming across peculiar takes – little plucks and drags – which I could not hook properly. It was daylight, and I found myself peering into the waters of the river just to see what was going on. I could see little. Then it occurred to me that these takes were like finnock at night, so I shut my eyes, imagined myself a couple of thousand miles away, fishing a sea trout pool in Scotland, and I fished by touch. I had no difficulty at all in hooking the takes after that. They were not trout; they were smallish whitefish – not much of a prize, but it did underline how different one's tackle handling is when you cut out the visual element and work by feel.

Secondly, in the take, I think it is often better to be a little bit of a salmon fisher and strike after the pull comes. In the deepest dusk and dark, you have no option. How well these takes are hooked! Like salmon fishing, it is sometimes a disadvantage to be a masterful man and act and it is a great benefit to let the fish do the hooking itself against the water pressure on the line. On the other hand, one becomes very sensitive to changes in the feel of the line when one is expecting a strike. I was fishing down a delightful glide on the Border Esk where the river breaks into two streams round an island, forming one fairly narrow, four foot deep glide which can be fished nicely from the grassy bank without wading. It was about two in the morning and I had been doing quite well with five or six nice sea trout for the evening. My senses must have become sharpened by the success, because I was fishing the fly round and I distinctly felt the line lighten in my hands. I can only describe it as that. I felt the weight diminish fractionally, and I tightened and foul hooked a sea trout in the dorsal fin. I take it the fish had come up to the fly and had brushed against the cast momentarily, probably with its head. I reacted to this and hooked it, a nice fish over 2lb (0.9kg). I think that characterises more than any other incident the importance of feeling in night fishing. You wait for the signal, which might be a firm pull or, in unusual circumstance, might be a stopping of the fly or something similar.

The demon or lure mounted on the tail of a sea trout cast affects how you fish it. I always make a lure work faster than a standard fly. It seems to me that the sea trout, fresh from the feeding of the estuary and probably only days away from the last natural sand eel or other darting food of the salt water, is in a mood to pursue and take all manner of wiggling, darting, swimming items. Sometimes the lure breaks the surface and might be described as a floating lure, but usually the lure is fished under the surface. That is, the lure may bulge or furrow the surface, without coming out. It is the wet surface lure which I like. Sea trout can sometimes pursue these lures with great gusto and take them with memorable power. At other times, in rivers and in lochs, they glide after the lure and engulf it, turning away in a controlled sweep.

I was once fishing Loch Moidart in the late evening and we edged the boat in past the weed beds. There was not much of a ripple and, really, if one had been orthodox, one would have abandoned the wet fly on the floating line and would have tried sunk line or dry fly. Well, I pulled the tandem lure (two No. 12 hooks tied with one long wing in a Grouse and Claret dressing), and it swam steadily off the weeds and was followed by a superb wave as a sea trout 'nailed' it and I was well into an excellent June fish which demonstrated how steadily some big sea trout take, rather like salmon.

I have always associated the sea trout with hard pulls in the take, recognising the soft takes as untypical. Charlie McLaren, that outstanding sea trout angler, has often spoken to me about soft takes, especially at night. Now the difference might be that Charlie may have lochs in mind more than rivers. He once spoke of the take being like touching weed in night fishing. Sometimes it is, but in Spey and Shiel and Endrick and Esk, in glides with some movement in them, the takes I regard as normal are powerful. Often the fish you hook, had it pulled and run and become unstuck, would have been thought of as a very large fish indeed. When it is landed, you sometimes look twice to verify its size, because the take and possibly the fight was so hard.

I hold my rod top fairly low when I am fishing at night. This is true of floating line and sunk line fishing, and it is the consequence of my handlining technique. I like to have a good direct line between my rod hand, with the line over the index finger, my hauling hand and the flies. I find that this has great advantages in striking well. You get the direct pull and you clamp the line to the butt with your finger and raise the rod. Having the rod low means that, even if the fish moves towards you in the take (and some do), you have plenty of movement to give the rod to take up slack at once and set the hooks well.

Floating line fishing is, in my mind, best suited to mild, warm evenings. The lower the water the better, provided it remains sweet. Balmy June and July evenings are marvellous times to be out. If the sky is very slightly covered with a fine filmy cloud, and if the wind is gentle or calm from the west, you are likely to have perfect fishing conditions. I do not like clear nights. Rivers in June and July steam in such conditions and it is often hopeless to fish in such conditions. Bright moonlight pleases some of my fishing friends, but has never pleased me. Even if you do not have a steaming river, you have sighting conditions which are poor for the fish. I think of it as a duck shooter. On nights when there is a 'ground glass' sky, lit perhaps by a moon above, you can see teal and widgeon and even passing snipe. On clear nights you have the greatest difficulty seeing anything, because you do not have the screen against which to pick out the duck. It is surely similar for sea trout. On cloudy nights they seem to see even the smallest flies and they take them well. On clear nights they seem to go off take. Perhaps they do, but it has often occurred to me that we think fish are off the take when they are merely unable to see and pursue our flies. Perhaps a bit of both.

Sunk Line Tactics

There are many degrees of sinking when you fish with your line below the surface. In a sense all our wet fly fishing for sea trout is to some extent sunk. The modern floating line is not like a greased silk line which floated on the surface; today's floating lines float in the surface, and the tip – and the flies beyond it – may be 6in (15cm) down, or perhaps more. It is also worth remembering that those of us who fished before modern floating lines came in fished with oil-dressed silk lines, such as the Kingfisher or the Hardy Corona. These lines fished down into the water and, in fact, would today be classified as slow sinkers. Bearing in mind, then, that fishing a sunk line for sea trout means something more than fishing a fly in the immediate sub-surface layers, a distinct technique can be defined.

I came to sunk line fishing early when I had regular access to the Endrick – Craigbel – which would not fish well with floating line, no matter how hard I tried. That pool held a heavy stock of big sea trout – fish in some cases into double figures of pounds. The heaviest I saw taken there was a thirteen pounder and my own heaviest on that prolific stretch of water was 9½lb (4.3kg). The embarrassing thing about that pool was that you would think you were fishing rather stylishly

with a floating line and you would get takes, but these were always the smallest fish. I would get fish of 1½lb (0.7kg) or perhaps slightly heavier on the pool on the floating line when my host, Mrs Elspeth Mitchell, fishing a Kingfisher silk line, would take fish of twice or three times the weight. I was converted early; I rapidly changed to a slow sinker – a much loved but now pensioned-off Cortland half-and-half line, whose sinking end was absolutely everything a slow sinking line should be. It cast nicely – like a silk line for sweetness – it had a fine taper and it sank well. It was also the most robust modern fly line I have ever owned. It did not crack for over a decade. With that line it was possible to fish a team of two ordinary sea trout flies very deeply over the pool and in the dusk and dark, touring, feeding sea trout liked the look of them and many a fine fish I took as a result.

On slow moving water – including lochs and lochans, it is, in my experience, far more effective to fish a fly well down in the dark than to fish it on or near the surface. Let me qualify that a little. When sea trout are in slow moving pools, say in a West Highland river, you can often do well with a floating line and a team of two No. 8 singles or small doubles when the wind is making a good wave on the surface transforming it, effectively, into a loch. The windier the conditions the better, up to the level of blow where gusts flatten the water and produce cat's paws of scattering wind. But when the wind is modest, or light, the floating line is often not successful at all.

I would add a further qualification. There are times in the evening when sea trout rise vigorously – like keenly feeding trout. At such times I have taken them on dry fly and on wet flies fished quickly over them. They will often take lures swum purposefully over them in these conditions. These risers in the Highlands are sometimes very fresh fish and that also helps when we try to take them on surface flies or on wet flies fished within a few inches of the top. I believe sea trout which are more than a few days in fresh water fear the surface; they lie during the day in the deepest and most secure parts of the pools and they only show feeding activity when the light begins to fade, and even then, often only when the light has really drained from the sky and produced enough gloom over the pool tails and glides to allow the fish to be tempted. Evening brings a reduction in light, but it also brings a reduction in wind. When that happens on a sea trout pool where there may be little or no natural current, the floating line does not work well.

A further point should be borne in mind. Sea

trout rise well in the dusk on many pools and then, after, say, an hour or so of activity, they go down and a kind of lull comes over the river. This midnight period often marks the end of activity to the floating line, or such a reduction in takes that many anglers might stop and go home. In my experience, that is the time you switch over to sunk line and go on taking fish. I have had nights on the Spey when sea trout were not very keen to take the wet fly fished on the floating line. One night in particular comes to mind, a night in early July 1978 when I could see fish moving everywhere on the big holding pool whose tail I was quietly fishing. I raised one, pulled one hard, then had nothing at all to encourage me. Suddenly I saw a spendid fish splashing in the tail of a ripple below the tail proper and I moved down behind a small wooded island and covered the fish. It took firmly and I was apparently well into the fish, but after a solid fight the hook hold gave out and I lost it. I came out of the water, somewhat demoralised and walked downstream to try my luck in a long pool below. An hour there with the floater took me to half-past one, and I had nothing in the bag at the end of it. Surface activity was by now minimal. I was tired, thirsty and demoralised. I went to my estate car, took off my waders and decided to turn into my sleeping bag. I drank a cup of tea and, as I did so, life began to come back. I finished the tea, pulled on my damp waders again (any angler knows what an unpleasant task *that* is) and, taking my rod with the sinking line on it, went back to the pool tail below. I had a take and landed the fish on the second cast. As quickly as I could I started again, and had a second fish, then a third fish ashore, then a further pluck and a fourth fish and by that time my blood was up. I had four nice fish on the sand beside me, the two best of them over 3lb (1.4kg) each. I would have fished on but light was already strengthening; a new atmosphere crept in on the scene. I could make out the plants on the far bank, monochrome, shortly to become progressively green. The trout began rising vigorously in the dawn; this time, the night was really over and I returned to my sleeping bag, four sea trout better off.

I fish either a slow sinker (which I prefer) or a sink tip line whenever surface-taking fish defy me, or go silent on me or seem to be not there at all. I fish the flies deeply and slowly round in gentle water where there is little or no stream. I try to show the sea trout the flies down where they are touring on their feeding rounds – that means the deep tails of pools, the 'dead' waters of moorland reaches, the peaty lochans on Highland rivers. I fish the flies like this on dams in the Lowlands and on the long gravel pools of the Border Esk, where fear of the surface or the end of the surface rise confine the fish to the deeps. I also fish this way on lochs, but that is another story which I shall touch on in another section of this book.

The technique of deep line fishing with wet fly is, at its simplest, a matter of fishing one or two flies (I prefer two) of what is often called 'sea trout size' – alias size 8 – working them slowly and positively over the fish in deep water. I imagine my flies are often four or five feet down during the retrieve on a long cast of over twenty yards. One principle in this form of fishing is to keep the flies swimming. It is very like my spring salmon fishing with sunk fly. The key is to lead the fly over the likely water, rather than let the fly be taken by the current and swum on a trammell over the lies. The art is to get the swimming right. Too slow, and you will hook the bed; too fast and you will not get depth or will present the fish with a fly which they might chase and miss. I am not so worried about working the fly too fast when there are fresh fish about. They are great chasers, and again, using demons – such as streamer flies, two-hook tandem lures with hackle wings, or trailing peacock herl – these flies can be fished fast and deep with success.

I was much influenced at one stage in the sixties when English midland reservoir trouting was coming into prominence. Richard Walker wrote about trout which would appear to take his fly when it was static on the bottom of the reservoir. Now around this time I had had some remarkable experiences on the Endrick when sea trout seemed to do the same. I left the fly on the bed of the pool for minutes on end and then moved it by an inch or two and often I got my take at that time. I had other fish which seemed to pick it up in the pitch dark when I was not moving it at all. I rather think, however, that in these cases the fish was touring near the fly, roving about the pool bottom as sea trout do and darting here and there. We see the 'vees' and bulges and ripples indicating such activity. It is my theory that these fish stir up the fly as they tour, and take it as fair-game. Reservoir trout certainly do this. They stir up nymphs and bottom food and turn and take it. Touring and disturbing bottom food like this is certainly reminiscent of estuary feeding, which the sea trout has lived on for many years. Would not shrimps and sand eels be disturbed in this way and taken by the sea trout? Possibly we are presenting our fly legered to the bed, in a way reminiscent of actual sea feeding conditions.

I am a great believer in reminiscence as a rationale in both salmon and sea trout fishing.

Both fish give up their feeding patterns when they come into freshwater. The salmon stops altogether; the sea trout may not completely cease, but the fish certainly does not get food in the prolific way, nor in the manner of presentation typical of the estuary. Thus, our flies, fished on the bed, or worked down near it may be reminiscent of more prolific feeding days. I believe streamer lures and tandems fished deeply touch off just that chord of memory, or putting it more behaviourally, just that response to a stimulus which produces a sincere take.

A Note on 'Roving' and Night Lies

It can be very confusing to an angler used to resident fish, like brown trout, to deal with a fish like the sea trout which has a strange, restless and itinerant character when it is in freshwater. It is true that there are pools which are known to be reliable holders of sea trout. These pools are often very clearly marked out because sea trout mass in them and show steadily – even spectacularly – during the day. I know several such pools, and as I write, one on the upper-middle Spey comes to mind. It is a great deep larder of a pool, lying near a sharp bend in the water and providing a great dub in which there is maximum security for sea trout and salmon alike, and a deep inscrutable eddy which, from June onwards, seems alive with fish going stale by the hour. This large sandy pool has only a slow current through it, and it is almost impossible to fish the main part of the pool without the help of a gale of wind, but that pool – and some others which are very similar – have taught me a great deal about the behaviour of the sea trout in freshwater.

To begin with, sea trout seem to feel unhappy in fixed lies. In this, they are very unlike salmon which like to tenant lies, often seeming to be like fixed furniture in the pools. You will see salmon seemingly static in many lies in rivers, waiting with apparent patience for the coming of the next flood to take them further upstream or, in some cases, waiting for the calendar to turn its slow cycle to autumn when spawning time will come with its crises. Sea trout forage about in the pools. On rivers like the Sheil I have watched them in low summer water gliding up through streams and turning warily in the margins. I have the strong impression when I see their grey shapes sliding through the water that they are eyeing me, and not the reverse. Pools which are well stocked with sea trout show fish for almost the whole day. The more fish – the more showing. Craigbel on the Endrick, for example – the main holding pool above the leap at Gartness – gives a steady and

spectacular show to watchers on the road bridge. Fish splash and roll and joust with each other and restlessly move up and down the dam.

As the light goes, activity eases. Fish seem to take a short break from their day foraging, and there is a noticeable calm – which may last only ten or fifteen minutes – sea trout move in the pools in a different way and, as dusk falls, they begin to rise to moths and flies and, happily, to our artificial flies cast to them.

During the evening rise, which is another name for the different form of activity I am describing, sea trout in the pools I fish, seem to move up and down the main stream, often travelling on the margins and at the head of the pool they turn and glide down the sides of the water to the tail. At a particular point or points in the tail the fish turn and hang in shallowish water and may lie there more or less located for periods of minutes. I have no evidence for how long they actually do lie there, but there is some possibility that the fish might lie there all night undisturbed. Certainly I would be prepared to believe that they would lie there for the whole part of the evening rise or for substantial parts of it. The key seems to be disturbance. Sea trout disturb each other. You can see this taking place on quiet pool tails. You may have noticed fish rising like trout in the tail when a great 'vee' will appear on the surface marking the arrival of another, possibly larger, fish. This incomer boils or splashes in the tail and it disturbs the steady rising pattern of the fish hanging there.

Anglers also disturb sea trout whether by casting their flies over the water, or, much more likely, by wading. Hooking fish naturally disturbs hanging fish too. It does not take long, however, for peace to return, provided the angler also settles and allows the fish to return and take up rising positions.

The key to good sea trout night fishing is this word *turn*. There are several spots in a pool where sea trout show as they are en route for the head or the tail and, to a novice, these must seem to be the productive lies. They are not. En route shows are totally unproductive and are often in deep water. So also are shows in eddies and backwaters, which may go on all night. What we are interested in is where the fish actually turn and hang. On the large Spey pool I mentioned at the beginning of this section there is an island dividing a fan-like tail in two. Each year it is of the greatest interest to the anglers to discover whether one arm or the other is the favourite hanging place since subtle changes in the sandy bed take place each year because of floods. Then, on a finer scale, the question is where the fish are likely to turn up. I found in 1979 that the fish were turning higher up the left bank tail glide than in former years. I had usually fished right down to the lip of the tail, where some large stones have caused the river to form a little holding hollow in the sand. In 1979 I found that I had to wade up from the point of the small island as far as I could go in belly waders and cast down and across into the left bank tail. The fish very clearly turned there and I had a night of six, including a five pounder, followed the next night by a night of five. There were fish in the tail lie too, but I had the distinct impression that the fish which were showing there were smaller.

Finding the turning points and, thereby the hanging lies of sea trout at night is of tremendous importance. Naturally we cannot see the fish in the water at night, but we can judge fairly accurately from the types of rise whether the fish are travellers or semi-residents. A travelling fish tends to splash or crash in making his presence known. These rises are normally in the deep glides, hard in under the trees or in places where the river is shaded by high banks or rocks. The rises you see in the tails of pools and elsewhere in shallow glides are of two sorts. The fish which are takers rise like trout, possibly showing more vigorously, but still giving the rise forms we associate with trout. Indeed, I will go further to say that the rises of sea trout remind me of the rises of salmon parr, but on a larger scale. The rise forms an irregular ring, often with a second disturbance in it. This is caused by the fish breaking the surface with its nose and following with a second break with the dorsal fin or even with a disturbance caused by the tail. Brown trout make all sorts of rises, but they are characterised by a sucking in of flies. Sea trout do suck in flies, but they also show fairly vigorously. I am sure many of the rises we see, even of hanging sea trout – the real takers – are not to flies at all. At night, it is often what you hear that guides you, rather than what you can still see in the gloom. Sea trout which are settled in the glides and tails often rise with a solid 'plop' making very little disturbance of the surface. I think these fish are sucking down moths and flies. They also show with the splashy or multiple ring which I have described as a parr rise, and again they are usually taking something, or are rising to drown a surface fly before taking it. Sea trout do rise like sedging trout on some warm evenings. They clump down on surface food and probably turn and take it as soon as it is in rather than on the water. This may well account for the predominant success of the wet fly over the dry fly even in evenings with massive sea trout

rises. Many of the takes I get are stronger than one would associate with fish sucking in flies and are much more like fish which are coming down on the flies, as I say, like sedging trout. A clear tip for night fishers is to act on feel and not sight. When a sea trout shows at your flies but does not strike, wait until you get the pull. Happily, some of the rises are not seen in the dark under the trees and the pull of the fish is the first indication of interest.

Sea trout also turn in the head of pools. For instance, on one long Spey pool where the river turns at right angles to form a great corner dub with a grand tail, sea trout range at night from the tail to the head, a distance of perhaps a couple of hundred yards. At the head there is a ridge in mid-river and the fish which turn all seem to do so on the left bank side of the ridge in the slack water beyond the gentle stream. It is worth the thigh-deep wade out to the knee-deep water over the ridge to fish the ten square yards of quiet water under the trees on the left bank. You do not need to move to the fish; the fish move up into the turning place and come to you.

There are times when taking lies are discovered in quite unexpected places, often by accident. I know of a taking lie discovered when an angler was afraid to wade onto the river in the dark – and for many there is deep seated, almost instinctive fear of stepping in to water when the bottom cannot be seen. We placed an angler on a safe bank of sand beside the stream of a sea trout pool because both head stream and tail were deep wades. He found a little sandy bay where sea trout seemed to pause in their roving. He had three for the evening rise – well upsides with head and tail fishers that night. It does happen, but I am not the best person to advise you on these lies. I go straight to the tails of the pools, settle in, and wait for the sea trout to turn there.

It is different in the deep darkness of the night, after the rising has apparently stopped. Then I have found that I can pick up sea trout on the slow sinking line fished in deeper water, even in the dubs of pools and the margins of eddies. As I have described elsewhere, sea trout fishing is a sandwich; we fish the floating line in the gloom of the evening, concentrating on the tails of the pools and on the known turning places in the head. When the evening rise wears off, and these places become more or less unproductive, we can sink the flies, or fish a sunk demon, searching for sea trout in deeper lies. It is almost as if the fish play in the half light in the thin water, then congregate in the deeper water in the quiet of the night, and return to the tails and headstreams in the dawn. Some

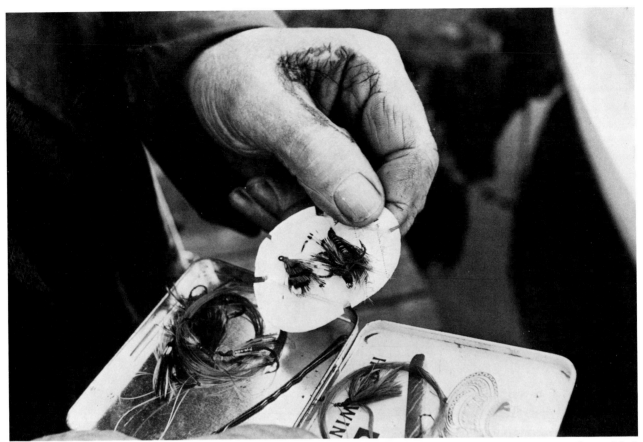

From an Irish boatman's fly box. These flies dressed on single and double hooks represent a typical selection for summer river and loch fishing for sea trout and salmon in Ireland (Michael Shepley)

anglers leave the river when the evening rise is over, saying the fish have gone down. They have, but they have not gone off. The all-night sea trout angler only sleeps after the sun is well up, and I can tell you that a week of night fishing – six nights in a row – can be a shattering experience. I am a sleep-by-the-river man, if circumstances allow it. I rig up my estate car with a sleeping bag, park it in some discreet place near the water and, after the dawn rise has stopped, I tumble in, and if I have to drive home the next morning, I do so after a reasonable period of sleep. But you can tell the addicted sea trout anglers on a week's fishing holiday on Speyside by the deep rings round their eyes!

Sea Trout in Lochs

A large percentage of our sea trout come from stillwater. In fact, there is a geographical factor involved of some importance too. Sea trout on the eastern side of Scotland, in the rivers of the Moray Firth, including the Spey, in the Dee, in Tay, in rivers of the Forth system and in Tweed make up the bulk of rod fishing for sea trout in rivers in Scotland. Many fish are taken in the rivers of the

west, but these fish are far outnumbered by the western crop of fish which run into lochs. Of course, excellent sea trout lochs exist in the west, and that is a factor of the terrain of the western Highlands. The rivers are short, tend to be spate waters, that is, given to quick high floods and failing to hold their flood well. The great lochs of the west lie in valleys in the hills and it is fascinating to note again that almost all the great sea trout waters of this region have a distinct north-west to south-east orientation. Let me list a few: Hope, Stack and Assynt in Sutherland all reflect this angle; Maree and Shiel reflect this too, with the latter taking up a slightly more westerly angle; Loch Lomond – the most southerly sea trout loch of distinction – again reflects the trend of north-west to south-east. It is interesting that even where there are large waters inland of rivers flowing east in Scotland, these lochs are not noted for great sea trout fishing, although they may produce some good days. Loch Ness is one such water, hard to compare because of its vast size with its neighbours. Loch Tay is too far from the sea for really good sea trout. Loch Earn does not seem to attract the stock. Other large waters in this category include Loch Shin which seems to have excellent characteristics – a short river, good

113

stocks of sea trout in the estuary (The Kyle of Sutherland) but never seemed to produce good catches, even in the pre-hydro days when access to the loch was easier. The Falls of Shin seem to be too high a barrier.

In lochs, sea trout take up residence which is quite distinct in area from either trout or salmon, and they behave in a way quite separate from the other game fish. Sea trout tend to lie in the deeper waters of lochs, in water from 12 to 20ft (3.6 to 6m) deep. Trout, on the other hand, like the shallow banks and bays of the loch, the water less than 10ft (3m) deep. Salmon overlap with trout, lying in water around 5ft (1½m) in depth. Since sea trout are deep water fish, at least during the day, in lochs, special approaches are called for in fishing for them. Firstly, wet fly fishing for sea trout in lochs is usually associated with a good wave and, partly because of this and partly because of visibility problems from deeper water, big flies are fished. The flies, which are broadly speaking trout patterns dressed larger, include the bulky spiders – the Pennells, the Palmers and the Cochybonddhu. In winged flies, the tradition of bulk is continued. We find that flies dressed with hackle round their bodies, palmer-style, are the most effective in Scottish lochs. These include Invicta, Wickham, Dark Mackerel and other flies some of which have a nice combination of dark natural feathers and bright tinsel bodies. The Dunkeld is a favourite and the Peter Ross. These flies are usually fished in No. 8 or No. 6 in the larger lochs. Indeed, on Loch Maree I have sometimes tied on a small dapping fly to my bob to give it bulk and presence in the loch. Often locally tied variants will have double hackling – the Kate McLaren is a Black Pennell with an overtied brown hackle – and this is towards a similar end – visibility and presence.

Fishing for sea trout in lochs is usually done from a boat. The option of wading and casting is there, but it is clearly limited to places where you can actually cover fish from the shore, and while these places exist, they are scarce. I do not include night fishing in this rule; clearly fish rove into shallower water after dusk, and I will deal with that later, but in day sea trout fishing on lochs a boat is essential. The water is fished in a way similar to ordinary loch trout fishing, but I like to cast longer lines and give the flies a good strong movement by handlining them back to the boat. Indeed, my index finger gets worn and sometimes becomes lined and raw after several days of wet fly fishing for sea trout. Movement is of the essence. Another feature of wet fly fishing where a trout tactic is employed but is concentrated on is

working the bob. Sea trout love bob flies, and I sometimes think that I could count on one hand the respectable fish which have failed to take the bob and have selected the tail fly. I exaggerate, of course, but there is a definite predilection for the bob fly on the part of the sea trout. But it is for a bob fly fished in a certain way. Sea trout love a bob fly, usually a big Pennell or a Dark Mackerel, cutting through the surface of the loch and dapping in and out with a wet look, like a great bedraggled moth. They love it when the wind pulls the fly line and makes the bob skid and roll a little, like a dapping fly. In fact, the bob action I am describing is really a kind of dapping, but with a fly dapped in and out of the surface rather than a fly dapped over and on to the surface in the conventional dapped way. I call this wet dapping and I think of it as presenting the fly to the underside of the surface, in reverse image to the conventionally dapped fly which presents the fly from the air on to the surface. My form of wet fly fishing daps a wet fly; conventional dapping daps a dry fly. I will describe dapping later in this section in some detail.

The rod which you use for loch sea trout fishing has, therefore, many functions to perform. It must be able to cast effectively, especially in windy conditions. It must carry a reel with good line resources, because sea trout can run large and can run far. It must be long enough to let you work the bob effectively and it must be light enough to fish all day without excessive fatigue. I use my favourite trout rods for sea trout fishing, my Pézon et Michel Sawyer *Stillwater*, my Sharpe's *Scottie* 9ft 6in (2.90m) two-piece, but I also use a 10ft (3.05m) T C Ivens two-piece *Lake* which is a rather heavy rod but gives me that little bit more control over the bob. There are all sorts of ways of improving your control over wet flies by selecting specialised rods for the job. I like Charles McLaren's solution which was to have a 12ft (3.66m) rod built for double-handed use, but with the emphasis on lightness and accuracy. He uses these long rods with great flair and they certainly are absolutely delightful to take fish on (having been given the chance to try them out on Loch Hope). I still feel that I want a single-handed rod for the job, and I realise that there are limitations imposed by this. Carbon fibre rods may produce the ideal single-handed 11 or 12 footer (3.35 or 3.66m), and I should like to try one of these, but I would hope that such a rod would be up to the rolling and punching required to fish No. 6 flies on a No. 6 line in a Force 6 wind on Loch Maree.

Wet flies for sea trout are fished on the drift in front of the boat, in a way similar to wet flies fished for trout. The take of the sea trout is also similar to its smaller cousin's rise, but because you are dealing with fish of three, four or more pounds, fish fresh from the sea and very powerful and fast, the rise can be much more spectacular. Some of the biggest fish I have taken on wet fly on lochs – my best so far has been 9lb (4kg) – have taken gently. I have noticed this about big salmon and sea trout; the big fish seem to be able to suck in the fly in a great gulp, while the smaller sea trout often seem to want to wallop over the fly, as if to attack it and drown it in the course of the take.

I wish I could describe what sea trout takes are like. I might manage to describe some of the main ways the fish moves – and I will try to – but the thrill of the rise, when the dark, peaty wave of the loch bursts open to give you a momentary glimpse of a silver flank, or a black head, or a curving high back . . . These are the indescribable moments of the offer. Equally indescribable is missing the offer, and I am afraid that it is inevitable in sea trout fishing that you will move fish and either not touch them at all or fail to get the hooks in properly. Sometimes it is one's own fault and sometimes it is the sincerity of the take which is suspect.

Let me begin with the swirling take. The fly is being worked through the wave and you do not see the fish, but there is a swirl to your flies, usually your bob fly. This is one of the least spectacular forms of take, but it is often a productive one. The swirl is formed when the sea trout swims fast up to the fly and turns as it takes before heading down again within far less time than it takes to read this line. You will miss this offer unless you are wide awake, have your rod and line under control, and can tighten on the offer. Sea trout, in complete contrast to salmon, need to be hooked by the angler. Salmon should be left to pull the line and then you can set the hook, if it is not already solidly in. Sea trout swirl at the fly, or splash at it, or rise head-and-tail to it and the key to the whole operation of the strike is seeing what the fish is doing. In wet fly fishing seeing is important, but not so absolutely crucial as in dapping, where the fish takes the fly in so many different ways that your strike must be gauged to each tempo and angle of the take. My principle in sea trout fishing is to strike as soon as I see the offer and, in the case of a subtle take, where I do not see the actual rise, to strike as soon as I get the least hint of the line tightening.

The strike should be fast and positive, and this implies that you must be ready to make it positively. As you fish your flies in, you not only gather in line with your left hand, keeping the line running in over your index finger as you do so, but you also raise the rod. This is necessary for several reasons, but the one which concerns us most here is that you must raise the rod to make the bob fly work well. Now when the rod is so raised that it makes the bob fly work in and out of the wave, the rod angle is high and that means that you may not have very much leverage left to tighten the slack line between you and the fish and to get the hooks home. I strike by pulling the line hard with my left hand over my right index finger on the rod butt, or, if I have enough rod lift left I use my index finger to clamp the line to the rod handle and raise the rod firmly as if to draw line in prior to casting. It is positive, but not violent. A sincere pull is required to hook a sea trout well, but it is not a savage pull. Sometimes people start up, galvanised into action by the sudden rise. There is a burst of adrenalin and in the surge of sudden action the strike is too hard and either the cast parts – often with a crack like rifle-fire – or the hook is pulled out rather than in, or worst of all, you break the rod.

It all sounds very dramatic when I write it down, but I can well remember breaking 9lb (4kg) nylon with a resounding crack on Loch Moidart when I was fishing there with wet fly on a June night. It had been quiet, and I was wondering whether there were many fish in the loch, when right under the gunwale of the boat up came a great fish to my dropper with a curving slashing rise which if I remember rightly scattered water over us in the boat. I tightened – and how! I was startled and my strike was uncontrolled. I smashed the nylon easily and I am delighted I did not smash the rod. I got a beautiful 6¼ pounder (2.8kg) later that night in the pitch dark (one of the few lochs I know well at night) and that fish leapt at the end of its long run and showed against the pale light of the west where there was a cleft in the valley – fish silhouetted in a pale glowing 'vee' between the outlines of the hills of Moidart. One of the unforgettable moments in my sea trout fishing life.

Sea trout sometimes rise very splashily. I have seen them lunging at the fly, but more often they wallop at it, if you know what I mean. They seem to demonstrate in their rise something which blends an excitement at the fly being there and a fear of it. The quick splash is a very common type of rise when fish are very fresh. It requires just as quick a reaction. When I was fairly new to good sea trout fishing in my student days I was invited up to fish Loch Eilt in Inverness-shire – a loch with a high reputation for its sea trout. On my first drift I hooked a nice slow, gentle sea trout of

5¼lb (2.4kg) which did everything right. It rose well, was not alarming or savage, and my tightening in the strike would have done an expert credit. The next fish, on the drift down by the railway, brought one fierce rise which I missed and immediately afterwards I had another wild rise and this time I reacted very rapidly and felt the hook going home well, then breaking and then taking again. I had broken in the fish which rose to my dropper and I had foul hooked it on my tail fly. This is not unusual. Breaking is unusual, but foul hooking a fish which misses your dropper fly, but which you think has taken is fairly common. There I was, firmly foul hooked into a very fresh good sea trout and, as you might predict, it went like a crazy thing. It tired eventually, but not before we had all debated whether I had hooked a ten pounder or not. The fish came to the net. In its jaw was my No. 6 Soldier Palmer which had broken off during the strike, and in its tail was my other fly, a Dunkeld No. 8.

I have, in the twenty odd seasons since that incident, sorted out my too vigorous strikes to sea trout which startle me. A sea trout rising as hard and fast as the one I have described would have hooked itself. All I would have had to do was tighten. A sea trout making less demonstration in its rise would need to be struck firmly. I have learned to make my strike inversely proportionate to the violence of the rise. Short line takes are the difficult ones. With long lines out on the wave, the fish has probably hooked itself and has started to leap about before we are really in control.

Sea trout also rise sometimes by nodding at the fly, as it were. It is hard to describe. The fish makes little show in the rise, but a head comes out and makes a powerful dab at the fly, usually the bob and so often this is as far as the encounter gets. These are very hard rises to hook. If you are using treble hooks (dreadful on the bob) you might find that the fish which nods or pecks at the fly is often hooked under the chin. Fish which do this may be trying to drown the fly. They sometimes do it in dapping, where the fly is obviously more lively and more aerialised than the wet fly. Sometimes a fish which nods at the fly will actually draw it under and take it at once with a swirl. I have seen this many times in dapping. It is also something I have come across in trout fishing and many of the impossible short takes we get from summer trout turn out to be drowning attempts and the fish take the fly the moment it is safely in the water.

Sea trout take in these and many other ways. I have had quiet draws, more like salmon than sea trout. My best sea trout (9lb (4kg)) in a loch

(Loch Moidart) took quietly in light ripple and drew the line solidly like a salmon. I had two five pounders on Loch Maree which drew the line like deep line sea trout at night, that is, with a solid, steady pull. One of the takes was at Salmon Point, and the gillie and I both called 'Salmon', but we were soon proved wrong, when the sea trout showed.

In lochs, look for sea trout in drifts offshore where the depth of water can be maintained. The larger lochs give you a chance to cover long drifts in this way, moving along the contours. At Kinlochewe, on Loch Maree, there are some lovely drifts in the top bay where there is a small island and certain columns of weeds. There are salmon there too, but that bay produces some good sea trout. On a strange loch, it pays not to be too afraid of open water. Once you know the best areas of a loch, you can plan drifts accordingly, but it has often struck me on Maree, for example, that the drifts were great sweeps of water, sometimes taking over an hour to complete. Dap and wet fly fishing in the same boat is an excellent way of exploring such water. The sea trout themselves map out their lies by showing to your flies.

What I have so far been describing is day fishing which depends on good Highland winds, producing good wave with a steady solid ripple. When the wind falls and the wave becomes small, sea trout can be very difficult to hook on the tackle I have so far described. As conditions get finer, you ought to change down and you will end up in the gentlest of conditions using 6lb (2.7kg) leaders and No. 10 flies or even No. 12. Err on the larger side for sea trout, however, but not for salmon. In fine conditions I like to use a small tandem fly, say a double Black Pennell No. 12 tandem, or a Worm Fly on the tail of a 6lb (2.7kg) cast with a Soldier Palmer, say No. 10, on the bob. I don't mind if the bob fly drags a bit and behaves a bit like a dry fly. Sea trout often love this dragging or scuttering fly. Taking sea trout in these conditions is often delightful. They do not splash wildly at the flies as they do in a Hebridean wave, but they sometimes come quickly to it, pushing a great ripple ahead of them, in a bulge. These takes are not unlike salmon offers and, indeed, the tackle I have described has taken several good summer salmon for me from the fine ripples of Highland lochs.

This form of fine fishing for trout gives you a technique for using on summer evenings when the wind falls and the loch becomes first like a ground-glass sheet, then a mirror. Sea trout will come into the shallows at dusk, roving in from their safe lies as they rove in pools from their day lies to the finer tails. I think the reason we do not hear more about loch fishing for sea trout at night is a simple one – most people fish all day, and get tired, stopping for a bath, a drink and dinner. When I first spent my summers in the Highlands I would often be invited to try a loch at dusk, while the tenant was recovering from his day efforts. These evenings were often astonishing, and they have set me on a course which has caused me to miss many a hotel dinner since. I have fished Loch Hope into the dark and it was there that I first noticed the change in location of sea trout as dusk falls on the loch. They move quietly into shallower water and may rise in the same region as trout. They quest and rove into burn estuaries, perhaps the very burn they will run up to spawn. As long as there is ripple in the evening, fish the floating line and use the lighter tackle I have described above. When the ripple goes, and with it the light, you can try the floating line by all means, but it is my experience that the slow sinking line will work best. Fishing from the bank, it is often possible to work the flies through water which shallows suddenly, say on to a shingle bank, or – a deadly place this – along the margins of a reed bed or a rushy flat. I used to prefer a light inch-long tube fly for this fishing. It has the qualities of fishing up off the bed as the line sinks. Incidentally the best line I have ever had for this was the Cortland half and half line – 40yd (36½m) long, 20yd (18m) double taper one end was a floater and 20yd (18m) at the other was a slow sinker. Instead of the tube fly, which I still sometimes use, I now prefer trout demons, that is a tandem dressing of No. 12 size of something like the Alexandra, or a hair wing dressing. In these dressings the wing trails the length of the tandem. In others, like the Worm Fly which I mentioned earlier, the flies are separate. A wonderful fly I have just acquired is my beloved Dark Mackerel dressed on a very small shank with a tiny treble at the tail. This gives a fly size equivalent to about No. 6, but gives a hooking power and a lightness associated with smaller dressings.

Some lochs fish well in the proper dark, rather than the dusk. I have some experience of this, using a boat to reach the fish. Then, in the calms of the night, one can be paddled around gently and cast either with floating tackle and a cast of No. 8 flies as for daylight – which sometimes works well – or with a slow sinking line and a larger sea trout lure, say a Black Lure or a Fitty Lure or a salmon tube fly. It works best, or perhaps it just feels best, on a still night. It is certainly amazingly exciting to hook a good sea trout in this way in the dark – out there on the black marble water with the reel going and a fish leaping somewhere, which you can hear but may not see, that is memorable. Sometimes your fish runs and leaps and you cannot believe that the fish you see is the one you are tied into. Lochs which fish in this way usually fall into the lochan, or enlarged pool variety. Often on the upper reaches of Highland rivers you find large boggy pools which may cover an acre or more and these fish well for sea trout at night. It is a kind of cross between night fishing a river pool and night fishing a loch. Some of the dead water of the middle and upper sections of some Highland rivers provide the best locations for this fishing, but the boat does help to provide movement. In certain strategic places such as the draw off where the river runs out or where a side tributary enters, the boat can be anchored and fishing is as from the bank. The boat often helps you to get to water where the banks of the lochan or large pool are boggy.

Fishing sea trout in lochs with a wet fly is for me a staple diet each summer. I sometimes think that the sea trout in these circumstances is a different fish from the subtle, difficult wary fish of the summer river, yet this would be misguided. The fresh run sea trout in a wave on a Highland loch is a fast slashing, muscular creature, but one which is in a very excited state. In a similar way, you will meet vigorous, fresh sea trout in rivers after spates. In lochs the fish comes straight into the fresh 'inland sea' and very often the river connecting the loch to the sea, as in many of the waters I have named, is short. Thus fresh fish move in the wave in that abandon which marks the first few days of freshness, and it is during this period that there is some wild and memorable sport. In rivers when the flood drops, the fish settle in pools, become timid and wary and take only in the dusk and dark – although some might be tempted during the day. Loch fishing has feelings and a dimension of sport entirely on its own, and I love it. It is a sector of sea trout fishing where the wind and the boat help you to reach the fish. Wind covers your approach and may help you to hook fish. The large acreage of the loch offers you a second chance when you have erred in a way that a river pool may not. It is thus, exciting, and forgiving and challenging, but in a different way from fishing a night pool on a river.

Dapping for Sea Trout

Dapping is at once an art with a strong natural logic in it and a streak of the fantastic about it. The natural part of dapping is that sea trout, and brown trout, at certain times of the year seize large natural windborne insects which appear on

117

Dapping for sea trout (and large brown trout) is a specialised art. A large artificial fly or a natural is fished on a floss silk line and made to dap and dance over the waves on the surface of the loch. Sea trout sometimes go wild over dapped artificials. A boat is shown here drifting a likely reach, a fish takes the fly and is hooked bending the long dapping rod well. Finally, the net is slipped under him. The water is Loch Corrib, Ireland

the surface of the loch. Jenny or Daddy longlegs (the crane flies), stone flies, moths, beetles and many other insects appear on the surface, usually blown there from the fields and moor on the lochside, and sea trout take them vigorously. It sometimes looks like a sport on the part of the fish. I have seen Jenny longlegs blowing from the reeds on to a Hebridean loch and the trout and sea trout have been lying in wait for them in the first ripple after the glassy calm in the lee of the reeds. Further offshore on sea trout lochs, I have also seen Jennies rolling and cavorting on the wave and sea trout have risen wildly to them.

It would be absolutely logical to dap for these fish, using either a natural fly on a special hook, or an artificial which would imitate the natural insect. You would use a long rod and a light line which would catch the wind well and roll and dap the fly over the wave in front of the boat. In fact, for a century or more in Ireland and in the west Highlands of Scotland, anglers have done just that. They have caught live insects – including the Mayfly in Ireland – and have dapped them using a floss silk line billowing out in the wind in front of the boat. Long and light rods handle this tackle best, and rods with whole cane butts and mid sections and often a greenheart top were developed, often being up to 16ft (5m) or more in length. This tackle can still be seen on lochs today but I can count on one hand the number of anglers using natural flies for sea trout dapping in Scotland. Ireland may have more Jennies, or more small boys to catch them, but the tradition of sea trout dapping in the Highlands and Islands of Scotland is now very firmly a sport of dapping specially tied artificial flies, fished on long rods, usually glass or carbon fibre, and dapping the flies with a variety of wind-sensitive lines which include the traditional floss silk as well as brushed nylon and untwisted nylon floss which is technically far ahead of the traditional lines.

The fantastic element in dapping relates to the flies used. They are dressed in bulky and conspicuous form, with multiple hackles, horns of deer's hair, tails, tail trebles, and flying trebles and they come in all the colours known to the art of dyeing. The artificial dapping fly seems to me not to represent so much the sober Jenny or the natural fly off the heather as to have taken the idea of the bulky bob fly from wet fly fishing and to have projected it into the sphere of dry fly fishing in conditions of wind and wave on the loch where visibility is a critical element in the presentation.

Dapping floats, dances, rolls and jigs these great flies out over the wave in a way which is memorable to watch. One can become mesmerised in a long day's fishing watching one's fly rolling and cavorting over the wave. But what is far more memorable is the reaction of the sea trout to the dapped fly. The fish splash at the fly and leap out after it; heads appear through the surface and large mouths open and engulf the dap; sea trout leap from the water and crash down on the fly and indeed, every aerial and aquatic acrobatic seems to be involved in sea trout taking, and very often missing, the dap as it skids and dances and rolls over the surface.

Thinking one's way through the art of dapping, one should begin, I think, by remembering the typical depths at which sea trout lie in lochs. They are medium depth fish, lying in water roughly between 10 and 20ft (3 and 6m) deep. Sea trout may be encountered in much shallower water and may be seen over much deeper water but you should take the 20ft (6m) contour as a guide. The best dapping lochs are large, mainly because the best sea trout lochs in Scotland are the large north-west facing waters which we have mentioned already – lochs like Maree. Large lochs between hills usually have good wind, and if there is any art which is wind hungry it is dapping. What one really requires for a good day's dapping is a long reach of the right depth with waves on it up to a foot high. You can dap right down to light winds, but the mechanical problems of aerialising the fly begin to defeat you when the wind drops. Further, sea trout move well to wet fly in lighter winds and, in my experience, there is not much point in dapping on when the wet fly can be made to work well. Dapping works best where the reaches cover good areas of water. Sea trout in a loch are not usually evenly distributed; they are either lying in patches, or travelling through, and dapping has the great advantage that it can pick up fish even over very deep water where sea trout are travelling. Indeed, one of the elements which can make dapping highly successful in some conditions is its ability to pick up fish which would not be on typical wet fly drifts, and it does this by bringing up to a large, wild fly, fish which would not rise to anything smaller.

Dapping is an art of the wind. You will find that you have only a small degree of control over the direction and action of the fly when it is fished on the billowing floss line. You can use the long rod to lift and lay the fly and you might be able to put some direction on the fly, leading it broadly to

Right: **Dapping Loch Maree, Wester Ross. This water is famous for its large sea trout taken on the dap. Dapping is an art of the wind, and the pictures here, taken on the same day, show a striking contrast between the flat calm at lunch time and the substantial wave which was produced by a sea breeze after lunch**

the left or right. There is, of course, an art in making the most of your low control over the fly, but in the end, it is an art of making the best presentation you can in very difficult circumstances. For instance, if your fly is moving to the left and a good fish shows behind it, you cannot move the fly to the fish although you might manage to stop it. In wet fly fishing you have to re-cast, but at least that can be done fairly accurately.

The sea trout reacts to the dapping fly in a whole variety of ways, some of which are controlled rises, and some of which are, as far as I can make out, wild shows which are not in fact offers. The fly sometimes has the effect on sea trout which a blown leaf has on a kitten, with the reservation that the kitten would likely catch the leaf. I have seen sea trout walloping through the surface after a fly, and apparently not really trying to take it. In the course of natural rises to flies, trout and sea trout may resort to pursuit and drowning tactics. I have seen trout do this with 'motorboating' sedges, bumble bees, flying ants and blowflies. There can be no doubt that sea trout chase with little intention of taking, and at other times take with a high degree of efficiency. In dapping, we can expect more showing than taking. This used to seem curious to me, but not now. If one thinks of it, a dapped fly attracts fish and almost every fish which is attracted will show to the fly or will appear at the surface near it. How often in wet fly fishing one sees a boil near the flies, sometimes immediately followed by a take. That is a clear case of a chasing fish. But in wet fly work, one does not see the scores of interested or following fish, the abortive swirls, the veering approaches. It is probably just that sea trout must show to the dap which makes it appear that the dap moves more fish than wet fly.

Does the dap take more fish than wet fly? In my opinion, well fished wet fly will hold its own with the dap in a big wave and will outclass it in a light wave. But it is difficult to fish wet fly really well. The bob must be fished consistently well up to the surface and through the surface, and this can be tiring. But wet fly will score where fish have to be covered accurately and well, perhaps at distances beyond dapping range. Wet fly and dap are not in competition, except in the simplest sense of friendly rivalry. They do not conflict with each other and indeed, are highly recommended at the

Left: **The author's boatman unhooks a 5¼ pounder which was one of two almost identical sea trout taken on wet fly on Loch Maree in August**

same time from the same boat. I love fishing wet fly when there is a good dap going in the boat, or in the case of Loch Maree, or some of the Irish lochs where the boats are large, I have fished wet fly with two other rods dapping beside me. It appears that the dap brings the fish up from the depths and for one reason or another the sea trout may not take the dap. Such a fish will often take a wet fly firmly. I have several times seen sea trout which have come up to the dap and have missed it, perhaps because the wind has whipped it away, lying at the surface for several seconds, seemingly bewildered by the loss of the fly. These fish will take a wet fly if one can be presented right away. The great difficulty in covering such fish is shortening line in time. I can remember many occasions when I have had to haul line in great pulls, in arm-long frantic draws, to shorten line quickly enough to cover sea trout on the hang close to the boat. The real problem with sudden shortening of line like this is that you cast to the sea trout before the line is short enough and you 'line' the fish, ie lay the line over or near it and frighten the fish, which is a real killer. Fish go down and bang goes an opportunity for sport. I suppose the wet fly rod fishing with dapping rods in the same boat should concentrate on short line fishing but should have immediately available about ten yards of line coiled on the bottom boards of the boat. This is not particularly good advice because line on the bottom boards snags the boards themselves, your feet, your bag, the buckle on your boots and absolutely everything there is to snag. Yet I do it all the time, taking maximum care to keep my feet clear, because those ten yards, immediately available is one of the keys to success. You can get ten yards of line into the air in two false casts and cover a showing fish far out very rapidly indeed. I have sometimes called this the best piece of bad advice in boat fishing.

When fish offer to the dapped fly there are several ways in which you can strike. It *is* a strike in dapping. The fly works over the water on a billowing, loose line. When the fish takes, you have to connect and this can be difficult. There is nothing more frustrating than seeing a great head appear and engulf your fly but you fail to tighten and the fish ejects the dap and is gone. But the problem of connecting with the offer is more complicated than that; sea trout have to be allowed to turn down with the fly. My own favourite strike on the dap is sometimes called the courtesy approach – you bow to the fish and then connect with it as rapidly as possible. Some anglers call out 'There he is!' or words to that effect, and while they are calling out, they hold their hand. By the time the phrase is spoken, the strike should be made. This is a device, a good psychological device, to stop our own systems from reacting too quickly to an offer. After all, we are waiting, perhaps tensely, and the rise comes as a sudden event. We may have waited all year for a day on Maree or Stack or one of the other great sea trout lochs and we may have had a dull, unproductive hour or two on the first drifts. Then, suddenly, up he comes, a great wallop as a good fish goes for the dap. It is incredibly easy to pull suddenly and pull hard and take the fly from its willing mouth.

There is a great deal of debate about the striking of sea trout and I can fully understand why. The kinds of rises vary and, with them, the speed at which the fly is taken and the speed at which the fish turns down from the surface. I have already spoken of sea trout hanging about at the surface when they miss the dap. They also do this sometimes when they take the dap. I think getting the dap is sometimes an anti-climax for the fish. The chase is the thing and the kill is dull. The best striker is the angler who best observes the fish. This is also true of wet fly fishing. I think dapping gives the angler the hardest time, both from the point of view of observation and striking. There are so many types of take and they are sometimes so dramatic that we are jolted by them. I've mentioned some forms of take already above and in the wet fly section. The wildest takes are often the misses and the simple swirls are often the most sincere takes. I love the head-out takes – great bluish black nebs appearing and the fly being engulfed. Sometimes the head appears vertically up out of the water. I have seen a yawning mouth appear in this way and close on a dapped fly. Fantastic, but difficult to strike. The swirls have the best chance of hooking themselves because the rise only appears when the fish has moved. What we see in the aerial takes are fish in the earliest stages of taking the fly, and we must give them time. The head-out takes require lots of time to let the fish turn down and take up a suitable posture in the water.

Many of our designs of dapping flies are made with hooking specially in mind. Dapping is very subject to so-called short rising, that is fish seeming to rise but either just tipping the fly or touching it. Trout do this in summer and drive us mad. Some dapping flies are dressed on single hooks, either standard shanks or long shanks. The average size I suppose would be No. 6 or No. 4 – quite large singles. I have tried daps on doubles, but they are unsuccessful because of the weight. For maximum hooking, some daps have extensions of the shank to carry a small treble, and this has merit. I have

seen good hooking on these extended flies. The extension is usually heavy nylon with a small treble whipped on. Sometimes the treble extension is attached to the head as a kind of flying treble way. I believe this also works well at times, but I suspect it of foul hooking fish and it is a menace in netting because it can foul the net and lose the fish. Dapping flies are also tied on tubes, mounted over the usual small treble and I have found these to be good patterns. The nice thing about this is that you can virtually build yourself a fly to the right specification – colour, length, etc. The disadvantage of tube-dressed flies is that it is difficult to tie on hair horns. I do like the way tube daps roll, however. They appear to me to represent the rolling, uncontrolled progress of natural flies in a high wind.

Dapping Tackle

The tackle we use for dapping has been mentioned in passing above, but it might be useful for us to list a typical outfit. I often use a 16ft (4.88m) glass rod which is fairly light to handle and is good in controlling the billowing line. I find that a long rod, even 17 or 18ft (5.18 or 5.49m) in length, has two distinct advantages in presenting the fly. Firstly, it can take advantage of any wind there is. The bugbear of dapping is lack of wind and the longer rod keeps you in action in winds which would not dap flies from 12ft (3.66m) rods. Secondly, the longer rod allows you to get the ideal convex curve on the floss when it is fishing. This convex curve, that is with the belly of the floss billowing out in a steady curve ahead of the rod, is the right line attitude for good dapping. In light winds you may find that the floss sags and forms a weak concave shape below the rod top. When that happens, it is time to try a lighter floss line or abandon the dap altogether. Also, when floss silk (if you still use it) gets wet, it gets heavy and sags and becomes concave as it droops towards the rod. Many of the nylon 'floss' lines (they are slightly different in structure from the old floss silk) resist water permanently and do not cause this problem. The modern nylon dapping lines are of untwisted strands of extremely fine nylon. The main advantage of such a line is its excellent sensitivity to light winds, but the difficulties are that it is very easy for hooks to become badly entangled with the multitude of fibres and this can be a little frustrating. I usually tie knots in my open fibre floss lines, to make them more manageable. There is a limit to how many yards of untwisted fibres you can handle. The efficiency of the line seems to me to be actually increased by knotting. Fibres which can be separated by the wind will not float out as

Above and below: **Dapping Loch Maree, Wester Ross. The dap is being fished over likely water about 10 ft (3m) deep when the fish sucks down the fly and the rod is bent into it. The 8lb (3.6kg) fish comes to the net after a solid, hard fight**

Right: **A 2½lb (1.1kg) fish takes the dap and the angler shows how well the large artificial dap has been taken**

well as fibres contained at certain points. My knots are simple half hitches tied in at intervals of about a metre.

Rods can be of different designs. I have a long telescopic glass 16 footer (4.88m) which is nice to handle but is difficult to thread the line through. I splice the floss – say 4yd (3½m) of it – on to thin nylon braided line of 15lb (6.8kg) breaking strain. This forms a fine running line which passes easily through the centre of the rod and out through the rather bizarre central tip ring which telescopic rods have. I think this rod started life as a French roach pole! It works, but it is the devil's own job to get the line through, since each section is 5ft (1.5m) long. I use some alasticum wire to make the first passage and with it draw the braid through. Then I splice on the floss and attach the short trace. When the rod is broken for transport, I leave the backing through it and I admit that this is an unsatisfactory compromise between dismantling the rod completely and having the job of re-threading it again in the morning. I much prefer spigot rods, such as a light glass salmon rod or better still a purpose-made dapping rod with rings down the rod in the usual way. At a pinch, my 14ft (4.27m) Milbro Verre salmon rod daps well.

We tend to use any old, large, spare fly reel for dapping, and this policy may be a mistake. The floss line is attached to the running or backing line, and I use only about five yards of floss. This is, in fact, another control over the wild floss in high wind. You can shorten floss and thus reduce the effect of a high wind on your dapping. The truth is that dapping tackle is very coarse. Any solid piece of running line or backing, say braided terylene of 20lb (9kg) breaking strain, may be used. The floss may be whipped or merely looped or tied on to the running line. The leader of nylon may be a short length of a yard or so of 12 to 15lb (5.4 to 6.8kg) nylon and the dapping flies are as I have described already. It is not purists' fly tackle. But it is extremely practical tackle and it suits the windy loch conditions in which it is used.

Possibly the most important single element in using the dapped fly is keeping the fly floating or at least buoyant. Remember that you do not have false casting to puff off the water and dry the fly out. I use an aerosol container of silicone floatant, but I also have a little bottle of Mucilin, and in my bag I have the same substance in cream form. Among the three preparations I usually manage to keep the fly floating for a reasonable time. One can also dry out the fly on a fleece pad or a piece of flannel or, if you are like me, by pressing it behind one's tweed jacket lapel. You should expect to replace flies regularly to get the best dry dapping effects, and this means that in your selection of flies you ought to double up, at least, so that you can keep going with a dry successful pattern.

Dapping is a great experience, but in terms of fishing technique, it is rather lower in my estimation than good wet fly fishing. It can, however, often wipe the eye of the wet fly, although I treasure the occasions when my wet fly has far outclassed the dap. It is an experience a sea trout fisher should have, and he may well become addicted to it. Dapping is visual, can be rewarding, takes place in magnificent areas on long scenic drifts and is usually associated in my mind with good lochside hotels and good company. It is a holiday art for most people since its main season is from mid July to the end of September. It takes place at a time when other salmon and sea trout fishing might be at a standstill because of lack of rain. Well worth a week's trial for the newcomer to the sport.

Section Four
The Pursuit of Salmon

The salmon, more than any other game fish is an all-the-year-round quarry. The first fishings in Scotland open in mid January – Helmsdale and Tay – and the last fishings close at the end of November – The Tweed. In between the mid-winter start of the Helmsdale (I have been frozen off that water) and the end of the Tweed fishing on St. Andrew's day in November, lies a bewildering array of conditions under which salmon can be fished for. It is useful, if a little crude, to divide salmon fishing into three: spring, summer and autumn, but these names are often misleading. The first fishings of the Tay in mid January are in mid winter; indeed, the worst of the winter is often February. If this is to be called spring fishing, how can it share the name with the May fishings on the Dee in Aberdeenshire, where we meet warm and fine conditions and fish for salmon with a tiny fly on a floating line in shirt-sleeve conditions?

In each of the seasons there are water and weather conditions which are extreme. Further, different waters have quite different reactions to spring, summer and autumn. For instance, autumn fishing on Spey hardly exists and I know keen anglers who would rather not take the coloured fish which come to the fly in September. Tweed may, in complete contrast, lie fallow after the summer and, with the first water after mid

September, bring in the great runs of clean autumn fish for which the river is famous. These autumn runs will go on bringing clean fresh fish into the Tweed until the last day of the season at the end of November. Indeed, I often pack up for the year on Tweed and feel that I should really like to go on fishing fly right through the winter until the sport merges with the spring runs of February.

In the parts of this section which follow, I shall try to set out the typical sport of each season and present the main approaches to fishing for salmon in a wide variety of different conditions and locations. Naturally, just as seasons blend, so do tactics, and it is right that they should. No wild creature can be boxed and classified precisely. In the end, after years of studying the salmon and fishing hard, one is conscious not so much of a series of different forms of fishing, but of a kind of seamless robe of sport.

Springers

The spring salmon is prized by anglers for several reasons. It is the first salmon of the new season, and is a beautiful fish – fat, hard in the flesh, usually high in the back and short, with superb silver sheen on its sides tinged with pink and blue hues. Further, the springer is a difficult fish to find. It does not run all of our salmon rivers. Most of the spring waters are in the north and east of Scotland, including Spey, Tay and Tweed. Several of these waters run fish very early in the year and sport can get off to a brisk start on Tay, for example, by mid January. Fishing the early spring runs on these rivers up north is, for me, a very special experience, a winter journey to what is often a fairly harsh environment. I have waded through ice to take fish, and snow is common and can cause the usual difficulties in getting to the waterside. But early spring is often quite different, almost balmy, often very sunny. It is fascinating to contrast these early spring conditions with the marvellous spring fishings of the Aberdeenshire Dee in May, when the banks are yellow with broom and temperatures can run into the sixties and higher. Then we are in a spring which is often more like summer than the summer which follows.

I do not believe springers are all that hard to catch. They are difficult to find, but that is quite a separate problem. Most springers are taken when they are very fresh and, like fresh fish in any season, they take well when you manage to

cover them with your fly or bait. Springers share the rivers with kelts, last season's spawned fish either dying or making their way slowly downstream to the sea, and kelts often take your fly or lure in the early spring river, raising your hopes. An early spring day can be quite active between kelts and the odd springer and I shall never forget a day on Tay when three of us took 56 kelts and one springer in an orgy of rod bending. Every kelt seemed at the moment of hooking to be a possible springer, and ironically, when my colleague hooked his 18½lb (8.4kg) springer, and called 'Springer', I pooh-poohed it and said something to the effect that it was another kelt pretending. Spring days are usually great days of hope, especially if you are fishing for your first salmon of the year.

In fishing for springers I have always found the key idea to be to look for sheltered lies. Springers lie in the gentlest places, in long gravelly glides on Tay, in the holding dubs of Tweed, in the tails of pools on Thurso and Brora where the water is slow. On Spey and Tay springers are often in the slack 'aprons' of water beside harder streams and

The salmon season on Tay opens in January, often in wintry conditions. The tail of the Meetings Pool at Stenton is a likely place for an early springer

The rewards of the midwinter-spring angler. These four excellent fish came from the Tay at the opening of the season. They took a Kynoch Killer harled from a boat, a method common to the river and much used in spring (Michael Shepley)

Above: Fishing the lower Tweed. Note the 'grue' on the water – ice crystals in clusters. This normally makes fishing unproductive but not for this angler (Arthur Oglesby)

Right: Two early springers from the Tay (Michael Shepley)

Below: Returning a well mended kelt. Some kelts take on a very metallic silver sheen as they linger in the freshwater, but they are unclean fish and it is illegal to take them (Michael Shepley)

Bottom right: A nice fresh run Tay fish from Benchil in early February (Michael Shepley)

On the Tay in January. The pool is spun through, in this case with a toby spoon, and a fish takes. As the fish is played and tires the question is how best to tail it out. After considering the use of the wire tailer, the angler decides to hand tail the fish, and brings ashore a well-shaped, but slightly dark, fish of 17lb (7.7kg) (Michael Shepley)

in lies behind boulders where the force of the current is broken. Fishing for springers with fly or with spun lures reflects this; you fish deeply and slowly. There are exceptions, of course, and I will come to them, but the tactics for springers for me relate to a slow hovering fly led deeply through the lies, or, if I am spinning, I like to present a gently fanning wooden devon which can be made to hang, slowly rotating over likely places and can be led sensitively through gentle glides.

These lies and these tactics are typical of cold water fishing. When the spring heats up, and it may happen in March in an early year, but is most likely to come in April, you change your tactics. In the warmer air and in the cold water as it gradually warms up, fly fishing with a floating line begins to take over. On Spey and Dee, for instance, as soon as conditions are right, we fish a floating line and small flies. Salmon rise to the small flies like trout. Back fins break the water when the fish takes, the surface bulges as a good fish turns on the fly, and salmon may show in the pools and streams like dimpling trout. It is still spring fishing, but it is a very different spring from the early days of the season on one of the rivers of Sutherland, or on the deep pools of the Tay.

Spring fishing merges with summer fishing about the middle of May. On Tay the spring boats are off from about the end of the first week of the month, and while fish still run the river, often in substantial numbers, that marks the change over to early summer fish. It is an arbitrary frontier.

Summer Runs

For many rivers, particularly those on the west coast of Scotland, in Ireland and in the south-west of England, the coming of summer fish marks the beginning of the main salmon fishing season. I was brought up in Ayrshire, and while, from time to time, we did take an early fish from the Ayr or Doon, we began to expect fish in May with the floods of the late spring and early summer. Further north, one finds on, say, Loch Maree that the spring tides around the third week of May bring fresh fish to the head of the loch at Kinlochewe. There, given water, they will run the river. These are summer fish, but they have the flavour of springers, partly because spring can be late in the Highlands and partly because the first fish of the year seem like early springers.

Summer fish run with spates on the smaller rivers of the west. Thus, in a wet year you may find that your catches are early and consistent. In

Spinning the Aitkenhead Pool of the Benchil beat on Tay in early February. The water is wide and heavy and casts of up to 50yd are common. The tackle is a 10ft (3.05m) two-piece glass spinning rod and a multiplier

Playing a good fish on the Spey at Castle Grant in May, the best of the floating line fly fishing (Arthur Oglesby)

many springs, May is a dry month, and fish cannot move into freshwater. In these conditions, a single spate in mid June can bring tremendous sport to the west – a burst after a spring hunger. But these fish are, again, anomalous runs, partly spring in character, yet summer in date. True summer fish run at any time from May to September. The earlier fish are ten to fifteen pounders on the west, but the average for a given river might be smaller than that. For example, on the Shiel the fish of May and early June, running with the first sea trout, are solid salmon in the teens and low twenties of pounds. In July, you expect seven and eight pounders. These smallish summer fish are excellent sport. I love catching

them on light tackle or in unusual circumstances. I have had them at night while fishing for sea trout on the Shiel, on the Endrick and elsewhere. They are usually taken on floating line, and they rise like trout to the fly. Often they follow your fly, quite visibly, and I shall always remember an afternoon on the Shiel in July when I was fishing Grassy Point, just below the great Garden Pool. At each cast I got bow waves as fish followed the fly with curiosity, but did not take. I was fishing from behind some low cover – I always try to hide from salmon, unlike the majority of anglers who seem to think the fish is blind, deaf and daft – and I had some heart-stopping moments when fish, sometimes in twos, followed· the fly and turned

Above: The springer is a much sought after fish

Below: Netting a fish is an art worth perfecting. Once the fish is bagged in the net it is safe. Slide your hand down the net shaft and grip the ring before pulling the fish ashore. A salmon in a net can severely strain the shaft if the angler attempts to lift the heavy fish out without supporting it

Fishing in summer conditions down a famous salmon and sea
trout lie off Grassy Point on the River Shiel

away. I did not hook any on that occasion, but later in the afternoon a wind got up and rippled the water at Grassy. This time there was no difficulty. I had an eight pounder soon after starting. Fish which follow may, in fact, not be takers at all.

Grilse come into many of our rivers in July and August, or even later. Technically, these are salmon with only one winter's sea feeding and they return to the river as small sprightly fish, 4 to 6lb (1.8 to 2.7kg) in weight. You can get 9 or 10lb (4 or 4½kg) grilse, but how are you to know that these exceptional fish are grilse unless you examine the scales? Scientifically, they are grilse, but for me, reacting subjectively as an angler, they are summer salmon. Grilse, for me, must mean a small, fitful, usually lean salmon of little more than sea trout size on average. They pluck at your flies and follow them tantalisingly and, sometimes, when your luck is in, they come so willingly that it is difficult to believe that it is the same tricky fish which baffled you yesterday. I have hooked two at once, in the Sea Pool of the Shiel, unfortunately losing one, but landing the other after a great, hair-raising fight which took me over the two falls into the sea.

When the droughts of summer come to large rivers like the Tay, reducing them to their bare bones, a whole new phase of summer fishing can emerge. The river shrinks, but does not diminish in an angling sense. The river within the river is revealed. Streams which were far too heavy to fish previously are wadable and fishable; great glides which are usually harled from the boat turn out to be streams and eddies and funnels full of lies and excellent for exploratory fly fishing. On the Tay at Brunbane, just below Caputh I used to pray for low water so that I could wade into the tail of Sparrowmuir and cover the 'vee' lie which was unfishable for most of the season. I remember wading deep one July day, leaning against the whole weight of the river to keep my balance and somehow managing not only to reach the 'vee', but hang the fly in it long enough to be effective. I had two fish in quick succession, both in the mid-teens, and both brilliantly fresh. Each salmon sped down the fast water below and took line and backing of several colours before I could stumble out of the river and pound down the shingle in my waders to get onto equal terms with the fish and play them out. That is salmon fishing of the best kind. That July day I lay on the shingle after taking the fish and savoured the blue of the sky, and the power and beauty of the quarry.

One of the delights of the summer is picking up a fish here or a fish there, often in unusual places

Above: Autumn fly fishing on the Tweed at Walkerburn (Arthur Oglesby)

Left: Two summer fish on floating line from the middle Tay. The first fish, 9½lb (4.3kg), took a No. 6 Blue Charm fished on a long floating line and its capture is shown on p. 140-41. The second fish was a 6½lb (2.9kg) grilse taken in fast streamy water on the same beat (Michael Shepley)

in a low Tay or Spey and the whole game becomes twice as satisfying if one can do it with a small fly on a floating line while the other rods are obsessed with bait. I speak personally, of course, when I say that half the game of fly fishing is wiping the eye of bait. It doesn't always work, of course, but when it does how you remember it! Simple rivalry is part of sport. I am not an exclusive purist; I do catch fish on devons, spoons and plugs and the whole array of luremongery, but in the last several seasons I have derived such satisfaction from fly fishing that I now fish fly on all kinds of water at all times of year, and it tends to bring just as many fish to the net over the season as bait. Regard fly fishing as the norm and spinning as the deviant for a whole season and see how you score. Don't give up spinning for summer fish, but decide to fly fish all morning, or for two hours before and one hour after lunch in any one day, regardless of conditions. It is astonishing how well the fly works, but many of us have forgotten this. Don't be stubborn about it; spin if you really have to, but

fly fish first. I caught all my fish on fly in 1978 and had my best season for thirteen years. I had two days of five, two days of four and doubles and singles spread throughout the spring, summer and autumn.

One of these days illustrates very well what the satisfactions are in summer fly fishing. I was fishing Stenton in very low summer conditions in August. The Meetings Pool, with its island at the head had only one headstream, since the flow on the right side of the island had virtually dried up. On the other side, what is usually an unapproachable torrent, was fishable, and while the great pool below was sluggish, the draw off at the tail was showing lies and attractive slicks of current, normally obliterated by several feet of gliding water.

I spotted a particularly nice funnel in the draw

off where a promontory of stones just under the surface near the left bank caused a nice purl on the glide. My colleague offered to boat me down to it and putting a No. 6 Blue Charm double on with a floating line, fished on my 14ft (4.27m) Webley *Glen* fibreglass rod, I covered first the water immediately above the promontory (a likely lie) and then the deep funnel itself, hard by the stones. On the second cast, up came a fish and with no uncertainty whatever, he was on. We towed him – just like walking him – up into the big pool and he played well. I was landed and at a sandy bay slipped the net under the salmon after a good fight, 9½lb (4.3kg), fresh, firm and a great summer fish (see picture sequence above).

After lunch, I concentrated with the fly on the one remaining head rush to the pool, and, using

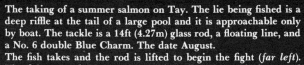

The taking of a summer salmon on Tay. The lie being fished is a deep riffle at the tail of a large pool and it is approachable only by boat. The tackle is a 14ft (4.27m) glass rod, a floating line, and a No. 6 double Blue Charm. The date August.
The fish takes and the rod is lifted to begin the fight (*far left*). The fish comes back up with the boat into the pool above and the angler is landed to fight the salmon to the net (*top left*). The net is in hand, already submerged with the bag extended, but the fish finds energy for a last burst of splashing (*left*). Tired out now and quiet the fish is drawn carefully over the submerged net (*above*). The fish is bagged in the net and the angler slides his hand down the net shaft to take the strain before bringing the salmon ashore (*right*)   (*Michael Shepley*)

two flies, and holding the 14ft rod as high as I could to clear intervening streams, tried to hold the flies in the glassy stream between the spouts of white water. They say salmon take slowly, and usually they do. What happened there was as quick as light. A small silvery fish arched over like a sea trout and solidly took the dropper. It stopped for a second or two, then turned and ran down the long white stream below into the Meetings Pool. The excitement of the rod bending and the reel making frantic noises, for what seemed a very long time, was amazing. I had to get out of the water, cross the diminished left-bank headstream and work my way down the bank to get level with the fish. He was still on and obligingly came back upstream again. It was a small fish, a clean grilse, and it did not have power to make the later runs

any more than local thrashing and twisting forays. It weighted 5½lb (2½kg), making two for the day. The other rods had predicted that it would be a splendid day for prawns, but, interestingly, not one fish was touched by 'old whiskers' that day. Two fish fell downstream to a Toby fished in a deep pot in one case and wiggled high in the water of a stream in another. Fish will take large and to my mind, unseasonal baits in low water, but I would not be weaned from the fly and the floating line by this chance.

In essence, that is summer fishing. Low water, a different riverscape, small flies (or comparatively small flies) and fish showing like trout as they take. But there is excellent fight in them, and one usually finds that one's flies take the freshest fish in the beat.

Fly fishing the Tweed for autumn salmon. The Tweed has a remarkable 'back end' season, extending to the end of November (Michael Shepley)

Autumn Runs

It is important to distinguish between catching fish in autumn and catching autumn fish. Our rivers have had spring and summer runs into them and the fish have lain in the pools and streams, getting potted and soft, for weeks or months. When temperatures drop in September and early October, these fish after being stale and uncatchable all summer, may be gingered up by a rise in water or another environmental change and may take your fly or bait. But these are not autumn fish, which are salmon fresh from the sea in September, October and November. Many rivers close in October. The Tay finishes in mid October and most of the other rivers close with the end of that month. Rivers up north, noted for their spring and early summer runs may close at the end of September. The message of this is that proprietors and river authorities may feel that it is not really sporting, nor is it good conservation to take black

fish (the hens) and while it may not do very much damage to take the red ones (the cocks) it may disturb the spawning to do so. I am not too worried about cocks, but hens advanced in spawn must be left to stock the river. I return potted hens from September on, but I have no objection to taking the odd big red cock, which can be a stiff fighter and can smoke well for the table.

As with the frontier between spring and summer, the line between summer and autumn is hard to draw. I think it is best to use a simple date definition. September fish and later are autumn salmon. It is also useful to identify waters for autumn fishing, since certain important characteristics mark out the best autumn salmon. For instance, the rivers of the Solway bring in excellent, large salmon in October and early November called locally 'grey backs'. In fact these grey backs are spoken of and caught in the rivers of Ayrshire, Galloway, Kirkcudbright and Dumfries, and not all of their rivers flow into Solway. Clearly, the

Fly fishing the Tweed for autumn salmon in the Beech Tree Pool, below Cardrona. The fish was well hooked on a medium-sized tube fly and duly came to the tailer – 13lb (5.9kg), in good condition, but slightly coloured

large, clean autumn fish is a phenomenon of the south-west of Scotland. It is also known in the western flowing rivers of England and Wales, identified by all sorts of local names, including 'blue back'. This type of salmon is obviously a race within a species. The biggest I have seen was a 27 pounder on the Doon, but Nith and Annan bring in better fish than this.

The autumn scene on the east coast is patchy. Most rivers close early, but the notable late running water is the Tweed. Its season is extended to the end of November and this late closing date is fully justified. I have taken shining clean fish in the last week of November, and, as I have written elsewhere in this book, I often feel I would like to fish Tweed right through the winter. The late runs on Tweed, called universally the 'back-end' fishing are spectacular and provide by far the best sport of the year on that great river. The runs begin as soon as the September floods allow it. The estuary nets come off in mid September on Tweed and this coincides with a fly-only rule for angling on the river. There might be a period of fly fishing with floating line in a warm September or October, but usually the floods are cold and we fish sunk line. The fish we are trying for are fresh, may run to 20 to 30lb (9 to 13½kg) (or over) and, indeed, it is unusual to fish the autumn run consistently and not get into one of the larger fish. Whether you will land it or not is another question. The largest I landed from the back end of 1978 was a twenty one pounder, a fine deep fish taken single-handed from the pot under the Kelso bridge, but I hooked and lost two far larger fish, one of which leapt and lunged in full view of two of us at Maxton before shedding the hook. That fish was possibly 25 to 28lb (11.3 to 12.7kg) in weight and was clean.

The winter overtakes the late autumn fishing on Tweed. Frosts come in November or cold high floods. The latter can ruin the sport, and drive you mad at the same time. Fish in their thousands run the caulds (weirs) on the Tweed and its tributaries. At such times it is the rods fishing in the upper Tweed, Manor Bridge and above, who take the salmon. If frost comes, fish run slowly, and water levels fall, since the trickles from the moors are all sealed up and surface drains in fields stop running. I love low water when I am lucky enough to be fishing the middle and lower Tweed in November. These beats hold the fish then, but given an inch or two of rise, the middle and lower Tweed can empty, and then the association water above Walkerburn – miles and miles of it – comes into its own.

I must not give the impression that Tweed is the only genuine autumn fishing on the east coast of Scotland. Don does well in some seasons and, fishing in the earlier weeks of autumn, I have seen some lovely fish off the North and South Esks. Interestingly, the Ness brings in good fish throughout autumn and winter, but I suspect that some of the later runs, which come long after the season ends for the rods, are really early springers, which the first rods on Morriston or Garry will take the following season.

Salmon run some of our rivers all winter. Tay closes with heavy fresh fish still running. Tweed closes with shining silver fish, lean and immature in spawn, in many of its beats. These waters clearly have a winter run and when we open on Tay in January, there is little doubt in my mind that some of the less silvery fish taken then, not kelts, are non-spawners from the winter runs. The winter run is one of Nature's insurance policies. It is not fished at sea because of the weather, nor in the estuaries, because it is the close season. The rods are off the river. In my view, a whole run of fish, unharvested except by occasional losses to the late autumn rods and the very earliest spring rods provides stock for the river. The waters of winter take them high into each river system and there they lie waiting possibly ten months until they spawn and continue their race. I have heard it said that winter runs are the reason for the amazing resilience of the Tay.

Salmon in Rivers

Where Salmon Lie

Knowing where salmon lie is vital to good fishing, yet it is one of the most difficult things to write effectively about. The topic embraces the whole river, and the life of the fish. We can start with a few generalisations, but on every beat I have fished there are local lies which either have to be pointed out to one or have to be discovered by experience. Salmon as a rule do not like deep lies. If your beat has a dub 15ft (4½m) deep, you will not find your salmon lying in the depths, although they may lie near deep water. Salmon like water 2 to 6ft (0.6 to 1.8m) in depth and this holds good for lochs as well as rivers. They like shelter in river lies, to conserve energy. They like places which cannot be

Top right: **An excellent lie for salmon on the middle Tay. The angler is spinning a wooden devon on a long, 10ft (3.05m) spinning rod with a multiplier and he is fishing his spinning bait round almost as if it were a fly (Michael Shepley)**

Right: **Spinning down the headstream of the Meetings Pool, Stenton, on the middle Tay (Michael Shepley)**

disturbed easily. Salmon like streamy water or glides and they may lie in, or near, the fastest streams on your beat, especially after the water begins to heat up. Streamy water is much more comfortable for the fish, provides protection and oxygen and it has always seemed to me that the stream itself offers an escape element. The fish is an excellent swimmer, and combined with the rush of the current, these powers can add up to a remarkable burst of speed and manoeuvrability, which are essential elements in survival.

On a strange river I look for lies in medium-current streams or in the long glides which gently deepen into pools. In most Scottish rivers it is the pools which hold fish, or rather, the headstreams and tail streams of the pools. Lies in the head-streams are usually summer and autumn lies. In spring, possibly because of the colder water with its higher concentration of dissolved oxygen, salmon like gentler lies. Headstream lies are dependent on at least two things: boulders to shelter the fish from the force of the current, to provide a respite from the endless pressure of the river; and, secondly, configurations of the bed which equally can form pockets of water sheltered from the stream – lies in invisible pockets of shelter caused by the variations of the stream itself.

A typical place to find a lie in a headstream would be where the stream itself is made up of two parallel currents. Salmon would lie close to the inside edges of these currents, gently fanning to hold their position in the run. Healthy fish do not usually lie in the slack water between streams. They like to have their noses in the faster water, yet be out of the push of the stream. Often these lies are marked out by a glassy appearance on the surface of the water where the heavily disturbed surface of the stream is softened by the shelter of a submerged boulder. Now, there is a lot of talk about salmon lying behind boulders, but it is only a half truth to identify the lies like that. Salmon do not lie hard behind boulders; such a lie would be uncomfortable for them. They are much more likely to lie either downstream of the boulder where the currents pouring round the stone meet and form a single stream again, or, as we described in the case of a headstream which is split, in the inside edges of the streams where current and security are right for them.

Turbulent areas in streams and pools are not liked by salmon. It is true you will find certain fish in great eddies where, in effect, the eddy is a large circular stream. I shun eddies. The fish in them are often stale or sick and are usually unfishable by fly. But I do like the draw-off from an eddy where the turbulent current is drawn

down into the main stream and the water steadies itself again and flows regularly, in contrast to the eddy itself which sucks water off into its whirls. Just below the Meetings streams on the Stenton beat on the Tay there is a very large and deep eddy. Most of us fish the stream above the eddy, then take the fly or spinner out of the water and walk down to where the stream finally sorts itself out and we continue from there. An eddy is rather like a knot in a plank of wood. It seems to push the regular fibres of the timber outwards. Watch for these round eddies on salmon rivers. Salmon will lie in the regular streams around eddies, but hardly ever in them.

Turbulence seems to worry salmon in a way I see as parallel to how turbulence worries us when we fly in light aircraft. It is very uncomfortable to go through lumpy air conditions. In heavy streams, salmon may seem to the untutored eye to be in the turbulent water, but closer investigation will usually show that under the surface marks of turbulence, there are lies, or ledges of rock or some other shelter where the uncomfortable effects of turbulence can be escaped.

It would be a mistake, of course, to assume that there would always be a visible physical reason for a salmon lie, like a boulder or a ridge of rock, or a bank of gravel. Rivers shape their beds according to the laws of physics. Water forms waves produced by the particular speed of the stream at a certain place, the nature of the bed, the presence of boulders and other features in the river and even the presence of boulders under the bed of the stream which cause the pressure waves to vary. A stream can dig out a substantial hollow with a pressure wave and that can deflect current up and over a patch of gravel immediately below. I have seen salmon lying in gravel streams obviously in shelter, yet without much in the way of boulders or rocks to be seen. I heard of two cases recently where a gas pipe line was laid under a salmon river and in each case the pipe was some 6ft (1.8m) down into the shingle. The pipe, however, produced a special pressure wave and a lie for salmon was created in the invisible shelter which formed below. These lies have to be pointed out to one, or discovered in the course of fishing – preferably by hooking salmon in them.

In the pools themselves, salmon usually let one know where they are lying, by showing. Seeing salmon is a very important thing. It encourages one in the long periods when salmon are not keen to take. Even kelts showing in spring helps psychologically. I do not like the days when I flog away on a river, never seeing a salmon, and never touching one. True there are days, especially in spring, when you can fish away and see little, yet from time to time get into fish. On my best day in the spring on the fly (to date) I fished one excellent pool in Sutherland, saw nothing except possibly a kelt in a backwater on the far bank, then hooked and landed a lovely twelve pounder. Further down I thought for some reason that a fish moved in the tail stream on the far side of a rock and whether I was right or not, hooked a seven pounder there to make it a double. A further fish walloped at the large spring fly but did not take hold. On a magnificent long 'lochan' pool below, we saw nothing, but I hooked four right in the tail, landing two of them and losing one large fish after a longish fight. You can have magnificent sport when nothing is showing, but it is nicer to see fish showing as well as feel the fish taking.

Where pools narrow and draw their waters off into a funnel-shaped stream at the tail you usually find a splendid lie. I love these lies, especially in spring when they can be fished steadily round with fly. Fish often show beautifully in them as they take, and seeing a take like that is the kind of bonus which makes fishing memorable. Greased line fishing over the draw-off to pools is tremendous fun in summer. Again it is a question of seeing the action as the fish takes. These lies are excellent running lies too. Fish will forge up the stream below and pause in the tail of the pool above (in some cases) and there they will take a well presented fly. In pool tails, you may find boulders 'veeing' the surface. These places often form marvellous resting and running lies. They can best be fished from a point well above them, if you can get to such a point on the water. Boat fishing over such lies is often good. I like the fly to hang in the glide and search out the sides of the 'vee'. Also, in autumn, gravel tails are places where fish take up redd lies, that is, lies related to the making of redds in which the spawn is placed. Cock fish often make a great territorial display of holding such places, and in autumn fishing you might find that a tube fly or a Waddington, usually in the large class, say 1½ to 2in (3.8 to 5cm) in length, can provoke tremendous shows. Great bow waves follow the fly round, possibly in the more violent cases followed by a great boil and a savage take as the fish 'eliminates' the fly. You can get some of the most spirited fights of the season in such circumstances. In autumn, one takes cock fish from lies like that, but hens are usually returned if they are heavy with spawn.

It is actually easier to explain, or try to, why salmon do lie in certain places, than to explain why they shun certain apparently ideal places. Possibly the answer is that there are, on a Scottish salmon river, more lies than there are salmon. Let me give an example. On some waters where there is a promontory causing an apparently perfect lie, you might find that salmon much prefer lying above the obvious shelter. Closer investigation may help to explain this. Boulders and promontories form marvellous lies above them because the water of the stream is pushed up by the back pressure from the obstruction. Yet why, in some cases, do the fish shun the luxurious shelter below? One or two 'vees' on a glide may be well known for holding fish, but others may never have a fish in them. The answer, I am sure, lies in the way the water actually flows there. We have already spoken of the way underwater changes in bad consistency may cause a lie where we can read nothing from the surface flow. Why should it not work against us too? We might seem to read perfect signs, yet find that a quirk in the bed causes a turbulence or a type of flow unacceptable to the salmon?

Running lies are fascinating. They excite me because of the fact of fresh salmon running the river, but they also provide places where the freshest of the fish may be taken as they pass upstream, bringing excellent sport and those shining, high-backed fresh fish to the bank which are a joy to see. Further, salmon may only rest in running lies for a very short time. A runner is often ambiguous. Is it technically running as you take it or does it rest and it is then that you catch it? It is a bonus fish; that fish would not have been in the bag in the normal way. My favourite running lie is in the neck of a headstream. Where a stream enters a pool there are wedge shaped areas of slack water on each side. Often these 'necks' are beautiful lies over shingle and stones, where the stream has cleared the bed. Where headstreams are multiple, often formed into a fan of streams, there are sheltered lies in the neck of each stream. 'Getting salmon in the neck' is a standing joke phrase among anglers. On Spey, fishing Delagyle near Aberlour, the keeper and I used to come back in the evenings after the day's sport had reached its normal end, with rods going back to the hotel at around six o'clock in a spring evening, and we used to fish fly through all the little lies, many of them lies in the neck. The gillie

Overleaf: **Fishing down the headstream of the Meetings Pool on Stenton, River Tay. The stream slackens below, forming a series of excellent lies (Michael Shepley)**

Fly fishing the Burnbane Pool of the Middle Tay in very early February. The angler has hooked a splendid 15½lb (7kg) fish, straight from the sea, in the 'scallops' of shelter in the gravel beside the stream

on Wester Elchies opposite did likewise. From the neck of Delagyle Pool the Wester Elchies gillie would take fish after fish in the evenings. He would hold his fly more or less at an angle in the first gentle water beside the rush. Salmon lying in the side of the fast stream, pausing as they ran, or, as evening approached, pausing for the night, produced excellent sport. On our side the neck was poorer but still produced salmon. Our best places were the neck of Pol Mo Chridh or the gentler Gean Tree Pool where salmon lay longer as the evening wore on.

Running lies differ from water to water, but one type which I have seen on several beats are what I call 'scallop' lies. On the margins of a long stream you will find that the shingle has been eaten back into bays. You might not recognise

Left: Fly fishing the falls pool on a Norwegian river. Fish are running, and this might mean that the population of the pool below will be unsettled, continually changing. At such times you might get plucks and pulls and lighty-hooked fish, or no offers at all (Jens Ploug Hansen)

these lies unless you had waded the stream and found the pockets in the shingle. These may be 2 to 4ft (0.6 to 1.2m) deep and salmon running up the stream will usually slide into such places for a breather as they face the ascent. In cold water in spring, these lies can hold places where fish will rest for long periods. There is no way of knowing how long a runner will stop in these conditions, but I have certainly seen fish moving in these scallops on Tay in January and February and have fished them hours later and have taken them on fly, or have been able to direct a colleague to a precise place where a springer was waiting.

On every pool there is a running route. Those who come to know beats intimately can trace that route, possibly showing that the fish follow a seemingly logical path from the tail to the dub, then, say, crossing to the right bank to run up the inside of the stream and perhaps cross again to go up the middle shelter between headwaters. On that lovely pool Pollowick, on Spey, I was fishing one April, not knowing the water well. I saw fish moving in the lie on the far right bank where I had been told salmon lay, but I was suddenly

151

aware of salmon showing close in under the left bank, near me in an eddy. Later I was told that the fish enter the pool and cross from the Green Bank at an angle of about 45° and commonly show in the eddy before re-crossing the dub of Polowick to the right bank again and following the pool up through the Sluggan above, where they rest in the stream itself, or close beside it. This is the pattern for only one pool, and I could give many examples, but it may serve to show that salmon have their own logic in running. Therefore, where we are looking for lies where running fish rest, we might sometimes have to look more deeply into the routes on some waters before we can make the most of our fishing. Of course, most pools are fairly obvious. Fish show at the tail as they enter and may lie there for short spaces of time, especially if there are boulders; they run the main pool, usually following the sides of the deep water. In the headstream, they take the inside of a stream rather than the main force, and they lie in shelter beside the stream, especially near the neck, with their noses on the gravel or rocks of the bar above.

I recall one September day on Almondmouth on Tay. That beat is just at the head of the tide, above Perth. Where the Almond joins, a great pool is formed with a wide shingly stream, deep near the Scone bank (the left bank) and forming a quiet sandy hold on the right bank, where the Almond has dug out a rather sluggish backwater. One wades down the long shingly stream and searches with a fly the shallow lies behind stones, trying the main current over on the Scone bank as far as it can be fished. Running salmon lie at certain times in great numbers down the Almond side of the stream, ie its slack side. I fished down that pool once and got bump after bump in water only a few inches deep and I couldn't work out what was happening. In fact the shingle was holding a huge weight of small fish, which run the Tay in autumn. I think my fly was too large. The rod following me down took two, then I fished the water again, after a short rest, got into one, and landed one, and on a subsequent fishing after lunch took a second salmon. The difficulty for me was that it was short line fishing in the stream. It was, really, ideal conditions for a short line and dropper fly, and my long floating line, usually a killer on the Tay, was not fishing the resting lies well. The other problem that day was that the fish were very fresh, just off the tide, and in that condition, like very fresh summer grilse, are liable to pluck at flies as they pass. We did well that day, however, once we had recognised the fact that we were fishing for running fish, and these runners were right under our rod tops.

Fly Fishing – The Basic Arts

Fly fishing for salmon is a curious art; it does not appear to be directly related to the feeding habits of the salmon in the way that, say, fly fishing for trout is. Yet, after years of fishing, one is very conscious of a very natural pattern in the art of presenting the fly and taking fish by it. I think I *want* to think of the salmon fly as food and the salmon taking it as such. I well remember reading with great identification a description of a formative moment in the development of greased line salmon fishing when A H E Wood* saw salmon taking down natural flies – white moths – in Ireland and conceived the notion that flies fished at or near the surface could take fish instead of the normal heavy line sunk fly tactics then common. I have seen salmon taking natural flies and I have absolutely no doubt that, from time to time, for its own reasons, a salmon will be attracted to a natural bait, such as fly or nymph, and will take it, albeit immediately to eject it. Salmon are non-feeders when they return to freshwater, and it is as non-feeders that we tempt them and catch them. There is a nice mystery in that.

It is probably misleading to think of fly fishing for salmon as one art. It is several. The tactics for fishing in cold waters, in spring or autumn, involve sunk lines, large flies and slow presentation which link fly fishing with spinning for salmon. The fly is probably best thought of as a fish in these cases. The tactics for fishing in the warmer waters of spring and summer are quite different. We fish with floating lines, small flies – often as small as trout flies – and we make the fish rise to our flies in a way which reminds one of trout fishing. I take salmon on my trout tackle every season, sometimes inadvertently, when a salmon in a loch or in a stream in the river takes my trout fly, but sometimes by design, when the conditions are fine and I do not want to wave a 12 or 14ft (3.66 or 4.27m) rod about. Also, on smaller waters in the Highlands, I would not want to trudge around with a great rod suitable for casting long lines on the Spey when the salmon fishing might consist, on these hill waters, of creeping up to a pool and gently searching it with a wisp of a tube fly.

I want to divide my description of the art of fly fishing for salmon into two parts – sunk line fishing and floating line fishing. My own thinking on these branches of fishing is strongly influenced by the idea that the salmon is somehow two fish rolled into one. It is a river fish, having spent two

*A H E Wood, 'Greased Line Fishing' in Taverner (ed.) *Salmon Fishing* (Seely Service, London).

Choosing the fly on the Tay in summer. Fly size and type become much more important as the water falls. A No. 6 Blue Charm double is chosen and before the day was done had accounted for two fish

years of its life as a parr living like a small trout in the river. Then it changes into a sea fish, spending, say, two years of its life in the sea living like a marine fish, pursuing the food of a sea fish. When the fish returns to our rivers, it seems to me that in certain water conditions the fish reacts like a sea fish and in other conditions it is stimulated to react like a river fish. Broadly, in the colder water of spring and autumn, the fish should be thought of as a sea fish, should be fished with sunk lines and fish-like flies. In the warmer waters of spring and summer, the fish is best caught on small flies in a way not dissimilar from wet fly fishing for trout. This rather crude theory seems to me to have some basis in fact. Equally, what we know about animal behaviour suggests that feeding behaviour may often be a reaction to stimuli from the environment. I think it is enormously helpful to think of the salmon's reaction to the fly as being a reaction to the stimulus of the fly in the behavioural sense. We stir something deep in the salmon's being. Although it is not actually feeding,

we can make it go through the motions. Arthur Ransome put it humorously in his book *Mainly about Fishing* when he likened the reaction of salmon to the fly to people chewing gum. Incidentally, in that book he also prints fascinating coloured pictures of creatures of the plankton – the small crustacea, squids and other forms of life which follow the drifts of plankton in the sea, and which are, in turn, fed upon by the salmon. He suggests that our salmon flies actually imitate these creatures. The idea certainly has merit. I take the view that I do not know what my Hairy Mary imitates, but I do know that when I get certain conditions on the river, and when I present it in a certain way, the salmon thinks it is food. I am therefore half committed to a pragmatism based on experience of the salmon itself. Perhaps, like the salmon I am two-fold myself; I like rationalising, but I am often prompted to cover a fish in a certain way, or present a certain kind of fly to a salmon on a basis of intuition, most of which is sub-rational.

153

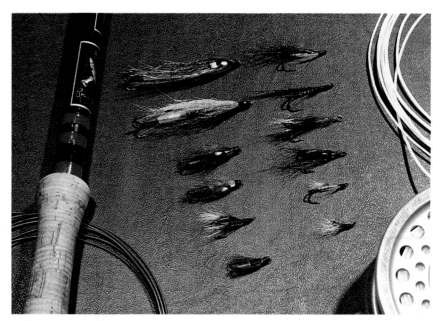

Left: Some salmon tackle. The flies shown represent the whole range of salmon flies from large Waddingtons for spring fishing to small greased line flies for summer sport. The larger flies would normally be fished on sunk line or on sink tip lines, and the smaller flies would be typical of floating line tackle (Arthur Oglesby)

Right: Playing a summer salmon on Spey (Arthur Oglesby)

Below: Fishing a floating line down the tail of a Spey pool in summer (Arthur Oglesby)

Fishing a Fly with a Sunk Line

Sunk line fishing for salmon is a form of fishing in which a fish-like lure is presented to the salmon in conditions broadly reminiscent of the sea. In February, March and part of April on rivers like the Spey, Tweed and Tay, most salmon fishers would be spinning the river. The water temperature would be anything from just above freezing to the mid-forties Fahrenheit (7°C). In these colder waters, fish move more slowly, running in a leisurely fashion and resting in sheltered lies quickly and unobtrusively. It is true fish do show in spring, but the frequency of shows is much below that of summer. It is almost as if the colder water reduced their vital force. In fact it is the other way round; salmon lose their zing in summer when the river heats up.

Let me describe the taking of a typical spring salmon on fly in a Highland river – the Brora in Sutherland in March. The river was running at 18in (45cm) of flood on the gauge and I had found several of the streamy pools on the lower Brora to be just too high to fish well. The Well pool was just too fast and the Madman stream was very heavy on my side (Gordonbush) and it was proving difficult to cover the sheltered lies well where any salmon in the beat would be lying. I went up to the Ford Pool when the beats changed over at lunch time and I found the water in excellent ply. The Ford runs a heavy stream down the right bank, opposite to the one I was fishing, and this fills a deep dub out of which a fine tail stream moves, gliding and broadening as it increases pace to form the headstream of the pool below. On our bank there is a great area of sheltered water, and in this area running salmon will lie, often right into our bank, easing upstream or just resting. I was fishing my Sharpe's 14ft (4.27m) spliced cane rod – my normal spring rod – throwing a No.10 wet cel line with a 9ft (2.7m) level nylon leader (16lb (7.3kg) strain) and a Black and Yellow hair wing lure tied on a 1½in (4cm) metal body with one treble at the tail – one of the locally-tied spring flies made for Rob Wilson of Brora.

I was fishing about 20yd (18m) of line, perhaps a little more. Longer lines help in spring, because the line sinks better and takes the fly down with it. The fly was falling nicely in the stream on the far side, but was not really fishing there. The stream was too fast to allow the fly time to sink and fish round. The idea is to get the fly down and swim it or lead it over the lies in a controlled way, making it hover and hang attractively near the lies if you can. The Yellow and Black came round beautifully as we neared the tail of the pool. In that height of water all the lovely lies of the headstream were unfishable, at least in cold spring water. I felt the fly touch bottom and I knew it was getting down well. Next cast I had a strong pull and was into a nice fresh fish which immediately after hooking came back up into the main pool for the fight – very obliging of it. It was a small fish, just over 8lb (3.6kg), but it was shining clean and fresh, showing those pinkish and bluish sheens which make springers magnificent.

In one story, that is the basic art of sunk fly fishing – a largish fly, a sinking line, slow presentation over sheltered lies. But the art does not stop there. Flies, for example, can vary a great deal. In my box you will find a concentration of hair wing flies mostly tied on wire bodies with a treble hook at the tail. Some are Waddingtons, that is, tied on purpose-made mounts with a long steel shank incorporating a treble hook at the tail. In my opinion, wire-bodied flies fish better than Waddingtons in the large sizes. Waddingtons 'butterfly' in the water and I have seen them make fish splash at them but not take them, where a heavier hair wing wire-bodied fly, fishing more compactly and sinking better, has taken the fish immediately afterwards.

The old traditional salmon flies used for generations in the spring were single large hooks up to 8/0 in size, dressed in rather elaborate mixed feather wings and with a tendency to tinsel and bright coloured feathers. I have had fish on these, but I do not find them as effective as the tube flies, which I will describe later, or as the superb wire-bodied Brora flies. Yet, two seasons before writing this, fishing in the far north in March, my companion fairly wiped my eye with a catch of two nice salmon and one other lost to my single fish, using a 6/0 Garry Dog. He had one out of the falls pool which was so enthusiastic about the big fly that it walloped at it twice before engulfing the whole 'meat hook' and being firmly hooked. He went on to lose one other fish in that pool and take a third from the flats above the first fall. But, in general, I find that large single hooks do not hook well and do not hold well. Some of my older colleagues talk about salmon fly fishing when there were no tube flies and no Waddingtons. One of them told me about his tactics of pulling the fly home when the fish took, and if he felt the hook was insecure, during the fight he would get well below the fish and lower the rod top under gentle strain before striking again, either to dislodge the

Right: **Fly fishing excellent streamy water on Tay in late summer. Although the Tay is traditionally fished by spinning, there is a distinct movement back to fly in summer and autumn, when excellent sport is to be had (Michael Shepley)**

A large cock fish is netted. Note the kype – the hooked lower jaw. As the fish remains in freshwater this kype develops and may cross the top jaw and produce a grotesque scissors effect (Jens Ploug Hansen)

hook and shorten the agony, or to re-set the hook in a better position in the salmon's mouth. Such tactics make my hair stand on end. I am used to hooks like No. 12 or No. 10 trebles which get a really good hold, usually in the scissors, and which do not usually come adrift.

Casting large flies is hazardous; they can hit you on the back of the head and stun you. One of my Tweed friends said that he was fishing the Ashiestiel Boat Pool one spring day, getting a good line out with a 'meat hook' on the end, when a bell suddenly rang loud and clear. It took him some seconds to realise that he had clouted himself on the back of his head with his great spring fly. I do not fish large spring flies much. I have a goodly number of them in my box, and sometimes I look at my old Dusty Millers and Silver Wilkinsons and recall using them years ago. I know one gillie who likes them on Spey in spring, but really they are ornaments now, not the kind of lure we would use in sunk line fishing, in the normal run of things.

Tube flies offer many of the advantages of the Waddington style of fly with certain interesting differences. They are better than Waddingtons because you can change the treble instantly; you can store and carry them easily and you can use two (or more) tubes to build yourself a fly of the right length and hue. The tube, as its name suggests, is a fly dressed on a metal or plastic tube. It comes in heavy and light dressings. At its smallest, the fly may be dressed on a tiny plastic tube with a wisp or two of the black hair from a stoat's tail, and no body except the tube. These tiny tubes, from a quarter of an inch up to, say, an inch in length, are typical of floating line fishing on the Aberdeen Dee in May and June. Spring tubes or autumn tubes, designed for deep fishing in cold water, are usually dressed on brass tubes lined with plastic and they may be up to 2in (5cm)

Right: **The Dee at Invercauld. The Dee is noted for its near-perfect greased line water (Arthur Oglesby)**

When the salmon fly is being fished, it is important to lead it round, to make it swim attractively. Note the way the angler's hands control the line. The retrieval is made by gently drawing line in a yard at a time through the sensitive index finger of the rod hand (Michael Shepley)

in length. On Tweed, the hair tubes they fish on the lower river in October and November may have weighted bodies, say, with lead wire wound round the tube, and will be dressed with dog hair or goat's hair or bucktail dyed to suit the pattern.

One disadvantage of tube flies is that they can hank up during casting and I have lost at least one salmon on Tweed through a salmon taking the hanked-up tube as I was retrieving it to straighten it out. The fish pulled the fly hard, but did not find the hooks. In hanking up, the fly doubles back on the nylon leader and snags it. To counter this, and to help to hold the treble hook out well – another problem with tube flies – we use little bits of bicycle valve tubing to provide a stiffening between body and treble. It works well but I find one has to check the fly repeatedly to make sure that the valve tubing has not slipped down or that the treble has not gone off line, or has not hanked up. I fish tubes and I like them. They often provide just the right compromise between a fat Brora type fly and a conventional single- or double-hooked fly. In their smaller sizes, one fishes them as standard with greased lines (floating lines) on Dee and Spey. I grumble about my tube flies, especially in their larger sizes, snagging the cast and doing unmentionable, tiresome things in casting, but I fish them a lot and like their hooking powers. During the fight, the body of the fly moves up from the hooks and keeps well clear of the salmon, leaving the treble hooks to hold well, unimpeded by the body of the fly, which might provide leverage to loosen the hooks. There is

much to be said for tubes, and I would not go to the river in spring or autumn without a box of them. But, overall, in spring fly fishing, I prefer the Brora type fly tied on a wire shank.

The standard way to fish the spring river with fly is, as I have outlined, to cover the lies with the fly well sunk and held hovering over the fish, or swum slowly round on an arc below you over likely water. But there are variations. North of Inverness (and on slower pools on Spey) you might resort to backing up. This is a technique of starting at the tail of the pool and as you fish the fly round on a longish line taking a step or two backwards and repeating the process. This causes the fly to speed up and pull attractively round the slack water at the tail of the pool and elsewhere where salmon might be lying. It is particularly suitable for Highland waters where long pools with rushy banks give you holding water without much stream in them. Backing up is a wonderful killer of salmon which have just entered a pool and are lying for a short breather in the tail of the pool, or in a flat. The fish usually pursue the fly and take it with a will. I have had four fresh fish in line take like this on one pool on the Thurso, and on Naver and Spey I have also had success using this technique. Interestingly, it does not seem to be favoured as a technique on Tay or Tweed. I dare say the swinging effect on the fly, caused in boat fishing the larger Tweed pools or the beats of lower Tay, would produce an effect not unlike backing up, but it is still interesting that this technique is restricted to the northern Highlands.

Those of us who try it further south, do so because it has performed so well for us up north.

Fishing a Fly With a Floating Line

The essence of fishing a floating line for salmon can best be set out in a description of taking a fish on the Dee. I fish a beat of that river in mid May and my turn came to fish the marvellous Lummels pool on the Birse water. It was just before lunch and the sun was gently easing its way through some fine high cloud. The Lummels flows round in a gentle curve and over the years it has cut itself into the base of a great clay cliff. Concrete walling has been put in to protect the bank and this forms a very handy fishing platform with the deep water curling past your feet and the pool shallowing out beyond the stream to form a gliding flat in which fish show regularly.

I was spey casting my way down the fishing wall when I saw a nice head and tail rise more or less at the limit of my casting distance. Twice I tried the fish, but in each case I seemed to be falling short. On the third cast I got the distance and the fish moved beautifully to the fly, boiling at it as it was brought round by the glide, but not taking it. I checked my fly quickly and cast again. This time the fish made no mistake. It took my Hairy Mary No. 8 with a fine black wave which parted to show the fish's back as it rose. Up went the rod and the hook was home. It was a splendidly fresh fish, not large, 8½lb (3.8kg), but it fought excellently, showed itself in a series of very strong lunges and leaps and eventually came to the net after a fight in which we had seen the fish repeatedly, both in the air and in the clear water. Fishing a floating line is memorable because you see so much.

Greased line fishing, or floating line fishing as it is more accurately named now, is an obvious approach for low water. But it would be a mistake to associate it with low water exclusively. Equally, it is a technique closely linked with the warmer waters of late spring and summer, but again it is wrong to stereotype it. A H E Wood*, who promoted the technique, and indeed may well have been the inventor, held that a salmon would rather rise to a fly fished just below the surface than to any other presentation, and he used to advocate using the floating line at any time from February onwards when the air was warmer than the water. I do not share his enthusiasm for cold water and the floating line. For me it is very much a question of water above a certain temperature with air still warmer.

*A H E Wood, 'Greased Line Fishing', in Taverner (ed.), *Salmon Fishing* (Seeley Service, London).

Fishing greased line down the Middle Narrows of the River Ewe in high summer. *Centre:* A fish moves to the fly in what seems to be a take. The angler does nothing but waits for the line to 'go' which would indicate a take. *Bottom:* The rings of the take spread and the fly comes round untouched. Not surprisingly, it is a non-taking rise, something experienced anglers are familiar with in high summer

161

The gillie ties on a fly for a lady angler on beat 15 of the Thurso. On a strange river the choice of fly can be critical

To be specific, Wood and his followers identified 48° (9°C) as the threshold. Water above this was obviously suited to the greased line. Water in temperatures below this might still produce good sport to a fly presented just below the surface, as the floating line does, but the fly size might be larger and the chances that the salmon would take a fly lower in the water were increased as the temperature went down.

Fishing the floating line is often associated with small flies. In the warmer waters of spring and in the summer river, small flies are universal. I use small doubles down to No. 10 in size and I have tiny Parker tube flies down to ¼in (6mm) in length, dressed on small bore plastic tubes. Often these minimally dressed flies seem to have only a wisp or so of hair on them, and they are usually dressed with no body at all. Yet, I have seen a spring fish come up to the surface for a Waddington 3in (8cm) long – a huge fly, fluttering its long hairs in a glide. It is true that on that occasion I was fishing a sinking line, but the glide was so fast that the fly was only fractionally beneath the surface. The fish followed, making a marvellous boil on the top and picked the large fly off the underside of the surface as neatly as any Dee fish in May. That was mid March with snow on the hills and a bitterly cold air chilling us as we fished.

That is by no means the only fish I have seen coming to a fly high in the water when all the theories say the best place to tempt the fish would be deep down, with a slow large fly. On Spey in early April, with cold water and spinning still dominant, I have often seen the persistent fly fisher do better than the spinners. I knew a gillie who would fish a dropper on his cast in April, presenting a large conventional fly on the tail and a small No. 8 on the dropper. That dropper very often took fish just as it was about to leave the water – right on the top. The salmon had the choice of a large fly fishing fairly deeply or a small one near the surface and it chose the latter. Now these instances do not prove a major trend. They merely remind us that we can become far too stereotyped in our fishing, and in this mood we forget that the salmon remains versatile. Very fresh fish will do remarkable things even in cold spring water. The gillie on Tulchan (Spey) told me that he had had his first fly-caught spring fish of the year on a No. 14 dry Greenwell in early April one year. I am *not* advocating that we all try this; I am merely trying to break the cast iron walls which seem to be placed around fishing approaches. The floating line will work in a vast range of conditions, but it is most likely to work in warmer waters, from the mid forties Fahrenheit (7°C) upwards when the air temperature is warmer than the water.

I had three salmon on my trout rod recently. Two of the fish were caught during the dusk rise for sea trout and excellent sport they were. I had had a good day on the Dee with four fish on the bank by mid-evening. At that point I laid aside my Sharpe's spliced 14ft (4.27m) salmon rod and changed to my 9ft 6in (2.90m) Farlow Sawyer *Stillwater* – an old friend, and far and away my favourite trout and sea trout rod. I put a small Stoat's Tail tube on the tail of the cast and I think it was a No. 8 Dark Mackerel on the bob. Oddly enough, the tail tube was larger than the one I had been fishing on my big rod for salmon during the day. As I re-tackled I took off my big Gye salmon net and slung on the smaller one and set off to the tail of the Quithel Pool to try for a sea trout.

I got a sea trout just after starting, but the evening blackened and things went off a bit. Fish, mostly salmon, were still crashing about in the gloom. In the wide tail of the Quithel at night one wades well out into a very still monochrome river and fishing is by feel – the rod in the hand and the line running over the forefinger. One does not move much, and a feeling of tranquility and detachment pervades. It was at this point that the rod suddenly bucked and the line pulled tight. There was an interval of about two seconds before the fish ran off across the tail of the pool at such a speed that I honestly thought my trout reel was about to disintegrate. It was obviously a salmon and a very lively one indeed. It leapt several times somewhere out in the gloom and all I could do was try to keep in touch. I got back out of the river, with difficulty, playing the fish somewhere out there in the dark. The fight was settling down a bit by this time, and it was just as well. I have seldom known such runs. But there was a problem. My small net was not right for a fish like this in the dark. My estate car was parked on the banks of the pool not far away and I decided to be bold and walk backwards up the steep bank and open the tailgate of the car to get the salmon net. I was half-way up and making good speed in the dark when the fish decided to run hard out across the pool tail. Where did it get the energy? I thought it was nearly dead. If my reel had screamed earlier it positively shrieked now. There was little I could do except hope that I had enough backing and get the net. Up went the tailgate and ninety yards out in the pool the fish stopped, pulsed in a tired way and began to come in. I brought him back on to the fly line before going down the bank, then got into the water and netted out a very tired perfectly silver 10½ pounder (4.8kg). A memorable salmon, an incredible fight and an overwhelming sense of achievement.

One might argue that that salmon was not a typical floating line fish at all; that it was taken when fishing for sea trout in the dusk. It is astonishing how many salmon will take a greased line fly in the dusk. During that short Dee week I had three salmon take in the dusk, and a companion, after a fishless day, took one on his salmon rod at half-past ten at night on regular floating line tackle. I like going up in size as the light goes, but the principle of presentation and handling of the fly does not alter. As the light goes, all sorts of subtle changes take place in the composition of the air and water. A gentle dampness comes down, and a calmness overtakes the evening wind. Fish move differently; salmon head and tail more and sea trout plop, making that attractive noise as they rise vigorously to evening flies and moths. What a marvellous time it is! I would willingly give up two hours of any salmon fishing day to get one such hour in the evening, and it brings perfect greased line conditions in May and June.

I think we start greased line fishing too late if we wait until the water is steady at 48°F (9°C) plus. Equally, we start sunk line fishing far too early in the autumn, thinking that autumn fish necessarily want it. On Tweed at Bemerside, the gillie had had not too good a day with his guests in October, and after they went he tried a greased line rather than the heavy line and sunk fly they had insisted on. He got into four fish in a very

short space of time in water which was high, coloured and getting cold, certainly below the magic threshold of 48°F (9°C). His fly, when he showed it to me, was astonishing. It was a summer tube fly with only six or seven black hairs on it. We delude ourselves into thinking that the salmon cannot see our flies, but an event like that shows how clearly a salmon can see and how willingly the fish will come up through 4ft (1.2m) of water to take the small fly, if conditions are right for it.

Of all the techniques in salmon fly fishing, greased line is far and away the most fascinating. It is an approach in which good reading of the water pays off, and in which good tackle handling makes all the difference between near misses and successes. The tackle itself is interesting in a special way, partly because of its lightness and partly because of its sensitive choice. Basically, any reasonably light salmon rod can be used. I think my 14ft (4.27m) Sharpe's spliced is a light rod, but naturally it is not as light as a fibreglass rod or one of the new carbon fibre rods which are ultra-light. I like the rod to be long enough for the river conditions you are likely to meet. I would not fish less than a 12ft (3.66m) rod where rolling, mending and casting a reasonable distance were involved. The lighter glass 14ft (4.27m) rods are excellent and I had several nice fish on my recently acquired Webley *Glen* rod last season. Trout rods are marvellous, but they do not have the casting power nor the mending power of the longer rods. Glass rods may spey cast fairly well, but for rolling and speying the spliced cane or the spliced Greenheart have no equals. The new glass rods have spigot fittings, and these rods have a much better spey casting ability than ferruled ones. Where spey casting is required (and I seem to use it almost everywhere in preference to overhead casting these days) a long responsive rod is absolutely necessary. Trout rods do not spey cast, although they may roll out line nicely within limits.

Modern floating lines are ideal for this form of fishing. As the older name 'greased line' implies, the earliest approaches were with silk lines, greased to make them float. Now a greased line floats on the surface and a modern floating line floats in the surface, a subtle distinction. For salmon, I much prefer the modern line. Mending and placing of the line may be better with a perfectly greased line, but I can well remember the trials and troubles of a greased line which just

Overleaf: **Loch Hope, Sutherland. This loch is one of the best of the sea trout and salmon waters in Scotland, well known for its dapping (Hamish Campbell)**

wouldn't float right, or got sand on it, or wouldn't dry out in time to be re-greased. I carried spare drums for my reels then. Now it is greatly simplified; a No. 10 double-tapered floater (AFTM 10 DT F) fishes perfectly, rolls and spey casts perfectly and covers water well. It is easy to mend, that is, to control by rolling a loop upstream to compensate for the uneven drag of an intervening current. On the open pools of Tay I often use a weight-forward floater on my Webley *Glen*, (AFTM 10 WF F) and it fishes well where long overhead casting is required. You cannot mend this type of line so well, and while you can roll it out, you do not have a spey casting capability because of where the weight is on the line – in the forward 12 to 18yds (11 to 16½m). The new 'long belly' salmon and trout lines offer a compromise between the excellent casting and shooting abilities of a weight-forward line and the rolling, mending and spey casting qualities of the double taper. One of my sinking lines is a long belly like this and is named 'The Speycaster'. It was produced by the Wet Cel people (Scientific Anglers) about fifteen years ago and it is still going strong – a remarkable achievement.

Terminal tackle in floating line fly fishing usually consists of a nylon monofilament leader which, in its simplest form, consists of a 9ft (2.7m) length of nylon monofil of suitable breaking strain, – say 10lb (4½kg) – provided with a reliable loop to attach it to the line. One can, of course, using the blood knot or the grinner or some other reliable knot for joining nylon, make up one's own tapered leaders or casts. I have never found tapered casts necessary for salmon fishing, except in special cases in floating line fishing where you want the cast to roll out very straight – say when you are fishing a short single-handed rod. Tapered casts are clearly more aerodynamically efficient than untapered ones. One feature of leaders which makes a great deal of difference to the aerial efficiency of casts is how the leader attaches to the line. The most efficient join is to use a needle knot or a small whipped end to attach a piece of heavy nylon monofil to the line. This, in turn can be looped to the fly cast or can be tied with a blood knot or similar knot to the nylon of the leader. This certainly saves the fly line from wear at the tip and provides a very sweet casting leader which passes through air and water with the minimum of disturbance.

Flies for floating line conditions are usually either lightly dressed doubles or singles in hair wing patterns – Stoat's Tail, Hairy Mary, Bucktail, etc – and these are likely to be No. 6 and smaller. The smallest fly I have taken salmon on is a No. 12 although, fishing trout tackle, I have lost salmon on No. 14 flies. It is very common today to fish small tube flies with the floating line. One of the series which has had great acclaim, justifiably, in recent years is the Parker Tube range produced by Sharpe (Farlow) of Aberdeen. These wisps of hair and feather, tied on light plastic tubes, are fished with tiny trebles, and overall may only measure ½in (12mm) in length. I have flies which have taken fish and which have only a tiny dressing of hair and no body. If these small tubes have a problem, it is their very lightness. They skate during fishing, showing in a 'vee' on the surface. We want our flies in floating line fishing to fish near the surface but under it. Low water doubles do hold down well into the water in fishing. They also do tend to have more reliable hooks than the smallest trebles. I speak with some trepidation about this subject. It seems to me that the quality of small trebles (indeed, trebles of any size) has fallen badly in the last decade. You find it hard or impossible to get trebles with forged bends, ie flattened or pressed shanks designed to give stronger hooks. Where are the outpoints of yester-year? Standardisation has set in, and many individual designs of treble have gone, and I have no doubt that angling is the poorer.

I tend not to change my rods for summer fishing. My Sharpe's spliced 14 footer (4.27m) is light enough for all sorts of tactics with floating line; my Webley *Glen* 14 footer – a spigot-jointed rod – is very versatile. I have a reserve rod in another ferrule-less glass rod, a Milbro Verre of the same length. This is a gentler, slower rod, and there are times one reaches for that in summer. My next step down in size in summer is a 10ft (3.05m) cane two-piece, a T C Ivens *Lake* which fishes well from boats on summer lochs. My much loved Sawyer *Stillwater* – a Farlow rod designed on the parabolic principle by Ritz and originally produced by Pézon et Michel in France is a tremendous killer of salmon. I have a small extension butt for it, which I slip on when I feel that salmon are likely. This keeps the reel off one's coat and allows free running. Although this is only a 9ft 6in (2.90m) rod, it packs great power. One must call on some 'bone' in a rod to move salmon to the net. I hate rods which bend and bend and move nothing.

Fishing the floating line is an accurate form of fishing. It has to be. You must cover fish, must react to rises and very often must set the hook effectively. In sunk line fishing or in mid-water fly fishing the first indication you get that a salmon has taken you is the strong pull as the fish obligingly pulls the hook home. Floating line fishing is clear water fishing and usually takes place in fine overhead conditions. My May fishing is typical. You can see it all, in and out of the water. Of course that adds responsibility. Excitement rises. You find yourself excitely fumbling casts because fish are showing and perhaps are moving to you. It can, at times, be the most memorable frenzy, which any number of years do not seem to dampen down.

Salmon in Lochs

In lochs, the picture is a very different one. Salmon in some lochs are very difficult to locate, and I have sometimes marvelled that no locals knew where the salmon lay, for example, in a Hebridean loch. They were regarded there as chance fish. In other places, salmon are fished for in precise places and the names on the map confirm that these places have been known as salmon lies for generations. We all know of salmon point, salmon rock, salmon reach, etc on Scottish lochs. Broadly, on a loch not familiar to me, I would start looking for salmon in shallow water, water between 2ft 6in (¾m) and about 6 or 7ft (1.8 or 2.1m). Salmon are definitely shallow water fish and they take up lies in water considerably shallower than sea trout favour. Sea trout seem to like the 10 to 20ft (3 to 6m) marks, although at times they will come into shallower water, notably during the late evenings.

The lies salmon take up in the shallow water are usually very practical; they are closely related to access to spawning streams. One obvious lie on every salmon loch I have fished is off the mouth of a known spawning burn. On Loch Maree at Kinlochewe, spring salmon congregate in mid May off the mouth of the Kinlochewe River. This typical lie is replicated many times in other lochs. The river has, in the course of time, brought down silt, and as the current slackens it drops this silt in the loch, forming underwater spits running out from either bank of the mouth. Salmon lie along these spits and may take up lies along the shore nearby. On Loch Brora in Sutherland there is a wonderful sandy reach where the upper Brora enters and on 1 May when boat fishing begins there I have seen the sandy beaches beside the river alive with salmon. They lie out over the sandy shallows in preference to taking up positions in the main channel of the river, or along the deep right bank where the river and the loch form their deepest reaches. You will see fish splashing in deep water, but these salmon are not in lies; they are moving round, restlessly, and showing here and there as they do so. On the sandy lies on the northern side (the continuation of the left bank of the river, as it were) salmon move in front of the boat like sheep, causing great bow waves if you are unfortunate enough to drift on to the fish, frightening them. People often think of the salmon as a rather foolish fish, not easily scared. This is not so; salmon in lochs are very easily put off and should be treated like feeding trout. You have nothing to lose by regarding them as sensitive, alert creatures. This approach may also bring you rewards in terms of fish raised and hooked where a coarser line of thought would rob you of the chance of rises.

In some lochs, especially the smaller ones on the upper courses of salmon rivers, fish lie all over the water. This is often because the loch is a kind of larder of the river, full of salmon, and it may also be because such lochs are generally shallow and weedy. I am sure we all have our prototype of such a loch. Loch Moidart, at the head of the small river Moidart on the west coast is such a water. On it, you fish the loch as if it were a single very large pool, each yard of which is holding water. A friend of mine who has had some remarkable success there for summer salmon described it to me recently as just fishing trout, steadily all day with a slightly heavier cast on, and smaller flies than you would use for sea trout. He had a marvellous week there just after a small spate. Salmon rushed up the river and lay all round the loch and took the smallest salmon flies readily, scorning the long rod, heavier line and larger flies completely. This syndrome of salmon preferring the smaller flies and the lighter tackle rings absolutely true to my own experience, and it has a bearing on the question of loch lies which I have mentioned above. Trout tackle allows gentler casting, more precise placing of flies, lighter leaders and, generally, a gentler style of approach. I do advocate such an approach – it will double your catches.

Debris in lochs, such as trees washed down by the floods and deposited in the loch, often form attractive, but very hazardous lies for salmon. On Loch Insh, on the upper middle Spey, there is a suicidal lie just like that. I was lucky enough to get into a salmon there on my trout rod late one evening in early summer. As soon as the fish took, my host moved quickly to the oars and we brought the salmon out gently and firmly in a boat version of walking up, that is, applying a steady pressure to the fish and leading it firmly but evenly from one bit of water to another. I do it often in river fishing when salmon are becoming difficult in one area and can be handled more easily on another.

That Loch Insh salmon came out of a veritable jungle of submerged branches and other debris like a docile, well-trained dog. It woke up in the loch itself, and made some spectacular runs, none of which, I am happy to say, took it back to its lie beside that jungle of branches, any one of which would have spelled disaster for my trout tackle, – or for any other tackle for that matter. Lies like that are a challenge, but are possibly not for the lone angler.

Salmon love weed patches. They form natural focal points for lies in shallow water. On the Manse Loch above Lochinver in Sutherland, salmon seem to lie under the fronds of weeds, and there is little doubt that shade does play a part in salmon lies. In many Highland lochs, shallow water, burn mouths and all the features we associate with salmon, co-exist with weeds. This helps us sometimes to pin-point a lie, and to check the drift line but it also adds a hazard to fishing. I have myself, never lost a salmon in weeds, and I believe this is because the salmon, unlike the trout or sea trout, is a leadable fish. Salmon also love those weedy pools which you get immediately below and often immediately above Highland

Left and below:
Taken on a trout fly in a Highland loch. This 7lb (3.2kg) springer is typical of the chance contacts a trout or sea trout fisher may make with salmon

lochans in the headwaters of salmon rivers. At the head of the Torridon river there is a strange little loch called Loch an Tasky – the loch of the fishers – and, although salmon lie in the loch itself and are caught from boat and bank, the main concentration of salmon is in the pool on the river immediately below the loch. One August day I found this out by wandering off from the loch, where sport was slow, and with my trout rod with sea trout flies casually searching the long, weedy pool which carries the waters of the loch down to the river. I raised four fish, one of which took quite well, unlike August fish in stillwater which have a rotten habit of just moving and not taking. It was a red fish I hooked and in the course of the early stages of the fight it shed the hook. I shall never forget that lie and the lesson it taught. Never approach pools like that casually, and never offer salmon what you would choose for sea trout. Change down in fly size; give the salmon mere wisps of flies, say No. 10 doubles light weight irons, dressed with light hair, sparse hackles and attenuated bodies. Or try a tiny Paker tube fly mounted over a No. 14 treble. In summer, think light for salmon, especially in these shallow lies between loch and river. Above all, keep out of sight; crawl and cast long, well-placed lines. These lies are very vulnerable to disturbance, and once moved, salmon might take all day to return to a catchable mood.

The shape and character of the bank play a very important part in helping us to locate loch salmon lies. Promontories often indicate reefs off shore where salmon would find rocks and ledges to lie beside. Tributary streams form silt beds and these may be in the form of 'horns' reaching out from the banks of the stream into the loch as we described earlier. These horns can be weedy or be marked by the odd sunken tree trunk, brought down in some mammoth spate in a past winter. Islands are also important for salmon lies, but one has to beware of assuming that every island is a salmon lie. The larger islands should be treated as if they were extra banks of the loch and the signs we have mentioned above for the main banks should be read for indications of likely lies. I am much more interested in sunken islands – those stony or weedy mounds on the loch bed where the water shallows to nearly catching the keel of the boat as you drift. If you fish the water for trout, you will know these places already as good drifts, and, indeed, if the loch is at all well stocked with salmon, you will have had rises or actual contact with salmon on your trout flies. This is especially true in the Highlands of Scotland in summer. Salmon take the smallest flies and unless treated

with skill at the time of the take, will break everything, generally carrying off the cast from the loop down.

Spinning for Salmon

We use the term 'spinning for salmon' to cover far more than the word spinning originally meant. In the first place, spinning meant presenting the salmon a revolving bait and that bait might be natural or artificial. The first lure which comes to mind when I use the term spinning is the devon – in fact the wooden devon – but a moment's reflection could produce a list of spun artificial baits which would include metal, rubber or plastic devons, wagtails in leather, plastic or rubber, the old-fashioned phantom minnow, various more or less realistic imitations of sprats, loaches, shrimps and prawns, and we would not be hard pressed to add to this so-and-so's favourite special lure – like the mother of pearl flashers I was sent to try out and which eventually proved excellent for mackerel fishing!

These are artificial baits, spun in the true sense. That is, they are made to turn round their traces, or to turn with their traces in the course of fishing out the cast. This is usually achieved by means of fins set like a propeller on the bait around its point of balance. Natural baits which are spun follow the same principle, except that they are usually mounted on a flight or rig which includes fins, or are set up within a scarab which has fins mounted on it and the bait is made to rotate as it is fished. One spins sprats of many colours in spring, and may in fact spin the humble minnow for salmon, either fresh or salted or preserved in formaldehyde, glycerine or some other suitable preservative. We spin fresh shrimps in high summer – a delicate art, which may involve catching your own fresh shrimps, dyeing them and hardening them. We spin prawns, usually preserved ones, but again they are presented to the fish in many colours.

I stopped off at a Stanley hotel after an August day's salmon fishing on the Tay recently and found one well known angler there with a catch of salmon which most of us would be hard pressed to match by any method. He had eight fish and all had taken the purple prawn. Red prawns had not worked, he said, and shrimps had failed. The fly had proved ineffectual, but his grotesque purple prawn had done the trick. It does happen. We might well find one day that someone would mount and spin a spare sausage left over from lunch and would have incredible sport. In salmon fishing there are no impossibilities.

Above: Salmon provide excellent sport in the shallow lochs which occur on water systems in the Hebrides and Western Highlands. Typically, they are to be found in lies between three and five feet in depth and they can be tempted to take a well-fished fly (Michael Shepley)

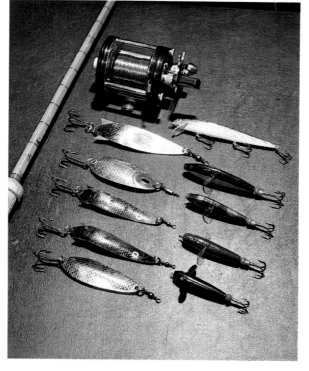

Left: Some typical baits for spinning for salmon. On the left are various designs of salmon spoon and on the left a Finnish Rappala plug and a selection of devon minnows. The reel is a Swedish Abu Ambassadeur 6000 multiplier (Arthur Oglesby)

Right: On the Pavilion water of Tweed, fly fishing for summer salmon (A. L. Hunter)

Above: The multiplying reel, usually just called the multiplier, is very popular for salmon spinning, especially with baits of over 20 gr. The reel in the picture is a Pfleuger Supreme (Michael Shepley)

Below: A 22 pounder taken from the Spey on a wooden devon, a 10ft (3.05m) Milbro Ghillie two-piece rod and a Pfleuger Supreme reel

But spinning refers to all sorts of presentations of lures where the motion of the bait is not rotary. Spoons, do not rotate; they wobble, flutter, wiggle, shimmy and do lots of things in the water, but do not, in any true sense, spin. Plugs dive and wiggle and shake but, again, do not really spin. Some spoons have a foot in both camps; they have a rotating blade which whirls round the body of the lure as it is fished through the water. The best known design of these whirling spoons is the Mepps. Among the best known of the wobbling spoons is the Toby, and on the Tay and Tweed I would not be surprised to find that the ⅝ oz (18g) Toby is the most popular artificial bait cast out.

I can well remember my own bewilderment as a boy on first looking at the range of flies and spinning lures in my local tackle shop in Ayr, and it may well be that every salmon angler at some stage suffers the same trauma. Looking back over years of spinning Tay, Spey and, to a lesser extent, Tweed, the striking thing about the lures I have used and have seen used is that most anglers settle for one or two types of lure and virtually ignore the rest. In my tackle boxes are lures of all shapes and sizes – devons, spoons, wagtails, and plugs – yet in the box I actually take with me to the riverside I have two main lures only, and it has been like that for the past fifteen years – devons and tobies. It is even more specialised than that; I fish wooden devons – Spey devons, and I fish gold or brass or black and gold tobies. Now it is perfectly possible that I have spun my beats unimaginatively over these years, but at the beginning of my salmon fishing career I very soon saw that salmon normally fall into two classes, the temptable and the impossible. The temptable fish are usually fresh, or are fish which have been stirred up in some way, say by a rise in water, and these fish, if they are willing to respond to your offer of a lure, will not make fine distinctions between one devon and another, and, indeed, between a devon and/or a spoon. What really matters is proper presentation of the bait. Devons and spoons have different swimming and fishing characteristics and you can select each bait to give you effective coverage of certain lies. Speaking generally, wooden devons are magnificent for holding and hovering, fluttering bait over lies in rocky water; tobies are tremendous for covering glides, flats, deep pools and similar open water. Of course each type of bait can be fished in different waters, and with skilled presentation can be as effective as the others, but, generally speaking, the type of bait determines the swimming and presentation characteristics of the lure, and it is this factor which is critical in taking salmon.

I am, of course, going to describe all sorts of exceptions to my rule, for instance, fishing from boats with plugs, but it might help if I set about describing the basic tackle and tactics for spinning devons and for fishing spoons.

Let me begin with my favourite spun lure, the wooden devon. The lure itself is simple; it consists of a metal tube with a moulded or shaped wooden or composition body roughly in the shape of a torpedo. Plastic perspex fins are fitted at the head, near the point of balance of the devon. You can get wooden devons in any length from 1in (2.5cm) to about 3in (8cm) but I have found salmon keenest on 2in and 2½in (5 to 6cm) devons. Again, you can paint your devons any colours you choose. The favourites on the Spey and Tay are undoubtedly brown and gold, black and gold and the noted yellow belly which is green on the back and yellow below. All sorts of lore relates to the painting of devons. One gillie on the Tay claimed that he and he alone had the secret mix of the right gold (it was actually a very successful mix); another Spey tackle maker assured me that his brown was red-brown, and without parallel as a tempter of salmon. It is fascinating and all quite amusing. Yet, if I look into my box, I have collected devons of a nice dark reddish-brown and I would reject others as unsuitable. I very much like a darkish gold on the belly, and I would not buy a devon with brassy or silvery gold below. I may think it slightly eccentric that others swear by this or that colour, but in my practice, I am half way to joining them. For instance I never spin a silver and blue devon now, although my first few salmon as a boy in Ayrshire were taken on a plain silver or a silver and blue metal devon. Either I knew no better, or the salmon knew no better. We all settle for the lure we have killed on. I have boxes of devons, all beginning to look the same, and boxes of flies, all looking like kith and kin.

I like the wooden devon for many reasons, partly because it is the spinning lure which can be fished more like a fly than any other lure. It might sound odd that I should want to spin in a manner similar to my fly fishing, but I do. I have a deep-seated aversion to fast spinning or, to use another term, forced spinning. I do not like to cast my bait out and grind it back across the stream, pulling it through the water in a mechanised way. I like, rather, to cast my bait out on a longish rod, let it settle in the stream, and by slow retrieval, or even by just taking up the slack and letting the water fish the lure, bring the devon or spoon round over the lies and under rod control and let the devon or toby move as naturally as possible through the stream, rising on pressure waves to cover under-

Above: Spinning for salmon on the lower Tay at Benchil. The rod is a 10ft (3.05m) two-piece and the reel is a Pfleuger Supreme. Nylon monofilament of 18lb (8.2kg) breaking strain is normally used (Michael Shepley)

Left: On some of the smaller waters of Scotland and Ireland good summer salmon fishing can be had, especially after floods (Michael Shepley)

Right: The rewards of early spring fishing on Tay – an excellent bag of salmon in very wintry conditions (Michael Shepley)

water boulders, hanging in natural pockets of shelter in the river, and hovering where the stream dictates it. My fly fishing is based on leading the fly in a natural way over the fish and my spinning is motivated by exactly the same principles.

This policy reflects in how I use the reel, and, indeed, on what type of reel I choose. I shall discuss the technical details of reels later, but the choice is broadly between fixed spool reels and multipliers. I am a multiplier man, fishing the reel on a 9ft 6in (2.90m) or 10ft (3.05m) rod. I like long casting in both fly fishing and spinning, and in spinning I regret the lack of a line heavy enough to mend during the fishing (ie roll upstream to control the speed at which the lure fishes). What I may be saying, is that I am a fly fisher by inclination, and that I fish fly wherever I can and whenever I can. When I spin, I do so because, for some reason, fly is not likely to be effective – and there are times and places where fly will seldom work – but when I spin, I am still in some way, fishing the lure like a fly.

The basic art of spinning for salmon is simple; you cast your lure out at an angle slightly downstream of right angles, you let the bait find its fishing level usually by pausing for a couple of seconds after the lure has landed and you have engaged the reel for recovery. Then, with a careful, controlled retrieve you bring the bait slowly round

with the current, covering the lies of the river in an arc below you. When the bait has reached a point where you feel that the fishable water has been covered – for example, when the bait has swung into the shallow water downstream of you, near your own bank – you lift the rod top and retrieve the bait quickly, to keep it off the bottom, and set up the rod and reel for the next cast. You might move downstream a yard or so before the next cast, or you might want to try a slightly different length of line over the same water as last cast, without moving your stance. The basic techniques of spinning for salmon are therefore casting the lure out, swimming the lure round with the stream and recovering the lure prior to the next cast. Of course you may hook a fish at any point during the fishing of the lure, or, more pessimistically, you might snag a rock or a sunk log or a similar hazard. Dealing with these eventualities will be discussed below. At this stage, I have outlined the basic art as if it were a fairly mechanical process.

Right: At the end of the cast when the bait has swum round over the lies, the devon is reeled in quickly up the slack water at the pool side

Below: spinning for salmon with a fixed spool reel. The devon is cast almost square across the pool, is allowed to sink a little, then is fished slowly round over the lies

Tackle for Spinning

What rod should one choose for salmon spinning? I have four salmon spinning rods, two of them glass and two of them cane. My old favourites are the following:

A 10ft (3.05m) Milbro Ghillie. This is a two-piece rod in hollow fibreglass, made in two pieces, jointed with a light ferrule. I have fished it for some ten years and, to my mind it performs splendidly. I use it with one of my multipliers, and during fishing I find that it behaves in a way which reminds me of a fly rod. The rod has excellent large rings, a 21in (53cm) cork handle and screw fittings which hold the reel well. I find this rod excellent for holding a bait over lies. The length is a tremendous advantage. I find that I can thrust the rod up and get my devon to hover and flutter over lies in a way which would be somewhat more difficult to achieve with a shorter rod. In fact when I see colleagues fishing with 8ft (2.44m) spinning rods I pity them. The shorter the rod the more the outfit becomes like a mechanised handline. Who wants to hook a salmon on a handline? Worse still, who wants to play a salmon on a short rod? The longer, more pliable rod lends subtlety to the fight, and when the end game comes and the fish is being brought over the net, or beached, or tailed, the longer rod is a magnificent asset. Fish can be steered safely to the net without putting extra strain on the hook hold. In some cases, this can mean the difference between success and failure in getting the fish ashore.

I have a cane rod with many of these characteristics. It is a slightly eccentric choice, since it was designed as a carp rod many years ago by Alcock. This is a 10ft (3.05m) two-piece ferruled rod with a sweet slow action. One might think of spinning rods being short and stiff, but this one is not so; it is gentle, long and quite soft. Indeed, I have once or twice used it as a fly rod and it casts a No. 8 fly line well. It fishes the baits round well, and I have found it to be a good hooker, despite its gentleness. It bends well into fish during the fight and gives one a lovely sense of feeling the pulsing, turning fight of the fish – something which is missing from the fight on short rods.

Top left: **When spinning large waters, such as the Aitkenhead Pool on the Tay at Benchil, long casts must be made, but the bait is allowed to swing round almost like a fly (Michael Shepley)**

Left: **The essence of early spring fishing. Two outfits with multipliers and one with a fixed spool reel. The heavy spoon is typical of January and February fishing (Michael Shepley)**

I have another old friend, with many salmon to its credit, an LRH No. 2 made by Hardy's in the early sixties. This rod is cane, 9ft 6in (2.90m) in length and is superbly ferruled with a patent Hardy ferrule with a spring-loaded pin which ensures locking and holding of the metal joint. The rings are agate and of high quality. The fittings are marvellous too, but the whole rod now strikes me as too stiff, slightly too short and slightly too heavy. It is the kind of rod which I admire as a kind of fishing furniture – prestigious, beautiful design, but now overtaken by glass and carbon fibre for practicality and lightness. Interestingly, I recently found myself at a sporting auction near Perth, and an LRH No. 2 came up. It did not attract excessive enthusiasm, and I debated whether to add it to my own collection, partly because mint items like this are becoming scarcer and scarcer. I did not bid, however, partly because I have a good LRH No. 2 and partly because I now spin very much less than I did. Fly fishing has brought me so much more sport than spinning in recent years and it suits the rivers I now fish up North where spinning is either not allowed or is not necessary. I still spin the Tay, of course, but even there I only do so when I positively cannot cover the fish with fly.

My fourth spinning rod is a 9ft 6in (2.90m) glass two-piece by Shakespeare, a Number 1518. I really bought this rod for one of my sons to begin with. He has started fishing for salmon with a fixed spool reel and he seemed happier with the shorter rod. I use it when something prevents me using a 10 footer (3.05m), or when the river I am fishing is smaller, or when I particularly want to use a fixed spool spinning reel. It is a competent nice rod, well up to knock-about salmon spinning and an excellent standby for pike spinning, or light saltwater spinning which comes my way sometimes on holidays.

To illustrate the art of salmon spinning as I see it, let me describe a remarkable morning on a beat on middle Spey. I was fishing Delagyle in April, with the river fining down after a cold flood. The fly was not doing well and we decided to have a morning's spinning. I was sent downstream to fish the Delagyle Pool which is a long streamy pool with a hard rush at its head. On our right bank there is little or no neck where runners might lie, but on the Wester Elchies side, opposite, there is a fine lie which extends in front of the hut. Using my 10ft (3.05m) Ghillie and a 2¼in (6cm) brown and gold wooden devon, I was able to hold the bait for long enough in that lie on the far side of the fast stream for the salmon to see it and take it. I hooked five and got four of them in a very short

A big day on Delagyle on the River Spey in spring. All the fish took a wooden devon fished slowly through the lies in the sheltered water beside the main streams

that a small line drum can be used. Modern multipliers are sophisticated pieces of engineering. They cast out with a swing of the rod – not quite so easily done as the word suggests – and the bait can be dropped or slowed down by means of the thumb of the right hand applying pressure to the revolving drum. The two reels I describe have governors in them to prevent the drum overrunning – a bugbear of rotating drum casting reels – and if these are kept in good order, and are set correctly, they do prevent overrunning and the awful tangles resulting, to a great degree. One has to practice at first, of course, to get this right, and I can think of some rather nasty overrun tangles which I had in the early stages. I have found, however, that monofilament nylon lines run better than the braided terylene we used to employ, and I have also discovered that if nylon does tangle on the overrun it comes out more easily, or can be cut and knotted for emergency repair much more effectively, than the braided line.

The Ambassadeur 6000 is one of a line of well-bred Swedish casting reels, and I would say it is the most common of the multipliers found in salmon fishing today, and it has bred into it the characteristics required for this fishing. It works on the free-spool principle. A small button on the reel releases the spool before the cast and a numbered dial on the governor knob means that you can adjust the anti-overrun governor accurately. When the bait enters the water at the end of the cast, you turn the handles and the free-spool release mechanism clicks out giving you geared drive between the handles and the spool. You can thus fish the bait in by a combination of rod movement and handle turning, giving the required bait speed and fishing level to suit the water you are covering. You turn the handles of a multiplier with the right hand since the reel is mounted above the rod butt, with the line running out, on top of the rod through the rod rings. The fixed spool reel handle is turned by the left hand, although right-hand handles are occasionally used and some reels provide for a right or left position of the handle to suit the user. In multiplier fishing, the left thumb is kept handy to control the reel drum and when you hook a fish the thumb can be brought down on to the drum to allow a direct pull to be given to the line through the rod, to hook the fish securely. When the fish is hooked (actually, most salmon hook themselves) the Ambassadeur drag system

space of time, and they were all fresh. Interestingly, after each fish, the 'opposition' followed me through the pool, but because of the nearness of the lie to their bank, they could not on this occasion fish it well. It wanted a long line and a hovering bait. On other occasions, especially with fly, the Wester Elchies rods absolutely wipe our eyes on the Delagyle side, but on this memorable day the 10ft (3.05m) rod and the hung devon did it. In this fishing, the line was hardly retrieved at all, except at the end of the natural travel of the bait, to retrieve it quickly and cast again. The rod was used like a fly rod throughout and the multiplier was used very much as a fly reel might have been used, more or less to store line on, during the fishing of the bait.

Multipliers

I have mentioned my passion for the multiplier. I regard it as the ideal reel for the rods I have described and for the kind of fishing I am most familiar with. I have two multipliers which I am very happy with, an ABU Ambassadeur 6000 and a Pfleuger Supreme. Broadly, multiplying reels are so named because they are geared up to give you a fast drum rotation relative to the rotation of the handle. This is excellent for quick retrieval after the bait has finished fishing. It also means

Right: A very popular multiplier in use on Tay. The Abu Ambassadeur 6000 has a free spool for casting, a star drag and variable casting governor. The rod is a Hardy built cane L.R.H. No. 2, 9ft 6in (2.90m) two-piece

comes into operation. A star drag set behind the reel handles allows the angler to adjust the tension on the drum to whatever pressure he requires. Thus, during fishing most anglers would have the drag set firmly to give a solid hooking resistance. During the fight, the pressure is released and the salmon can take line as freely as required. The star drag system operates through a slipping clutch. That is, the clutch will allow the handles to turn the spool up to a certain pressure, and above that pressure the fish may take line. This is a safeguard against sudden hard runs by the fish.

I once had a 16½lb (7½kg) fish on the Tay seize the bait with uncharacteristic force and tear off without allowing me time to release the star drag. It ripped line off the reel and made the ratchet produce a fantastic buzz. Had I not had a slipping clutch that salmon would certainly have smashed me. I have never had such a fierce take from a fish before or since.

The Ambassadeur reel works on an anti-reverse principle. That is, the handles of the reel can only turn forwards. Thus, if a fish needs to take line, it does so by making the spool turn against whatever drag there is on it. The Pfleuger differs from the Ambassadeur significantly by allowing the angler to select whether he wants his handles to turn forwards or backwards with the reel spool or whether he wants the anti-reverse switch on which gives the reel the mechanical characteristics of the Ambassadeur. The ability of the Pfleuger to run more or less like a direct drive reel, say a fly reel, endears it to me. It gives me the feelings of playing the fish as if on a fly rod – or at least it goes some way towards my own eccentric principle which affects my choice of bait, my method of casting. It guides my tactics in swimming the bait round and it certainly colours the way I fight the hooked fish. I suppose you could identify the same principle in my fly fishing, but viewed the other way round. In deep line fly fishing in the cold waters of spring and autumn, when I use my 14ft (4.27m) rod, a No. 10 sinking line, a heavy leader and a 2in (5cm) heavy tube fly or Waddington, you could say that I was spinning with a fly rod. There is obviously a difficult line to be drawn between heavy fly fishing and spinning. That is, we know which is which, but their fishing characteristics are strikingly similar. Of course the fly is cast by the fly line, whereas the spun bait is cast out by the weight of the lure and its leads, and it is retrieved and re-cast from the reel on each occasion. But having said that, I am still very conscious of fly tactics when I spin, and my selection of tackle reflects this.

Fixed Spool Reels

The fixed spool reel is far and away the most popular spinning reel in salmon fishing. Its principles are well known. The spool of the reel is mounted at right angles to the axis of the rod and casting involves line running off the side of the fixed spool in coils. The line is picked up for retrieval by a spring-loaded bail arm which clicks over the spool to gather the line and coil in on to the spool by rotating round the line spool, which remains fixed – hence the name. A refinement which modern fixed spool reels all have is that the spool is made to reciprocate, that is, move in and out during the retrieve, thus allowing even laying on of the line during the retrieve. Multipliers of the Ambassadeur and Pfleuger type also have a level wind mechanism to lay the line on evenly. Even winding of the line is vital to good casting.

Fixed spool reels are fitted with slipping clutches, which allow the fish being played to take line by overcoming the resistance of the setting of the clutch. Thus line can be given to fish without the handle of the reel turning backwards. Some fixed spool reels have handles which can turn backwards, allowing the reel to give line by means of the bail arm turning backwards under the pressure of demand from the fish as it pulls, and the handles of the reel can be allowed to turn backwards, appropriately. An anti-reverse switch is provided on these models and most anglers, I think, would use it for much of the fight. I have a Mitchell with reversing handles, a ABU Cardinal and a Daiwa. I think the first reel I ever saw with this two-way action of the handles was an Intrepid produced in the early sixties and, for me, it produced a reel with a far nicer feel than the older type with one-way turning only.

Both multipliers and fixed spool reels, with their slipping clutches, require special 'pumping' action to bring in the fish at certain stages of the fight. If your clutch is set very firmly, so that the action of the handles can draw line in and move the fish (a horrifying way to do it) the clutch would have to be set far too firmly to allow the fish to take line should it suddenly pull out, or plunge – as salmon often do. A smash could result. The way the fish is brought in, with the 'pumping' technique, is that the angler begins with his rod fairly low, pointing with a low bend towards the fish. The line is clamped to the rod, or to the reel by the finger and a firm gentle pressure is applied to the

Right: A reconstruction of tailing a fish out. The fish is played to a standstill and is led into shallow water with its nose towards the bank. Then the fish may be lifted out in one clean strong motion by gripping it by the 'handle' above the tail (Michael Shepley)

Into a fish with a fixed spool outfit. The angler is adjusting his clutch on the fixed spool, so that there is sufficient pressure on it to retrieve line

rod by lifting it, drawing the fish in towards you. When the rod is as high as it is safe to take it (say approaching 90°) the finger pressure on the line is released and the reel handles are rapidly turned, and the rod lowered as the reel is operated. Thus, line is recovered as the rod lowers and some yards are 'won' during the pumping.

In playing a fish on a fixed spool reel, there are several hazards which do not exist for multipliers and these include what I call the organ grinder's syndrome. Since the reel has a slipping clutch which will give line out to the salmon when it applies more force to the reel drum than the clutch will hold, it is perfectly possible for the angler to go on turning the handle as he plays the fish and if the fish runs during the fight the turning of the handle does not retrieve line, but merely causes the slipping clutch to slip. This is a dreadful technique, and should be avoided at all costs. Firstly, it wears out the clutch, but that is not so immediate a problem as the kinks that the perpetual turning of the bail, backed by a slipping clutch, produces during the fight. If you want to produce a real ball of kinks, which will ruin your line, just

grind away against the pressure of a salmon. Swivels, which are designed to keep kink to a minimum, will not work because you are adding the kink above the swivel. 'Organ grinding' is a sign of rotten tackle handling, lack of experience and sheer lack of mechanical aptitude in using fishing tackle.

Spinning Rigs

The rigs I like for fishing tackle are the simple ones. To begin with I make a trace on the nylon monofilament itself by tying in a swivel, usually a high-quality, ball-bearing swivel, about 1ft 6in or 2ft (0.5 to 0.6m) up from the end of the line. If I am fishing a wooden devon, I merely attach the end of the spinning line to the eye of the devon mount and, provided one can cast the light devon out, one can spin quite acceptably with the rig. Wooden devons, however, are light, and I find an unweighted devon very difficult to cast with a multiplier. One could make a shape at casting one with lightweight nylon line on a fixed spool reel, but even then, the longer distances required for salmon fishing would demand some weight up the

Playing a fish on Tay in January. The angler is in the process of 'pumping' the fish in. The reel is stopped and the fish is pulled in by a gentle, steady pressure as the rod is raised. The rod can then be lowered while line is reeled in, and the process repeated (Michael Shepley)

trace. Metal devons are heavy enough to cast on their own, and many of the spoons I use, including the ⅝oz (18g) Toby and similar spoons are eminently castable without extra lead, but wooden devons require it. I like spiral leads, the old Jardine spiral with its helical groove on the sides of the lead 'torpedo' and the soft brass wire twist at each end. This type of lead is easy to wind on and is a secure lead. It does not foul snags readily and it is highly effective in casting, having a good profile, and little air resistance. It does not affect the fishing action of the bait adversely – very important for wooden devons – and finally, it is available in a whole range of sizes and can be changed at a moment's notice, either to match lighter currents encountered as you fish down a pool, or to adjust depth of fishing.

Probably the most important function of the spiral lead, however, after its sheer weight for casting, is its anti-kink potential. If you take a spiral lead after running it on to the line just above the trace swivel (the ball bearing swivel I mentioned using), you can anchor one end of the lead to the eye of the swivel. Then, taking the lead in

both fingers, bend it into a shallow banana shape. This will keep the lead down in the water and make it very difficult for kink to pass it into the line above. It will, in effect, make the swivel work. There are lots of anti-kink leads on the market, and most of them use this principle of producing a lead which is difficult to turn in the water, because it offers more resistance than the kinking effect of the devon could turn. Of all the anti-kink leads I have used, however, the bent spiral is the simplest and most effective.

Spoons are not usually leaded. They carry their own weight in their materials, and in the case of spoons like the Toby, they can be bought in appropriate lengths and weights. For salmon fishing, I would regard the ⅝oz (18g) Toby as the standard size. The same size of Toby can be bought in 1oz (28g) weight, and a slightly smaller 'heavy' design of Toby comes in ¾oz (21g) weight. The ⅝oz (18g) Toby is a marvellous swimmer and has a remarkable property of fishing across streams where a devon would have to turn its head upstream and sidle across the same water to fish effectively. I have repeatedly hooked salmon across

185

the mouth with Tobies, and on some occasions have hooked salmon on the outside of the jaw, near the angle, proving this. I used to wonder why salmon could take the Toby and be hooked outside the mouth, until it occurred to me that the fish were taking the large spoon across its length, and were being hooked with the treble still outside the salmon's mouth. Certain baits have this strange effect; the salmon take them in a special way. For example, the Kynoch Killer, a plastic diving plug, carries its single treble just under its head. Fish are often hooked around the nose as they take, and I have even had a salmon hooked in the eye socket as it took the wobbling, plunging Kynoch. Actually, I am no lover of the Kynoch, although I recognise that on the Tay it is a remarkable boat bait for harling, that is, fishing from a rowed or gently motored boat, swinging the plug round behind the boat as it crosses and re-crosses the pool.

Whirling spoons, like the Mepps, hook just like devons. They carry their weight in their body, either in bead form, or in some kind of weighted metal shank on the wire spine of the Mepps. I have not fished a Mepps for salmon for many years. It is a tremendous killer of all sorts of fish, but I am not desperately keen on it for salmon. It sets up a large profile in the water as it whirls and I incline to baits and flies which form slim, tapered profiles in the water.

In a guide to fishing, it is impossible to cover all matters relating to spun baits. What is probably more valuable is to set out the principles of salmon spinning and to invite the reader to try his own variations on baits and presentation. My own experience is so firmly linked with wooden Spey devons, fished with a spiral lead, and to Toby spoons, with small ventures into Koster spoons, and into plugs like Kynochs or that remarkable fishy diving plug from Finland called the Rapalla, that it would be misleading to discuss other lures in detail. The angler should fish the baits which suit his water, and should suit his tackle to the length of casting and the baits selected. But I do feel that the principles I have outlined, of spinning slowly, or letting baits settle to their best fishing depth, and of holding them to allow the stream to wash them and fish them over boulders to let them hover and flutter over lies, is the right approach.

Spinning from Boats

Spinning from boats is quite a different business. Spun baits or spoons are trolled behind boats in early spring in some of our salmon lochs. This used to be done behind a rowed boat, but in these days of smooth, slow revving outboards, trolling is now usually done under minimal power. The natural sprat is often used for January fishing on Loch Tay, for instance, and I have rowed and trolled these baits on Loch Naver and elsewhere. Tobies fish well in this way, but are rather heavy for the shallower reaches. Salmon are shallow water fish, as we discussed in the part of this section dealing with lies, and effective trolling for salmon depends on being able to follow the right contours of the bottom, fanning your large baits, preferably light ones, over banks 2 to 6ft (0.6 to 1.8m) under water. Salmon love the bait which is swung, that is which turns and changes direction as it fishes. I row in a zig-zag when I troll, coming in on salmon holding banks and turning out so that the bait reaches the lie, hovers for a second or so, and then turns out again as if leaving the bank for safer water. But I have to say that I do not really like trolling. It is boatsmanship rather than angling. A spring day trolling may be a long slow sail, punctuated by the odd moment of excitement as the rod suddenly dips and the stone or other weight on the line bounces off, hooking the take. You grab the rod, get into contact with the fish, and play it, in much the same manner as you would hook and play a pollack on sand eel.

I have the same objection to harling, which you will find used most extensively on the lower Tay. The two anglers sit in their boat with their spinning rods out over the back of the boat, trailing lures which might include a Toby, a devon or a Kynoch Killer. The boatman does most of the fishing, and, indeed, in some of the worst cases, the boatman uses his rod, his lure and the angler merely plays the fish. Some of the tackle used in harling appals me. It is heavy, horrible and coarse. The whole thing smacks of commercial line fishing, not unlike that employed in the Pacific, off British Columbia, where trolled baits are attached to lines on winches. Bells ring and buzzers sound when the fish takes and it would not surprise me if they winch the fish in under power.

Boat fishing Tweed is much more sporting. You are held in position, either by a roped boat under the control of your gillie or in a rowed boat. You cast to the lies and you have to work your fly round by a combination of your own tackle handling and adjustment for the movement of the boat. I find this combination of angler and gillie a close and interesting one. A good gillie knows how to hold the boat well over lies, allowing the angler

Right: A good Spey fish of 15lb (6.8kg) taken on the Finnish Rappala plug. This plug is of floating plastic shaped like a fish, but it has a diving vane under its chin which allows the current to take the bait down

the maximum chance to cover fish. When the fish is hooked, the boat is carefully handled and is set ashore and the angler plays the fish from the bank. I have done this on Tay also, on beats where the gillies appreciate the subtleties of fly presentation and coverage. On waters where the boat merely harls baits or flies over the lies, I would far rather be left on the bank, picking my way by wading to points where I can cover lies myself.

Shrimps, Prawns and Worms

There is one branch of salmon fishing which I have said little about – shrimp and prawn fishing. Shrimps can actually be fished on a floating line cast by a normal fly rod. The salmon will come to the shrimp fished in this way in much the same way as it would come to a fly. In fact, I ask the question, 'Why fish fresh shrimps with all their difficulties for mounting and casting, when a good shrimp fly imitation would probably do as well?' There are theories that the scent of the fresh shrimp is vital. But is it? The restrictions on coverage of the lies probably reduces your chances

Left: **Harvest time on Almondmouth, River Tay. These two excellent fresh fish were taken on spun bait from the boat**

a great deal and any advantage stemming from the scent of the bait is cancelled out. At least, that is how I see it. Shrimps can be very effective fished in a trotted style, that is, cast into a stream and allowed to bump and trundle down over the bottom. I have seen fish after fish come from a low summer pool of the Tay in that way when fly was only able to take a couple during a day's hard searching. Shrimp fished in that fashion is rather like worm fishing for salmon, where the single large lug worm or the bunch of worms is bumped down with the current right on to the noses of the fish. This too can be a particularly effective way to take summer fish which are not keen to take either spun lures or fly.

Again, shrimps can be spun, mounted on their own trace with fins, or mounted in a shallow hoop on a trace, with a single treble hook at the tail. Shrimps and prawns are mounted with their whiskers pointing to the rear, and indeed, shrimp flies are dressed with pheasant feathers tied to simulate this. This long-standing method of presenting shrimps and prawns has always fascinated me. Does the salmon expect to meet shrimps in the sea with their whiskers facing him? Shrimps do propel themselves backwards. I have waded the

Below: **Shrimping for salmon in low summer conditions (Michael Shepley)**

pools of Scottish beaches and have often seen the fish shoot off backwards in this way. We know of the method of shrimping with a net where the fish are encouraged to jump back into the net, but how does this affect the way a salmon would take the shrimp? It is presented to him in an uncharacteristic manner, anyway, being trotted down stream. I suspect the salmon takes it for much the same reason as it takes a worm – for interest, stimulated by some remote feeding mechanism, and not because the lure perfectly simulates the shrimp in its natural environment. Maybe the shrimp is taken for the Arctic Krill, or another crustacean met in the sea, whiskers first? The fish, remember, takes worms which it has not seen before, except possibly as a parr in the river. Nevertheless, spinning fresh shrimps is a delicate art because the fresh shrimp is a delicate creature.

Shrimps and prawns can be spun, but they can also be fished sink and draw. This is best done on a spinning rod. The prawn, say, is mounted on its flight with a needle (or the flight may include a metal pin to form a spine). It is then bound with red thread to the mount, whiskers to the rear, and is fished, usually weightless by casting it out over the stream and allowing it to sink and fish round very slowly. I have seen prawns virtually legered in this way, ie left lying on the bottom, and taking salmon regardless. Salmon go quickly for prawns in the summer months, or become disturbed by the prawn being fished over them. It is fascinating, but I recognise that it is a rather unpopular method of fishing because it does disturb fish. Salmon often take prawn suddenly and unstoppably, fish after fish. I have heard of double figures being taken by one rod on Tay in a great bout of hooking, playing and landing. Sometimes the prawn must be a certain colour; for instance, I have come across the purple prawn being enormously successful when the undyed prawn or the red one was no use at all.

You will gather that I am not too keen on 'old whiskers' the prawn. I share Tay beats with anglers who swear by it and if I can match their catch on fly, or better still, can take a fish where they do not, I am cock-a-hoop. Happily, the areas likely to produce salmon in summer to the prawn are not the areas I would choose for fly fishing. I prefer the streams and the glides; the prawn and shrimp people like deep, quiet lies. It is usually a Jack Spratt situation, and this makes it tolerable. I can sympathise, however, with those beats which ban shrimp and prawn fishing entirely, and I am sure that it is only where catches are vital to estates and tenants, that prawn fishing is allowed indiscriminately.

Playing Salmon

Much of this book has been concerned with tempting the salmon, and getting the hooks home. But when that has happened, usually in a moment of great excitement for the angler, what remains to be done is the important business of fighting the salmon into submission and grassing him. It is often a fight in the sense that the fish is strong, and puts one to the test physically – making the angler run down the bank, negotiate bankside trees, wade streams and generally move about on the bank in at least as active a way as the fish does in water. These cases are the exception, however. Playing a salmon is much more often a case of controlling one or two runs, mastering the fish as it lunges, twists or turns during the fight, and more or less waiting until the pressure of the rod tells and the fish weakens.

The first thing a salmon does after pulling the fly or bait and hooking itself (they usually do) is to pause. Some anglers say the fish takes, turns, hooks itself and returns to its lie. I suspect the fish does not always return to the lie. I have seen fish taking the fly and moving off with it to deeper water. Whatever actually happens at this moment of truth, is that most salmon stop for a couple of seconds. You raise the rod and bend into the fish, and during those seconds of grace, if you have any presence of mind at all, you make sure that the reel is clear and that you are ready to give line to the fish. If I have time early in the fight after hooking, I get the slack line off the water and wait for the first run.

I would like to discuss further this slack line between hand and reel. I fish with the line going out over the index finger of my right hand (the rod hand). As I fish the fly round, I may wish to alter the speed of the fly by handlining a little, or I may wish to give myself more loop forward of the rod tip for mending, or to allow the fly to sink further. Or I may wish to shorten line. Handline control is vital in fishing, and this means that you are likely to have anything from a yard of slack in a loop at your hand to five or more yards of line lying at your feet on the water or in the bottom boards of the boat, or on the bank. One must be constantly on guard against this slack fouling feet, twigs or boat boards. I check after every cast to see that all is well, usually by running my left hand down the line from my rod hand to see that there are no tangles, and by giving the reel a little half turn just to ensure that the drum is free and no loops have fouled the handle.

When the fish takes, I feel the fly stopping, or I may feel something like the rod altering in

Bringing a good fish to the net on fly in Norway. The fish is tired out by the fight in the heavy stream and the gillie submerges the net. The angler draws the fish over the net and the fish is bagged. The angler is over-bending his rod as he draws his fish in. A rod at this angle actually exerts a very low pressure on a fish. A lower rod is both safe and firm (Jens Ploug Hansen)

Tweed sequence

Above: A good fish is hooked during autumn fishing in the pot under Kelso Bridge. It runs downstream and fights in the fast water below

Left: The fish is brought out of the heavy stream as soon as it will come and the net is made ready

Left: The experienced gilli
puts the net into the water
and waits while the angler
brings the tired fish over it

Below: The net is lifted in
one steady sweep and a fine
fresh autumn fish comes
ashore, taken on fly

weight in my hand. It is usually subtle in that split second of the take. Then the slack line on the water outside of the rod tip, the fishing loop, straightens and one gets the pull. Usually this slack is enough to give the fish line enough to hook it well. Lots of Tweed fishers then give the fish a couple of yards of line from their hand to hook the fish well, probably by forming a belly below the fish in streamy water. I don't often do that, unless the line is very short at the time of the take. I usually bend into the fish, transfer the rod to the left hand during the pause after the take, reel in the slack like fury and with my left hand up the butt, with the rod well bent into the salmon and with my right hand ready to work the reel, I wait for the fish to run.

A cardinal principle in playing salmon is to let them run. Salmon may run two yards or twenty yards in their first burst. Twenty yards will seem to you to be very much longer. In fact I kill most of my fish without any more than the fly line being out, that is, no more than thirty yards out at any time during the fight. There are many exceptions, however, and these are the ones you remember. I have braided terylene backing on my floating line, and this consists of new green backing, bought with the line and older white backing some forty yards further in. Thus a fish takes green backing plus the fly line and has some seventy yards of line in all, but several fish go much further than that and get on to my white backing of which I think there is some sixty yards. I have seldom seen the white go out, but twice or three times this year I have had well over seventy yards out. I do not think this is always with large fish. My 5½lb (2½kg) grilse from the heavy stream at Stenton on Tay took at least ninety yards out. It used the stream and I could not follow at the time. I know of an estimated forty pounder on Tay which fought conventionally for ten minutes, then ran down a long stream into Brunbane Pool and took fully two hundred yards off the fixed spool reel. The angler was run to a standstill and he decided to hang on. All the line went out and then the

What a 20 pounder can do to a fly. This fly with its treble heavily distorted came out of the mouth of a good fish taken in fast water on Tweed. The fly had hooked into both jaws and the fish exerted very heavy leverage on the treble as a result (Michael Shepley)

great stretch began as his sixteen pound stuff gave and gave. It broke at the drum, despite the frantic efforts of the angler to hold the nylon and keep the pressure on the knot down. It broke with a great crack, and off went the largest salmon that angler had ever hooked.

Let me describe a typical fight with a good fish, where some trouble had to be overcome. I was fishing Tweed in early October in 1978 on the Junction beat at Kelso. Fish were running, and I had managed to take one by wading the stream above the Junction itself, and two others from the boat on the Kelso Bridge Pool below. A superb day already. My turn then came to wade the Bridge stream. At the height of water then prevailing, this was difficult, but there is a little pot under the main arch of the bridge, which one can fish with a long line from well above the bridge, where there is shallowish, even water over shingle. I went well upstream and sidled out towards the main arch and, using a twenty yard length of line, which helped the fly to get down in the fast water, I rolled the big waddington Black and Yellow out to search the lie.

I had a soft, but definite pull on my second cast under the bridge and I was into a salmon. The fish cruised round the pot allowing me to shorten line and wade down over the craggy boulders piled round the stanchion to protect it from floods. All was nice and simple to that point, then the salmon, having toured the little pot pool several times, turned and ran down the fast water below. Line went out and backing followed and I worked my way to the downstream side of the bridge stanchion, where there is a small grassy landing with a deep pot of slack water between the streams.

I had to walk the fish back up. That is, I clamped the line to the rod, lowered the angle and walked back up through the arch. Then, reeling in as I walked forward I recovered line and fought the fish in the pot again. The salmon toured the pot again, then ran out, repeating the performance. I walked the fish back four times, and it was hard work. By this time I realised that the fish was large and fresh and it was not giving up easily. It refused to come out of the stream into the slack water below the bridge stanchion, yet that was the only place I could use my net. The boat below on the pool saw my predicament, and tried to come up to help, but could not. It was myself and the salmon, and that was that.

I held on and the fish tired. Twice I eased it into the slack and twice the fish summoned up the energy to get back into the stream. I was now worried about my hook hold. There had been some heavy pressure on it and it must have been chewed

somewhat by such a strong fish. At last the fish came in, and I got down into the water with my net off, came in behind the fish as it wallowed between me and the bridge and slid the net under. The fish was so short and thick that it would not bend, and I was greatly perplexed by this, then, as I waited with this great solid silver fish lying still over the net, the fish moved slowly and tried to turn, and in so doing it collapsed into the big Gye net and was bagged. It was difficult to get up out of the water with the load there, but it was achieved. The fish was killed, and admired. What a splendid short salmon! It weighed 21lb (9½kg). The nicest salmon for shape and size I have had for several seasons. I have never seen a fish with a higher back, nor a thicker breadth between its flanks. Later, when it was smoked, we all marvelled at the depth of flesh to cut.

The principle to keep in mind in fighting salmon is Shakespeare's 'give him line and scope'. But there are limits. I do not like to see a fish playing the angler. Some tackle is to blame for this. Some of the weaker glass used in salmon fly rods is soft and much too flexible and does not provide enough bone to move the fish at the end of the fight over the net, or into beachable water. One must be able to move fish safely and effectively, and cane is a marvellous material for doing just this. Glass, unless it is well graded, just bends, and to get pressure on the fish you have to lower the rod top and imperil the hook hold. I believe that some early carbon fibre had the same problem. It was sweet to fish, but hopeless in moving fish about.

Do not try to be too masterful in the fight, especially at the early stages. Salmon are enormously powerful fish and if you haul them about while they still have strength, you will have some nasty surprises. Let fish hold in a stream, pulsing and pulling. The water will help to kill them. Let fish move about in the stream; let them run up – the best way – and let them run down, but follow them quickly. Watch for fish which edge down and down and make you follow without your eventually getting opposite them. These are often good fish, but don't be scared of them. Try stopping them firmly and walking them back up to better water. It is a time-honoured method of bringing even large fish back up to manageable water.

When the fish begins to tire, it will signal this by showing at the surface. These shows might be boils at first, then a kind of head and tail show in streams. That fish is tiring. At a later stage, the tail will come up and may abortively flap at the cast. That fish is within a minute of netting. A beaten fish lies inert on the surface of the water,

Left: Using the Gye salmon net. The net is on a strong metal ring mounted on a sliding, squared fitting on a duralumin shaft. The net slings neatly on the angler's back and is easily released from its harness when required. Note the way the angler supports the shaft of the net when he lifts the fish out of the river. This is a safety feature of netting

Above: A fine 15 pounder from the Tay comes ashore after taking a small tube fly in May. Again, note how the experienced angler is handling the net. The weight is supported by putting the hand up to the net – with a fish of this weight the strain on the net can be seen (Michael Shepley)

A Norwegian netting sequence. *Above:* The fish has been brought in, but it finds a new lease of life and struggles out again. *Right:* No doubt about it this time, the fish is on its back, and can be drawn over the submerged net. *Far right:* The net is raised partly out of the water to 'bag' the fish. Note how the hand is slid down the shaft to support it, even with a very robust net (Jens Ploug Hansen)

or wallows weakly upright or turning over on to its flank. A fish which has been allowed to wallow too long may turn over and lie apparently dead upside down, with its white belly upwards. It may even sink. This is to be avoided. A weak but mobile fish can be made to swim into your net, or can be allowed to beach itself.

In netting, I use a Gye net which is slung on my back in a leather harness. When I want the net off, I tug the lug of the harness and the net swings away from my back and the handle can be slid out of the harness ring. The net head can then be moved down the squared aluminium shaft and it locks firmly at the head. I pay great attention to bagging the net out right. There is no point in trying to net a salmon with the net stretched over the frame like a tennis racquet. Get the bag free and get it wet and sunk. Then, with the rod in the left hand, where it usually is during the fight,

Above: The author discusses the successful fly during an autumn session on the famous Junction Pool at Kelso on the River Tweed (Michael Shepley)

Right: Three double-figure salmon from the Tweed in November (Michael Shepley)

move the fish to the sunk net. Try not to move the net at all. Submerge it and bring the fish to the net. Then, when the fish is properly over the net, raise the net and fold the fish into it. You do not need to lift the net high out of the water at that moment; indeed, you might break the net. I usually move my hand down the shaft and grasp the ring of the net, turning it so that the fish is bagged and the entrance to the bag closed. I then walk ashore, getting as far from the water as I can, and finding a flat, manageable place to handle the fish. I kill it, usually with a stone or stick, but in the absence of either, I often use my fist to quieten the salmon before walking further, still holding the net, looking for a suitable priest. Of course it is best to always carry your own priest – I have had several, and have unfortunately lost them all!

Beaching a fish merely means leading the fish to a gently shelving shingle or sandy margin, and there, with the rod held high, maintaining gentle fighting pressure on the tired fish, allow the fish to 'swim' up out of the water. Each turn and slow

twist of the salmon can, with your help on the rod, move it up out of the water. This is a safe and sure way of landing fish and if the hook is seen to be weak and to fall out you might have enough time to reach forward and hand tail the fish, before disaster sets in. Hand tailing a salmon consists of grasping the fish firmly by the 'wrist' above the tail and lifting the fish out. This takes a good grip and I have seen some horrific mistakes made by people who thought they could tail fish out but have failed. Such 'helpers' drop fish back into the river.

I have sometimes got behind my fish off the beach and have used the arch of the long rod to help the fish to beach itself. Then, when the fish is well up out of the water, I merely reach down and push the fish up the shingle and tail it out by hand. It is a gentle process, and is leisurely. It takes coolness and deliberation. Those who panic help the fish to escape.

Right: **Hand tailing a large Tay fish in spring. The fish is played out and drawn with its nose towards the shore. Then, without losing rod bend and steady tension on the fish, the angler picks up the fish and walks ashore. This fish was hand tailed in preference to using a mechanical tailer (Michael Shepley)**

Below: **Casting a heavy spoon into an early February water running cold with snow 'bree' on the Tay (Michael Shepley)**

The angler puts pressure on the salmon, thumbing the multiplier in case of a sudden run; the net is released and tucked under the right arm ready for use (Michael Shepley)

The net is ready now, with the rim held below the water line; the salmon makes a desperate cartwheel in an attempt to break free (Michael Shepley)

The fish is drawn over the waiting net NOT the other way round, but still manages a rush for freedom (Michael Shepley)

Over and into the net as the angler turns, keeping the rod high and holding the fish in place until it slips deeper into the net (Michael Shepley)

The net rim is turned and the fish safely bagged ... note though the spoon caught in the left-hand corner of the net, which could pull the bait out the fish's mouth (Michael Shepley)

On the way to the bank with the net supported under the arm and held close to the net rim (Michael Shepley)

The sense of achievement ... *note the spoon again* still in the net, and the salmon has unhooked itself. The greatest care should be taken in netting lest the hooks snag the net before the fish is safely in (Michael Shepley)

205

Left: The Sharpe's telescopic tailer in action on the Dee. The noose has been put round the tail of the beaten fish and it is then pulled tight (Barry Welham)

Above: A magnificent Spey fish of 26lb (11.8kg) beside a Sharpe's telescopic tailer

My advice is never to allow a stranger to net or tail a fish for you. I sometimes do not allow a gillie to land a fish for me, if I suspect him of being inexperienced, or clumsy. Never let a helper scoop out a salmon. As soon as you see any assistant waiting for the salmon with the net held down into the water like a shovel, give him his instructions to get the net out and level. A net may be allowed to bag out in the stream, but may not be used to follow a fish round in the water to try to engulf it.

I used to use a mechanical tailer a lot, but I now much prefer the big Gye net. The wire tailer consists of a kind of snare of steel wire which is slipped over the tail of an inert, beaten salmon and is pulled tight. This is a safe and effective method of getting fish out, but there is a possibility that if the loop is not properly set, or if it fails to grip the tail 'wrist', it has to be re-cocked. I once re-cocked my loop three times before the obliging salmon was tailed out. That can be heart-stopping stuff. Tailers may break – rarely – but when it

happens, it is ghastly. I know one chap who eventually played and landed his fish, an eighteen pounder, after his tailer had parted and left the handle and the loop on the salmon's tail. It was a bewildered and panic-stricken salmon which he had to deal with, and it could so easily have broken loose in all the activity.

Playing fish is, of course, marvellous. I love the feel of the rod bending and I lie awake at night imagining the pulse of a hooked fish. Of course the strike is superb, but the handling of the fish in the fight gives me marvellous satisfaction. It takes skill to play a big fresh fish well. The fish may leap, or lunge, may roar off in a long fast run, may porpoise and slash its tail, but, with skill and not a little luck, even the largest and liveliest salmon can be subdued. And when it is and the net slides under the fish, the cycle is completed. We have tempted the fish, hooked it, fought it and grassed it – an inexplicably satisfying set of operations in which hope and skill, anxiety and deep satisfaction all mingle.

Loch Assynt, with Quinag behind – home of excellent salmon, trout and char (Michael Shepley)

Section Five
Other Game Fish

A Note on **Fontinalis** (Chàr)

Salmo salvelinus fontinalis has many names beside its Latin classification. In the United States it is usually called brook trout and sometimes the fuller name of eastern brook trout. Lots of American and Canadian anglers just call it trout. Canadians like to refer to the fish as the speckled trout or *Truite mouchetê,* and in Maine and other northern states of America I have often heard the nickname 'squaretail' used but I think this term is specifically applied to the larger (often male) *fontinalis* in and around lakes. There is a sea-going variety of *fontinalis* in New Brunswick and the maritime provinces of Canada and in Maine and when I fished for them in brackish reaches of rivers such as the Miramichi (New Brunswick), the local anglers referred to them as 'sea trout'.

This fish is the local trout of the north-eastern states of America and of Quebec and the maritimes in Canada but, technically, it is not a trout in any European sense; it is a char. Its nearest relative in my home waters is the red-bellied Scottish char *Salvelinus salvelinus*. When I found myself with the eastern brook trout as my local game fish for two years, I very quickly discovered that a European trout fishing mentality was not always the best frame of mind in which to fish for them. I found myself using approaches which I had tried out for char in Lapland, in the north of Norway and in my home Highland waters of Scotland. In

Europe, the char is a dimpling difficult fish, one which many anglers regard as something of a mystery. After some years of experience of them, I still feel that the mystery remains. I find some techniques work well, but I regard *fontinalis* particularly as a difficult, highly interesting game fish, more difficult in stillwater than in streams, a fish which tests the skill of any fly fisher.

I was lucky enough to begin my fishing for speckled trout in Maine on the Kennebec River and on the little forest ponds which lie in the Maine woods between Jackman and Caratunk. This is a marvellous region of mixed woods with whole series of lakes linked by forest streams and larger rivers. Some of the rivers are alive with *fontinalis*, eg the Dead River at West Forks just above its junction with the Kennebec. The river brookies, however, are usually small. I found them seldom over 10in (25cm) in length and somewhat easy to tempt in the streams to wet or dry fly. In the ponds, however, the fish ran larger and were extremely selective feeders. On calm summer evenings they could be frustrating and difficult fish, and to tempt fish of a pound (½kg) or over was an event.

I had an evening on Ellis Pond, near West Forks, Maine in mid-June. We arrived in the early afternoon after an eight mile (13km) drive over extremely bad track which took all the power

of our four-wheel drive truck to negotiate. We disturbed a rather drugged looking cow moose on our way in. She looked balefully at us, shook her head to disperse some of the billion flies which were pestering her, and slouched off into the woods.

We studied the water during the afternoon. It was entirely surrounded by trees and in several places the shoreline was a jumble of fallen timber. Above the waterline the woods were impenetrable, or nearly so. I noticed that the lower branches of the trees were all eaten away up to about six feet (1.8m) where deer, feeding from the ice in winter, had browsed the foliage away. Waters like these – clear deepish ponds or lakes (ponds may be thirty or forty acres in extent or more) – are typical of the north-eastern states of America, and in Quebec they proliferate. They are boat fishers' waters. Even if there is a shoreline from which

Left: **A nice brook trout (*fontinalis*) taken from the waters of the Chateauguay River, New York State**

you can cast well enough, it is seldom productive. I tried shore fishing in other ponds in Maine and I never managed to take more than a fingerling or two. Further the wading was terrible. A fine silty bottom filled in the gaps between fallen logs. You had to test every step, just as you would have to in traversing the woods themselves. You could find a log 'raft' under a foot of fine silt and feel that it was solid, and in two steps you could put your foot through the lattice of logs and into several feet of silty water. Horrible. This is canoe or boat country. It is also four-wheel drive country and it is a region where camping and forest know-how are essential to safety and survival. I happen to love land like this, full of the spirit of the wilderness and full of a sense of hunting the fish, but I could sympathise with people who might feel that this was too difficult for the smallish fish rewards it offers.

I turned over three fish in the course of the afternoon and landed one of them. It was 8in (20cm) long and I returned it. We saw a few rises, but really, there was very little surface action. This disappointed me, as it always does in lake fishing in North America. *Fontinalis* do not show well except on still evenings. Then they move around the surface of the still pond in feeding shoals going down at the least whiff of wind. It is tantalising and difficult fishing reminding me of smutting or midging trout (browns) in Scotland or, worse, on English lakes and ponds in summer.

On Ellis I judged the fish to be nymphing – taking the gnat and midge hatch just before the nymphs broke through to the surface. The tension of the surface film probably held millions of nymphs struggling to break through and the feeding was not so much a series of rises by the fish as one long sucking operation as the tiny larvae were taken. I used a largish midge nymph on a floating line and a tapered leader. The technique I tried first was the British one of allowing the nymph to sink gently through the surface film and then with a tiny movement of the rod, checking the sinking and just holding the nymph steady for some seconds before twitching it as if it were about to make for the surface in the hatching process. I have found that even when the natural fly is very much smaller than the artificial, trout (browns) are often tempted to take a gobbet of nymph meat with their midge soup. It worked on Ellis and I took one nice *fontinalis* of a 1¼lb (0.6kg). Taking that fish showed me just how strong a 'brookie' is. The fish made excellent deep runs, showed little and never seemed to tire. I had the impression of drawing the fish still fighting to the net.

But taking that first good speckled trout misled me. I thought in my innocence that I could go on using brown trout tactics and taking the better class of fish in the forest ponds. I little realised that a fish of this size taken on my first outing had also spoiled me. It was a full season before I took anything as good. I *played* one which would have run 2lb (0.9kg) in the north branch of the Saranac in New York State, but I lost it.

I say that first evening misled me, because I was to discover that evening *fontinalis* around 10 to 12in (25 to 30cm) in length. I was using a canoe on that occasion and I found that the best way to take the fish in the evening was to use a really light 8ft 6in (2.59m) with a No. 5 floating line (well tapered) and the finest leader in my box (3lb (1.4kg) on this occasion). I attached the smallest 'Footballer' nymph I had (No. 16; alternate turns of black and white horsehair for the body and a

turn of peacock herl for the thorax). With this tiny offering I stalked lines of sipping *fontinalis*. I would glide up, lengthening line in the air and placing the nymph with accuracy in the path of the shoal. I did not allow the fly to rest long. I used a Scottish midging technique. As soon as the nymph landed I lifted the tip of the rod and made one long steady draw. This seemed to excite the brookies into taking. It was not, obviously, what the nymphs themselves were doing. They were inert or nearly so. My nymph was larger and I made it suddenly appear in a brookie's window (*very* small when the fish is at the surface) and move in a determined steady way out of reach of the fish. Call it what you will; it is temptation. Fish, even the subtle brookie, fall for this even when the nymph you are presenting is much larger than the natural food which pre-occupies the fish. I took my limit very quickly that evening and I went on to fish for and return many more trout – thinnish, extremely hard-bodied brookies of 10 to 12in (25 to 30cm) in length. It was superb for about an hour-and-a-half. The lake was almost completely still and the knolls of trees reflected in arches of darkness on its glassy surface. The gliding canoe was just right for the conditions.

Fontinalis go off the take when dusk really deepens. Browns will go on rising quite well into the dark and in the gloom you might take a really large one. My experience of speckled trout is that the fish prefer daylight feeding and love the calm waters of the evening, but do not feed seriously after that.

Fontinalis come in interesting local varieties or races. In appearance the fish usually remind me of the European char. They are dark fish with a scattering of whitish or yellow spots over their sides with a number of red spots, often with an aureole of a whitish or bluish colour behind each. On the back there are dark green kidney-shaped spots and irregular barring over the fins and tail. The fins themselves are beautiful, each one reddish or brownish and piped with creamy white. Brookies' bellies are whitish in the females and orange or red in the males, especially near spawning time. Many of the fish I caught were dark, especially in forest streams, with mahogany brown backs, but the lake fish were usually greenish.

Brookies are cool water fish. I have had my best numbers of fish between April and mid June, but numbers of fish may be taken throughout the summer, especially if you sink your flies by day down through the upper bands of warm water to the cool waters 10ft (3m) or more down. I am not terribly enthusiastic about this form of fishing, but in the lakes of the Papineau-Labelle park in

Quebec I have sometimes found that this is the only way possible to take the trout.

The sea-going variety of the brookie is a fine fish, running in size from 1 to 3lb (0.5 to 1.4kg) in weight. My only experience of these fish was in late May and early June on the tidal reaches of the Miramichi. The fish have a very short peak taking time. The locals told me that they run upstream in spring for about a fortnight and then they may be taken in smallish numbers upstream. The main taking time is late May and the main place for the fishing is the head of the tide. In the case of the Miramichi, this is twelve miles (19km) from the mouth. There, the waters 'back up' under the influence of the tide rather than share in the brackish water itself.

These 'sea trout' take large trout flies or Scottish sea trout flies in the streams and glides. I found them roving fish. Some were in obvious lies in the streams, but some were apt to rise once here and once there as if they were strangers (as they were) in the water and did not quite know where to feed. I found dry fly often better than wet. Unlike Scottish sea trout (which of course are related to browns) the sea-going brookies did not like night fishing. They would go off feed as the dusk fell and that was that. They are daylight fish. These are lovely brookies – hard fighting and beautifully marked. The brackish water affects their colour. Some I took were almost silver in colour but still with the characteristic spots and back markings (the mackerel bars of the *fontinalis*).

My travels in Quebec and the north eastern states of the USA have led me to feel that there is a serious lack of good brookies in accessible water. Many lakes are in danger of being fished out by worming (in Quebec), and in other waters of easy public access, although there are good stocking programmes, there are far too many fish of the 6in (15cm) class which are taken as fair game by visiting anglers. In my view, it would be better to leave such fish until they were at least 8in (20cm) in length, as indeed certain fishing authorities demand. My own limits are that a trout must weigh 6oz (170g) at least if it is to be taken. Even then I strictly limit myself to a couple of pan fish (if I am camping) and work for larger trout to make up my limit – often failing miserably in the process. But I do feel that many waters in Quebec are in danger of becoming wildernesses of tiddlers because of indiscriminate worm fishing and size limits being ignored. The larger brookies are still to be found in the woods of Quebec and Labrador however – fish in the 2lb (0.9kg) class and better. There, sheer remoteness and the shortness of the fishing season protects the stock. *Fontinalis* has the name of being a slow growing fish, but interestingly enough, an experiment in rearing them at Loch Fitty in Scotland produced several fish which outstripped fed rainbows. This suggests that it is food supply which limits the forest stream or pond.

The brook trout is a splendid fighter, deep rather than showy. It is a tricky taker of fly and a real challenge to brown-trout-minded anglers. It is fished for, or shall I say, hunted, in some of the most exciting woods and loveliest hill country I have ever seen. That is not without significance in the taking of any game fish in its natural habitat.

The **Ferox** of Scotland

The name *Salmo ferox* was given to large loch trout which seemed to our forefathers to be so different from the ordinary run of brown trout that they were identifiable as a separate family. I have a great deal of sympathy for anglers who feel that they want to label the obvious differences in trout type, race or variety they discover, although the other half of me knows that biologists will not have it so. The position is that we now give only one name to the brown trout and the sea trout, *Salmo trutta*, and we have abandoned the practice of giving Latin names to the Loch Leven trout (*Salmo coecifer* or *levenensis*), the Gilaroo or Gizzard trout (*Salmo stomachius*), and the large loch trout (*Salmo ferox*). Biological enlightenment is one thing, but there is something of a mystery surrounding the great trout of our lochs and, as an angler, I am intrigued by this. The *ferox* of our lochs in Scotland are much bigger than the average run of trout; they look different, are taken by

Left above: Loch Rannoch, a famous water for *ferox* (Michael Shepley)

Left below: An 18lb 4oz (8.3kg) trout from Loch Quoich, near Invergarry. This is a record fish from a water which has a famous name for growing large trout (Highland News Agency)

Above: An excellent 10lb (4.5kg) *ferox* (Michael Shepley)

Right: Mr C C Mann of Glasgow with a remarkable catch from Loch Quoich. Included in a large bag of normal loch trout was a *ferox* of over 9lb (4kg) which was landed after a long fight. The fish was foul hooked in a fin, making it very difficult indeed to bring to the net

'Eighteen pun' an a face like a bothy cat' was how one Highland gillie described the ferox he had caught. This Loch Rannoch ferox displays all the ugliness of a large male loch trout in the teens of pounds probably beginning to go back in condition (Michael Shepley)

different angling techniques and, in brief, are sufficiently separate in these ways to warrant at least a nickname.

The real age of the *ferox* was the second half of the nineteenth century. The Victorians were great sportsmen and at that time much of the Highlands were just being opened up. Shooting lodges were being built and the railways were slowly reaching key points in the north of Scotland. The *ferox* was one of the trophies hunted, and round the pursuit of *ferox*, like the pursuit of royal stags, a great many stories were woven. One comes across them even today. In Lairg I heard the story of a boatman who used to specialise in taking anglers out on Loch Shin to troll for the legendary *ferox*. After a successful day the gillie was regaling his friends with the tale of the tussle, the hooking of the trout, the strong, hard fight and the suspense before the net was finally slipped under the fish. They swung the bulging net aboard and looked at their catch. It was a *ferox* all right. 'Eighteen pun' an' a face like a bothy cat!' the boatman described it. This tale is typical. The *ferox* is usually

described as large, strong and ugly. It was thus very interesting to discover, in a mid-nineteenth century account of Scottish fishing, a plea for the *ferox* to be regarded as two breeds, one ugly and one beautiful. Stoddart, in the *Angler's Companion* (1853) wrote:

Of the *Salmo ferox* of Sutherlandshire, there are two distinct varieties. The one is a coarse looking fish, having a huge head furnished with rapacious jaws. The tail is broad and square formed. Its external markings are numerous and irregularly distributed. The colour of its skin is not inviting. It wants freshness and transparency ... The other variety includes fish of captivating build, deep in the flank with curved backs and small heads. The teeth, more than the size of the mouth, announce them to be of

Right: Two Rannoch ferox. The larger fish is in slightly poor condition and has a large kype (hook on the lower jaw) (Michael Shepley)

A char, taken in Canada. Char are found in Cumbria, Wales and Scotland as well as in various parts of northern Europe and North America (John Darling)

predatory habits ... Its flesh is redder than even that of *Salmo salar*, although by no means so relishable.

Mystery number one then seems to be that the *ferox* is sometimes a rather horrid looking fish – actually terrifying to some who have caught it – but some are most handsome fish and one has almost to make an excuse to account for its cannibalism. Niall Campbell caught a magnificent fish on a rapala plug in Loch Faskally Pitlochry. It was, for some years after the revision of the original record lists, the record trout for Great Britain and it weighed over 17lb (7.7kg). This trout looked, said Niall, like a scaled up two pounder in perfect conditiion. It cut like a salmon, had a small head and was in every way a most beautiful fish.

Left: **Spinning Loch Rannoch in the early season for its *salmo ferox*. This water holds some very large trout which are normally only taken by spinning or trolling (Michael Shepley)**

One explanation of this is that we may catch *ferox* on their rise to condition, or at their peak, just as we may catch specimens over their peak – indeed, in poor condition and probably in old age or wasting away from disease or other reasons. I am also sure that some of the accounts of *ferox* caught in the past are accounts of the taking of large kelt salmon. I think the British Rod Caught Records Committee was right to purge its lists in 1959. I have seen spawned salmon (and large spawn-bound fish) which to the casual glance might have seemed trout. They were brown and spotted and not unlike *ferox*. I have seen a large spring trout, for example, taken from Loch Maree and entered in the hotel register at Kinlochewe which I had not the heart to point out to the captor was almost certainly an egg-bound coloured sea trout. I suspect that many a bottle of sherry has been sent to anglers reporting a record brown trout in September when a closer laboratory investigation would have declared it a sea trout.

Loch Rannoch, a water famous for its *salmo ferox* (Michael Shepley)

There is a further class of fish which must be confusing to anglers at times. The brown trout which live in the brackish lochs of Orkney, for example in Loch Stennes, and which have in the past produced trout of anything from 18 to 29lb (8.2 to 13.2kg) cannot be regarded as ordinary brown trout at all. They are either sea-going fish which are technically sea trout, or are estuary fish (slob trout) and not true freshwater loch trout. I am not saying that these Stennes fish (and others) are under par in any way. On the contrary they are fabulous trout, deep in the flank and magnificent in every way. I have seen casts and photographs of these fish and I have nothing but praise (mixed with appropriate envy) for their captors. But they are as the Americans say, 'something else'.

The fact that *ferox* have widely different appearances is not very mysterious. What is, for me, more of a mystery is why one trout breaks through the growth barrier and vastly outdistances all the other trout in a given water. Some reference books merely state that the brown trout grows to different sizes 'according to the abundance of food in the environment in which they live. This species has been known to reach a weight of 40lb (18.1kg) although fish of over 10lb (4½kg) are considered exceptional in most waters.' (McClane's Standard Fishing Encyclopedia, 1965.)

The best fed fish I have ever seen were in the river at Calne in Wiltshire where the little chalk stream flows through a pork sausage factory. These trout fed on the waste and they grew big, possibly 5 or 6lb (2.3 or 2.7 kg), but even with what seemed to be a super source of protein, none of them reached anywhere near 20lb (9kg). A trout in the upper teens of pounds in Faskally in Perthshire lives in a mildly acid water and, although there are plenty of small trout and salmon parr and perch to feed on, it does not seem to me to be such a food-rich water that the breakthrough was one of food supply only.

Think also of fisheries like Grafham. This reservoir is one of the richest trout environments in England. It can produce rainbows of 6 to 8lb (2.7 to 3.6kg) and browns in much the same class. It is a stocked fishery with what might be described as plenty of protein around in many forms, including coarse fish, and smaller trout. Yet there are no records of huge trout there. Perhaps there will be *ferox* in Grafham through time, but I doubt it. At the moment it appears to be a stable fishery with a range of trout from 8lb (3.6kg) down through the five and six pounders to the regular three and two pounders. It would be safe to say that no Scottish water exists with the vast food

resources of Grafham, yet there are lochs throughout the Highlands – Rannoch, Ericht, Ness, Shin, Assynt and Fionn, etc – which, although much poorer waters, biologically speaking, produce from time to time considerable numbers of large trout. For example, a hundred years ago, Loch Rannoch produced 25 *ferox* to one rod in one season. Loch Rannoch is a splendid water for trout, but no one in his senses would call it food-rich. Equally, Loch Leven is a splendid loch with plenty of food, which can produce a range of brown trout from 1 to 3lb (0.9 to 1.4kg) or more, but does it ever produce a fish of *ferox* size?

I would therefore dismiss the 'presence of enough food' argument. It is true that just as you cannot make omelettes without eggs, so you cannot produce a *ferox* without enough protein there to convert. But the mere presence of food does not imply the presence of *ferox*. Some other factors are implied. Trout fed in wells and garden ponds do not grow huge, although they may become large in ordinary angling terms, like the Wiltshire trout which fed on bacon waste.

What causes the *ferox* breakthrough? I would like to make three suggestions. Firstly, there must be a genetic directive; there must be something in the genes which creates a potential *ferox*. Secondly, there must be an environment which allows the fish to live long – for example, a deep Highland loch. Thirdly, there must be food for the fish which does manage to break through the growth barrier, and, generally speaking, this food is in the form of small trout or coarse fish. Thus, Loch Rannoch is an ideal place, or was until recently when it was subjected to far too high rod pressure. Loch Ericht still yields *ferox*; so does Shin. These are safe places, and that seems to be critical. They are also deep places, but I take it that this is merely a component of safety, and not a separate factor. There used to be a suggestion that the char of some of our deep lakes formed the food of the *ferox*. This may well be so, but I am sure that char do not form more than a proportion of the food; small brown trout would seem to me to be much more the staple diet of their gargantuan brethren.

Ferox are usually caught by spinning or trolling for them, but there are some interesting records of large fish in this class being taken on fly, which suggests less than a taking interest. The huge 39lb (17.7kg) trout taken from Loch Awe in the nineteenth century was said to have been foul

Right: **An excellent bag of grayling taken on the trotted worm from Driffield Beck, Yorkshire**

hooked. In our own times Charles C Mann, the well known former Glasgow fishing tackle dealer, foul hooked a 9½ pounder (4.3kg) in Loch Quoich, Inverness-shire. But there are records of nine pounders on fly from Shin, twelve pounders from Ericht and Loch Garry and a host of impressive smaller fish taken occasionally on fly in many of the larger lochs of the Scottish Highlands.

Possibly the best description of a technique for taking *ferox* was written by Niall Campbell. In essence the tackle was deep trolling tackle with either a ¼lb (0.1kg) trout mounted on a flight, or a large spoon. The interesting feature of the rig, however, was a flasher mounted 10ft (3m) ahead of the bait itself. This flasher served to bring the fish near the attractive flasher, the trout would take the bait behind.

Trolling a deep loch is not every angler's idea of brisk sport. The fishing is usually slow, and one strike a day would be good going. The boat is (or used to be) rowed and while that was at least a steady occupation, it was usually done by the boatman. The better outboards today operate well at trolling speeds and (my prejudices are showing) you can now be mechanised and bored all day in comfort. Occasionally salmon fishers trolling sprats in spring will take a *ferox*. Worm anglers also take some startling trout from Scottish lochs. The legered worm (which again, I confess, I despise), or bunch of worms, lies on the bottom and every thousandth trout which finds it turns out to be larger than average and, with luck, much larger than average. I have had reports of some of the Glasgow worm brigade having their card games on the banks of Loch Rannoch interrupted when a fish of size and power has stripped their reels and usually made off with worms, traces, lines and all. But just once in a while, one of these trout is landed and it runs into double figures.

It is really quite rare to find a trout fisher who pursues *ferox* to the exclusion of other forms of trout. I know quite a number of specimen hunters but not one who has *ferox* mania. This is probably because there are comparatively few waters left where *ferox* exist in numbers sufficient to justify a total or near total concentration in this sport. But there is something else too. I do not think this age is especially *ferox*-minded. The methods used to catch *ferox* are really rather coarse ones. Trolling deep in lakes is often a branch of light engineering compared with fly fishing, and it is my feeling that we are showing all the signs of becoming much more fastidious about our trout fishing. There are waters in Scotland where one might take a 6lb (2.7kg) trout on fly (Linlithgow Loch or Coldingham, for example). In England there are reservoirs in which a rainbow of this weight or even heavier might be taken. These fish are there to be stalked and hunted with 9ft (2.74m) rods, normal reels and more or less normal lures. I say 'more or less normal lures' because the terror and the bottom seeking lures common on midland and southern reservoirs in England are very far from being traditional flies. They are far more in the order of demons or terrors and when you fish them you are not really conscious of being a fly fisher. Nevertheless, the tackle is, apart from the terminal trace and lure, normal fly tackle and the lures I have just described are in fact legitimate and useful 'flies' in the rules of most waters. Now, if *ferox* could be hunted with streamer flies, like the big rainbows of Britain and America and New Zealand, they would, I think, sail back into acceptability. I can see difficulties in handling the tackle in such a way that the right depth is reached, and I'm afraid, it is likely that trolling would be resorted to (as it is in New Zealand) to fish the fly at the depths necessary. A 9ft (2.74m) fly rod competent to cast out say an AFTM 8 sinking line would not be a convenient weapon for handling the fish in the initial stages of the fight. A *ferox* pulling hard and fighting deep would put intolerable strains on the fly rod. A specially built 9ft rod would not be a suitable casting tool. We are caught in the typical forked stick of our sport; a rod which presents well may be wholly unsuited to striking and playing the fish, yet if we design a rod to handle the strike and fight of a *ferox*, for example, we have little better than the trolling rods of our forefathers.

Right: **A good grayling (*see* section overleaf), ready for the net** (Michael Shepley)

Grayling

Grayling co-exist with trout in many British streams and, thinking more geographically, grayling are to be found throughout the whole northwestern arc of Europe where trout are to be found. They seem to thrive in the colder and more barren rivers of the Arctic better than trout and, indeed, some of the largest grayling I have ever seen or caught have been in waters close to the northern limit of trout. Grayling have also made an excellent home for themselves in the north and west of Canada, again in waters where trout are either absent, or use the lakes to give them food and protection throughout the hard winters. I have caught grayling in one Arctic lake where a tributary entered, but it is reasonably unusual for grayling to live in lakes anywhere else. I know of no lake grayling in the UK, for instance.

Co-existence, in the case of the grayling means competition with trout, but there is a strong element of grayling and trout being complementary fish. Grayling spawn in the spring when trout are recovering and showing their best angling form; trout spawn in winter when grayling are at their best. A cynic might say that this merely means that trout eat grayling eggs and grayling eat trout eggs. To a degree this is true. But trout eat trout eggs also, and salmon eggs and roach eggs and fry, if they can get them. Where grayling would adversely compete with trout would be where they take more of the available natural food than trout can bear without losing condition or average size. Equally, grayling would be decidedly unwelcome in streams where they began to dominate, spawning more efficiently than trout and adapting better. I have heard it said that some waters have been badly affected by grayling ousting trout in this way – the Isla in Perthshire has been held to be an example. I have heard these arguments in many parts of Scotland, usually advanced locally to account for a poor trout season, but usually I find the case based on too short a span. It is this year and last year which people are talking about, probably fortified by a reminiscence of days of yore. What I am much more aware of is that grayling in certain rivers such as the Teviot or the Nith can extend the fishing season for clubs and individual anglers and in cases where this does not adversely affect sea trout and salmon fishing I

Left: **Fly fishing for grayling exends the trout fisher's season by several months (Michael Shepley)**

think this is a good thing.

I remember being a grayling addict as a young trout fisher, really because I was a fly fishing addict and the law was inconsiderate enough to have a close season. I used to fish for grayling in the Ayr, and its tributary the Coyle, in February and I got some nice sport in before the trout season ended. I also fished them in November and what I remember most in the late forays was that my flies were taken as often by gravid trout and by parr as by grayling. While salmon fishing in November on Teviot I have seen anglers trotting worms and fishing maggot for grayling and while I am glad that the fishing season is extended for them in this way, I do shudder lest sea trout or spawning trout succumb when we would hope the law would protect them.

Grayling are beautiful fish. Their appearance is that of a scaly silvery fish with black fleck marks along their armoured sides. Game fishers are used to fish which are small scaled and are softer to the touch than grayling. They feel as if they are metal clad and their great squarish scales make them feel like coarse fish. But I find them delightful fish to see, interesting to fish for and challenging to take on fly. I cherish memories of autumn fish taken in the Tarn in France, in the Cévennes, where they were better to fish for than the trout, mainly because the grayling were catchable – a little bit sillier than trout, and they liked my dry flies. In Finland and Lapland where I have fished extensively, grayling run large and in the lovely glow of the midnight sun in the Arctic rivers of Lapland, big grayling roll over on the surface of the forest streams and can give you wonderful wet and dry fly sport. I think I have valued the grayling more out of the UK than in it. I took several large grayling in Lapland, and indeed, my only ABU record gold pin came from a remarkable piece of good luck with grayling which I think is worth re-telling.

I was fishing the Poroeno river in Lapland, a tributary of the water system which makes up the Tornio river which flows into the Gulf of Bothnia right at the north of the Baltic. This is an area of fells and tundra and the rivers flow crystal clear over sand and gravel. It is (or certainly was when I fished there in the late fifties) the home of the biggest grayling I have ever seen or heard of. We took food for a fortnight, loaded it, and barrels to carry the salted fish, and we rendezvoused with a Lapp family two days' march inland and hired

Above: Grayling fishing on Tweed, trotting a worm in streamy water (Michael Shepley)

Left: A good Tay grayling

Right: A nice Tay grayling taken on fly is gently beached (Michael Shepley)

In the waters of Finnish Lapland, grayling grow large and reach weights of up to several pounds. These fish came from the Lataseno river. The best fish weighed nearly 4lb (1.8kg)

one of their long, canoe-like boats. There were grayling everywhere, but one great fan of streams below a lake was outstanding. I waded out and fished wet fly down them and I chose large flies on a sea trout cast. In one hour I had nine fish weighing 27½lb (12½kg). I wish they had been sea trout, but what sport they brought! They erected their great dorsal fins in the streams and it was hard fighting to get them to the net. But thereby hangs the main story. I was on the eighth stream out from the bank and my bag was heavy, but I decided to try my cast down a nice deep run rolling over golden sand. I had a heavy take and this one fought strangely. For a time I wondered whether I had hooked the European record fish, but I glimpsed one of the grayling and saw that it was something like a three pounder, but on the tail fly was something much bigger. It was hard to get them anywhere near the net and I would have liked to net the tail fish first, as the books all say, and scoop the dropper fish in immediately after, but I couldn't get near the tail fish. So I decided that the only way was to net the dropper fish and hope for the best. The fish slid into the net and the fly snagged. There I was, a hundred yards from the bank, snagged in my net with a good big grayling hanging down inside the bag of the net and a whopper walloping on the tail.

I whipped out my sheath knife, severed the dropper and with the first fish hanging in the net played out the tail fish and soon had him ready for netting too. The dropper fish weighed 3lb (1.4kg) and the tail fish, 4lb (1.8kg). I had landed 7lb (3.2kg) of grayling on one cast. If it had been in one fish, I would have claimed some kind of record. As it was I managed to take a 4½ pounder (2kg) from that same river and it won me some form of recognition!

These great Arctic grayling are much larger than the grayling one is likely to find in British rivers. There are records of fish over 4lb (1.8kg) from the chalk streams and three pounders are not uncommon, but if you take grayling of a pound (½kg) or over in most northern streams, you have done well. The bags of grayling we see these days in Scotland are of fish from ½lb (0.2kg) upwards, with some over the pound (½kg). I have the impression that grayling average sizes are going down, but records are few and far between and this is only an impression.

Grayling like gravelly, reasonably gentle reaches of rivers. There they shoal and rise to the fly.

There are times when you would think the river was empty of grayling, but when you find a shoal and when it decides to rise, you can take many fish in one standing. The grayling, unlike the trout, rises from a position low in the water to take surface food. I have seen fish doing this and missing the fly hopelessly as a result. The most productive way of taking them is, as I have mentioned, by trotting a small brandling worm down the reach, or by using maggot – neither of which appeals to me. The grayling will take nymphs and small wet flies, especially fished downstream. When the fish are on surface flies, dry fly fishing like trout fishing can do well. What is nice is that you can get some fly fishing in frosty November weather in the middle of the day when it is a delight to be out. This, I believe, makes the fish complementary to the trout, and it is this form of sport which I recommend.

The grayling is an introduced fish. The Clyde and Nith in Scotland were stocked in 1855 and 1857, and the Tweed was stocked in 1880 – the same year as the Tay. In England fish were planted in a tributary of the Thames, the Windrush in 1859, and in a feeder stream of the Exe in 1866. Rivers in Yorkshire were also stocked about this time and the Cumberland Eden also had grayling introduced. Our forefathers clearly felt positive about grayling, and well they might. It is a charming fish and can be very sporting. It is good as a table fish and it seems hardy enough to withstand our winters and to hold its own against trout and sea trout.

Tackle and tactics for grayling are similar to those for trout. Only the time of year is different. But striking the fish which takes you has its peculiarities. Grayling peck at the fly, probably because of the way they rise and because of their peculiarly shaped, hard, leathery mouths. Be positive and strike rises far more vigorously than you would trout. I also find that small flies hook grayling better than larger ones, and I regularly use No. 14 for grayling where I might have settled for No. 12 for trout.

So when you are out with the trout rod and find your flies taken by a sprightly, silver fish which fights a solid but quivering fight in the stream, look for the great, beautiful back fin erected like a sail in the water. You have hooked a grayling. Note the place well; they are seldom solitary. With luck you will creel half-a-dozen without moving ten feet from the first encounter.

GAME FISHING SEASONS (UK)

Rod Fishings (Scotland)

	Open	Closed
Salmon*	1–10 February	31 October
Sea Trout	1–10 February	31 October
Trout	15 March	6 October

Rainbow Trout not covered by present legislation.
*There are numerous local variations. The most important of these are:
Awe, Beauly, Nairn and Spey:
Conon, Cree, Dee (Aberdeenshire), Findhorn, Naver, Helsmdale, Hope, Nairn and Spey: 30 September

Exceptionally early openings include:

Helmsdale	11 January
Thurso	11 January
Halladale	12 January
Naver	12 January
Ness	15 January
Tay	15 January
Conon	26 January

Exceptionally late closings include:

Tweed

Rod Fishings (England)

	Open	Closed
Salmon	1 February	31 October
Sea Trout	1 February	31 October
Trout	1 March	30 September
Char	1 March	30 September
Rainbow Trout	Not covered by current legislation	

Note: There are numerous local variations, which anglers should enquire locally about.

Index